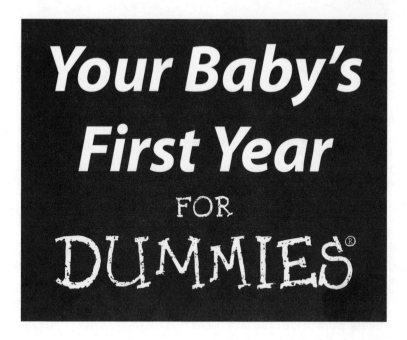

by James Gaylord, MD and Michelle Hagen

WILEY

Wiley Publishing, Inc.

Your Baby's First Year For Dummies®

Published by
Wiley Publishing, Inc.
111 River St.
Hoboken, NJ 07030-5774
www.wiley.com

For general information on our other products and services, please contact our Customer Care Department within the U.S. at 800-762-2974, outside the U.S. at 317-572-3993, or fax 317-572-4002.

For technical support, please visit www.wiley.com/techsupport.

Wiley also publishes its books in a variety of electronic formats. Some content that appears in print may not be available in electronic books.

Library of Congress Control Number: 2005923786

ISBN-13: 978-0-7645-8420-6

ISBN-10: 0-7645-8420-0

Manufactured in the United States of America

10 9 8 7 6 5 4 3 2 1

1B/RX/QW/QV/IN

WILEY

Your Baby's

21 DAY LOAN ITEM

Please return <u>on or before</u> the last date stamped above

A fine will be charged for overdue items

CITY COLLEGE NORWICH

About the Authors

Dr. James Gaylord has a dual Board Certification in Pediatrics and Internal Medicine and has been in private practice in Burnt Hills, N.Y. since 1997. He is a 1988 graduate of Albany Medical College, where he also served as an assistant professor from 1993 to 1997. His training includes a residency in Pediatrics and Internal Medicine; he also spent a year (1992-93) as chief resident in Pediatrics. He continues to train medical students in his private practice.

Dr. Gaylord and his wife Diane live on a horse farm in Greenfield, N.Y with their three children: Abigail, 11; Brendan, 10; and Margaret, 7.

Michelle Hagen is a freelance writer and editor and the author of 8 books. She has a degree in literature from Empire State College and lives in Wilton, NY with her husband and three sons.

Dedication

Dr. James Gaylord: To my children: Abby, Brendan, and Maggie, who taught me so much about parenting in the first year of life.

Michelle Hagen: This book is for my babies: Sam, Hal, and Nolan (who truly aren't babies at all anymore). I'm constantly amazed by the fact that I'm raising three incredibly amusing, interesting, and good-hearted young men. I love you, I love you, I love you.

Authors' Acknowledgments

Dr. Gaylord: I would like to acknowledge my wife Diane whose networking made my participation in this project possible.

Michelle Hagen: First, to my co-author, Dr. Jim Gaylord, I appreciate your input, guidance, and patience throughout this long process. I know how incredibly busy you are with your practice and with your own family, which makes me even more grateful that you agreed to take on this project in the first place.

Thank you to Mike and Diane Young, who introduced me to my wonderful co-author. Thanks to Jessica Faust, my agent at Bookends, for all of your support and assistance. To Traci Cumbay and Jen Bingham, my editors at Wiley, I enjoyed working with both of you more than I can say. Not only are both of you outstanding at what you do, you're both fun, funny, and fair. You made my job that much easier.

Thank you to Dr. Mary Elise Hodson, technical editor on this project, for your helpful suggestions during the editing process. Thanks to Tracy Boggier, Acquisitions Editor at Wiley, for your assistance in getting this book off to a solid start. Kathryn Born, thank you for your outstanding illustrations. Each one is an asset to this book.

And last but not least, thanks to my husband Mike and to my boys, all of whom have played a vital role in my interest in and love for babies over the years. Thanks also for being so proud of my work, especially when the truth is that without you guys, I'm nothin'.

Publisher's Acknowledgments

We're proud of this book; please send us your comments through our Dummies online registration form located at www.dummies.com/register/.

Some of the people who helped bring this book to market include the following:

Acquisitions, Editorial,
and Media Development

Project Editor: Traci Cumbay

Acquisitions Editor: Tracy Boggier

Copy Editor: Jennifer Bingham

Technical Editor: Mary Elise Hodson, MD

Senior Editorial Manager: Jennifer Ehrlich

Editorial Assistant: Hanna Scott,

Cover Photos: ® BananaStock/PictureQuest

Cartoons: Rich Tennant (www.the5thwave.com)

Composition Services

Project Coordinator: Maridee Ennis, Shannon Schiller

Layout and Graphics: Carl Byers, Andrea Dahl, Lauren Goddard, Stephanie D. Jumper, Julie Trippetti,

Special Art: Kathryn Born

Proofreaders: Leeann Harney, Jessica Kramer, Carl William Pierce

Indexer: TECHBOOKS Production Services

Publishing and Editorial for Consumer Dummies

Diane Graves Steele, Vice President and Publisher, Consumer Dummies

Joyce Pepple, Acquisitions Director, Consumer Dummies

Kristin A. Cocks, Product Development Director, Consumer Dummies

Michael Spring, Vice President and Publisher, Travel

Kelly Regan, Editorial Director, Travel

Publishing for Technology Dummies

Andy Cummings, Vice President and Publisher, Dummies Technology/General User

Composition Services

Gerry Fahey, Vice President of Production Services

Debbie Stailey, Director of Composition Services

Contents at a Glance

Table of Contents

Introduction

· ·

*W*hen you're pregnant and preparing for the future with Baby, it's so easy to nail down a "schedule" for feedings, for naps, for your own return to work. And then your dream child becomes a reality and you find that — well, she has her own ideas that don't quite coincide with your best-laid plans.

For some people, bringing a baby into the home is no big deal — their child is quiet and mellow, and just a joy to behold throughout the first year and beyond. For the parents of a fussy, sleepless infant, however, the experience is completely different. And because you'll be talking to other new parents at the doctor's office or at a playgroup, the parents of the restless baby assume that the parents of the quiet infant have a line on some secret method of raising a laid-back kid. Enter parental guilt and feelings of inadequacy.

There are bound to be times during Baby's first year when you feel as though you've got the world by the tail: Baby's sleeping and eating well, she's hitting those milestones right on time, and you're balancing childcare with work or with housekeeping. Then again, for every action, there's an equal and opposite reaction; it only makes sense that there will also be times when you feel like you don't know what the heck is going on, and wonder why you ever thought you could handle this huge responsibility in the first place.

Give yourself a break during those moments. The first year is one big learning experience — for you and your child. Baby will be conquering new territory every month (detailed in the pages of this book), and you'll be right there, cheering her on and adjusting your own life to meet her latest wants and needs. There will be days of triumph (as when Baby smiles, coos, and laughs for the first time) and days that you'd rather just forget (teething — 'nough said). *All* of the days go by so quickly, though, and before you know it, Baby will be 3 months, 6 months, 9 months, and then 1 year old. It all happens without your realizing it — Baby's a toddler and you're a confident, veteran parent.

This book was written with the intention of giving new parents a realistic look at what Baby's first year may be like. Think of this as a time to become acquainted with your child as she grows into her personality and you grow into parenthood.

About This Book

This book was written by a pediatrician with a booming practice and two great kids of his own, and a writer/mom who's raising three boys — and all of these kids were completely different during their first years. We've left out a lot of scientific research on why babies behave the way they do and have mostly focused on the practical and emotional aspects of seeing your child through the first year.

For example, you won't find statistics in this book, because, quite frankly, it isn't all that helpful to know that a certain percentage of infants sleep through the night at 3 months if *your* 3-month-old is still waking up three times between midnight and daybreak. Knowing how to encourage her to catch forty winks is far more helpful than comparing your experience to phantom families around the country, so in this book, you find no-nonsense advice given in the simplest terms and presented in an easy-to-find format.

We know that parenting is hard work — we've been there personally, and Dr. Gaylord has listened to many, many, many parents' concerns about the first year. We've laid out information in plain language and with a twist — we took off our rose-colored glasses while writing in an effort to let new parents know that the first year, while magical and wonderful and glorious (and far too fleeting), inevitably has its moments of confusion and frustration. We want new parents to know that they're not alone, and that feeling this way is normal — it doesn't make you a bad mom or dad. It makes you human.

Conventions Used in This Book

To help you navigate through this book, we've established the following conventions:

- ✔ *Italic* is used for emphasis and to highlight new words or terms that are defined.
- ✔ Monofont is used for Web addresses.
- ✔ Sidebars, which are shaded gray boxes full of text, consist of information that's interesting but not necessarily critical to your understanding of the topic.

Baby math can spin a parent's head around at times. We tried to keep the months and the chapter titles in sync in order to eliminate confusion. Please bear in mind that when we refer to, for example, a "1-month-old" or an "almost-1-month-old," we're talking about a child in the first month of life and approaching the 4-week mark.

What You're Not to Read

Sidebars included in this book are "extra" information — a more in-depth look at areas of concern during the first year. Some focus on development, others focus on recent studies — none of them are crucial to your understanding the rest of this book. Read them if you want, and skip them if you aren't into that kind of thing. No big whoop.

Foolish Assumptions

We assume that you've picked up this book for one of several reasons:

- ✔ You're pregnant and wondering what Baby's first year will be like.
- ✔ You've given birth and are reading everything you can get your hands on regarding the months ahead.
- ✔ You've given birth and you wanted a book that doesn't talk down to you or make you feel as though there's something wrong with you if you're having a hard time making the adjustment to parenthood.

We go on to assume that you're looking for advice on making it through the first year, that you know it's not always going to be easy, that you want to be the best parent you're capable of becoming, and that you're willing to give up preconceived notions (read: fantasies) of how these first 12 months with a child *should* be. That's all.

In a nutshell: If you have a baby in the house, we want to talk to you.

Other titles in the *For Dummies* series that you may want to check out include *Breastfeeding For Dummies* by Sharon Perkins and Carol Vannais, *Choosing Childcare For Dummies* by Ann Douglas, and *Parenting For Dummies* by Sandra Hardin Gookin and Dan Gookin — all published by Wiley. These books will give you a great overview of various aspects of child-rearing.

How This Book Is Organized

We've broken this book into 24 chapters. Each of Baby's first 12 months is addressed in its own chapter, including a list of milestones for each specific time period, a discussion of what happens during each well-baby visit, and tips for ensuring Baby's safety and well-being at every stage of development. The chapters are grouped into sections.

Part I: Giving Baby a Healthy, Happy Start

These debut chapters focus on preparing your house for Baby, what happens in the maternity ward, deciding on a method of feeding your child, and actually transporting Baby home. We also discuss the production of traveling with an infant in this section, along with information to guide you in making the decision to return to work — or to stay home. Diverse topics, yes, but issues you want to know about and consider so that you're not forced to make decisions on-the-spot.

Part II: Introducing: Baby!

These chapters focus on Baby's infancy, including an honest discussion of a new mom's recovery from childbirth and how Baby may or may not be settling into her new home. Look for the milestone markers at the beginning of each chapter to know what Baby may be up to during this time.

Part III: Moving, Shaking, and Growing

Months 4 through 6 are covered in this section, a time when Baby's personality begins to blossom and he starts moving of his own accord. Each chapter in this section contains information on adding solids to Baby's diet and how that may affect his sleeping and nursing routines. A discussion on whether to let Baby "cry it out" is also included in this section.

Part IV: Discovering the World Beyond Mom

Baby becomes more mobile during the second half of the first year, and she also begins to grasp the true concept of communication. She's becoming a real person now, and these chapters focus on encouraging her language development and keeping her safe when all she wants to do is explore. We also discuss the other people in Baby's life — your friends who love to compare your child to theirs, and your relatives, who refuse to follow your directions when they watch your child. Tips for dealing with these well-meaning but frustrating pals and relations are included in this section.

Part V: Keeping Up with Baby

Baby really starts moving during the last three months of the first year — in fact, he may be up and walking by his first birthday party! He may also have a handle on real language at this point, or he may be quite happy to sit on his blanket without saying a word. Tips for staying sane while parenting an active baby are given in this section, along with advice for parents whose children haven't hit the big developmental milestones just yet. Weaning becomes an issue at this point, and advice for making it a *less* uncomfortable experience for Mom is included here. There's also a list of toddler-loved toys (just in case you need some help buying for the big party).

Part VI: Protecting Baby's Health and Safety

These chapters give an overview of the first-year immunizations and common illnesses, along with advice on comforting a sick child and when to call the doctor. Basic first aid and baby-proofing measures (to prevent injuries in the first place) are discussed in these chapters. We also give you some insight into how to care for a special-needs baby.

Part VII: The Part of Tens

A standard feature in all *For Dummies* titles, the Part of Tens includes short, to-the-point chapters focused on presenting need-to-know information in the most efficient way possible. The Part of Tens chapters in *Your Baby's First Year For Dummies* include advice for making it through the first few weeks after Baby's birth, what a dad can do to survive the first year, and what kinds of situations or illnesses warrant an immediate call to the pediatrician, plus advice on which ones don't.

Icons Used in This Book

The icons used throughout the book are bits of information that can make your life easier or protect your child from harm.

Some situations call for advice from a pro. We use this icon to let you know when something merits an expert medical opinion. Or when you should consult your doctor to put your mind to rest about a situation.

This icon points out words of wisdom that we feel are particularly important and likely to be valuable as you brave Baby's first year.

When we go into medical details or delve deeply into a topic, we use this icon. Rest assured that you can skip this information and still come away with the facts you need.

This icon highlights advice on how to ease Baby into a new situation or to make less work for yourself.

The Warning icon points out situations in which you or Baby may find yourselves in harm's way.

Where to Go from Here

All *For Dummies* books are written in *modular* form — that is, each chapter stands on its own. You don't have to read the introductory chapters to understand the chapters toward the end of the book. Heck, you don't have to rely on any *one* chapter to explain another. Each chapter contains advice specific to that particular month or topic, so you can dive in wherever you need to and you won't be lost. Start wherever you're at during the first year. If you waited until the fourth month to buy this book, skip right to Chapter 9. If you're still pregnant, start at the beginning and decide what you need to know at this point. We know that new parents seldom have loads of spare time to spend reading, so we didn't include information that will bore you to tears or put you to sleep — wherever you choose to begin, you find pertinent information that you can use at that particular time in Baby's development.

Part I
Giving Baby a Healthy, Happy Start

The 5th Wave

By Rich Tennant

"And this from a woman who's too embarrassed to use a cell phone in public."

In this part . . .

Preparing yourself for what lies ahead can help make the changes that occur during Baby's first year a heck of a lot easier for you and your child. Find out how to get your home ready for Baby, how to make the best travel plans for you and your child, how to find the best daycare for your infant, and discover what really happens in the hospital.

These are diverse topics — but believe it or not you may find yourself dealing with each of these issues over the course of Baby's first month. Just imagine what you'll encounter over the span of the first year!

Chapter 1

Preparing for Baby

- -

In This Chapter

▶ Making plans

▶ Remaining flexible

▶ Paging Dr. Wonderful

▶ Parenting the adopted baby

▶ Summing up Baby's big moments

- -

*W*ondering about how life will be when Baby comes into the fold? Go ahead and make plans, but give yourself a lot of wiggle room. Counting on a baby to follow the plans you make months before delivery (concerning work, or vacations, or sleep, or even having a pleasant day) is like picking a random date and planning on having nice weather. You just don't know. You can't know until the time comes. Make several contingency plans for Baby's first weeks at home — sort of like having an umbrella handy.

The first year is an amazing time of growth (something your pediatrician will officially track at every well-baby visit) and development. When you hold your tiny infant in one arm, you'll hardly be able to imagine her balancing on her own feet in a matter of just 12 months' time, when she may also be learning to talk, eating real foods, and displaying signs of her true personality (which, to your delight or dismay, may mimic your own — or your partner's).

Adoptive parents face the same issues and challenges (along with some concerns unique to their situation) when it comes to seeing Baby through the first year — and beyond. This book is meant to be a guide for everyone who is taking on the total commitment involved with raising a child.

This chapter gives you an idea of what lies ahead — and where to look for information in this book.

Bracing Yourself for the Changes Ahead

So, you're all set to bring Baby home and jump into this gig known as parenting. You've thought about this for — well, what seems like forever; you've prepared yourself mentally; you know that your life is going to be different — but different in a *good* way.

No matter how long you've been dreaming, planning, and discussing this particular phase of life, you really can't ever know what it'll be like until you're actually going through it. You may bring home a mellow, quiet, easy-going child, or you may bring home someone who seems to have been sent to punish you for all the grief you gave your own parents.

Equipping yourself

Having all the right equipment can make life a heck of a lot easier, as can having the right people around to lend a helping hand. In the event that you've had a difficult delivery, or that your child just isn't sleeping the way you thought he would, having a good support system and accepting the fact that you need to take it easy for a while (as discussed in Chapter 5) can really help to ease your transition toward taking complete responsibility for this one little person.

Make your checklist (or wish list) early and keep track of what you have, what you don't have, and what you absolutely *must* have before you go into labor. Chapter 2 lists the necessities of new parenthood, from car seats to co-sleepers.

Keeping an open mind

The best advice for new parents may be this: Be flexible. Although you do want to educate yourself on life with a baby during your pregnancy, try not to settle on one particular idea of how things are going to be.

Babies are unpredictable. You could have a terrific first week at home, resting while Baby does little more than snooze in your arms only to find that Baby becomes fussy during the second and third weeks for no apparent reason. Maybe you're planning on going back to work after a month, but after a week of broken sleep and long days at home nursing your child 'round the clock, you're beginning to wonder how the heck you're going to meet that goal. Chapter 4 tells you about returning to work. Running even the simplest errands with a newborn in tow can take twice as long as you may expect, and when fatigue and frustration (discussed in Chapter 5) hit, they can make you feel like you're down for the count. It's really not the case — you just need to regroup and recharge and figure out what works — and what doesn't.

Becoming a parent

Bonding with Baby (covered in more detail in Chapters 2 and 6) can often take two forms: immediate and absolute from the moment of this child's birth or gradual and intermittent. Nothing's wrong with you if you fall into the latter group. Sure, you may have been expecting to feel an instant connection to your child, but remember — he's a stranger to you. Don't berate yourself for not feeling like a parent immediately. The feeling *will* come to you — you can bet the farm on it — and after it does (or even before), you may wonder how you can be trusted to care for this beautiful child.

If your baby comes with special needs or if he gets sick or injured, you have an even more challenging set of circumstances to handle (but, trust us, you can do it). Turn to Chapter 18 of this book to find out more about how to care for Baby when everything isn't perfect.

Parenting is sometimes an overwhelming responsibility, especially in a year filled with firsts. Although countless changes are headed your way with the introduction of a child into your home, there won't be anything you can't handle. Repeat this mantra every morning, noon, and night if you need to — because it's the truth.

Planning for Life with Baby

Setting up Baby's bassinet and swing are good starts to preparing for the big day when your family welcomes the little one home — however, many other issues are worth discussing before Baby takes center stage, such as:

- ✔ Are you breastfeeding or bottlefeeding? (Read Chapter 2 for an overview of each.)

- ✔ Which partner is going to be the primary caregiver? If both of you are going to work full-time, who's going to take charge of feeding and clothing everyone? Will there be an equal division of household and Baby duties or will another arrangement work better? (Chapter 4 discusses some of these topics.)

- ✔ Is there anything you can do to prevent sudden infant death syndrome (SIDS)? (Chapter 20 has advice on this.)

✔ Do you expect to make frequent trips with Baby? (Chapter 3 offers some tips for smooth traveling.)

✔ Do you know the Heimlich maneuver for babies? How about infant CPR? (Chapter 20 goes over this.)

✔ If you're returning to work, what kind of day-care arrangements should you make? (Chapter 4 again.)

✔ Who do you accept help from, and who do you turn away at the door? (Chapter 5 advises you in this matter.)

✔ How do you deal with family members who happen to disagree with your parenting philosophies? (See Chapter 14.)

✔ What's your take on spanking? How about your partner's view of it? (Chapter 17 gives advice for handling discipline in an age-appropriate manner.)

✔ When do you begin preparing your home to be baby-safe? Before you know it, Baby will be rolling, crawling, mouthing, and pulling up on *everything*. (Chapter 20 gives advice for baby-proofing your house.)

Of course, you must consider much, much more to prepare yourself — and your life, and your home — for the arrival of your child. These major concerns are really just the tip of the iceberg, as you'll find after the first year really gets rolling.

Choosing a Pediatrician

Planning on choosing a doc from the Yellow Pages? Don't. Buying space in the phone book isn't an indication of how qualified a doctor is — no matter how big and fancy the ad. With just a little research, you're much more likely to find the right pediatrician.

The first thing you want to decide is what kind of doctor you're looking for. You have two options:

✔ **A pediatrician** specializes solely in children; he followed up medical school with three more years of training in the care of babies, children, and adolescents. Board-certified pediatricians have taken an exam demonstrating their vast knowledge of the health and well-being of their prospective patients.

✔ **A general practitioner** sees a much broader range of patients and may, in fact, be able to take care of your entire family (a big bonus if you're frequently ill). On the downside, he may not know as much about less common conditions in an infant (though if he sees a lot of infants in his practice, he may be very informed on the latest issues).

Ask your friends, neighbors, co-workers, and obstetrician — anyone you know who has kids and/or *whose opinion you respect* — for the names of good baby doctors.

Make sure the doctors on your short list accept your insurance, and then set up an interview with one or more of them. Some doctors don't charge for this meeting; others do. Ask about the fee when you make the appointment.

During your interview, you need to find out the following:

- ✔ **What's the doctor's educational background?** Did he attend medical school in another country, for example? You need to do your research and make sure that the requirements for graduation there are as stringent as they are in the U.S. Also find out whether the doctor is board certified. A doctor who isn't board certified in pediatrics isn't necessarily incompetent; certification simply means that this physician has completed extra training and assessment (beyond the minimum requirements) by a board of experts in the field.

- ✔ **What's his child-rearing philosophy?** Does it mesh with yours?

- ✔ **What's his take on the use of antibiotics for infections?** Some doctors nowadays are taking more of a wait-and-see approach to ear infections, for example, to allow them to clear up by themselves. You may love this approach to medicine, or you may be completely opposed to it. It's best to know *now* how an ear infection will be treated so that you don't find yourself at odds with your doctor when the situation arises.

- ✔ **How many doctors are in the practice?** Will you be able to see your doctor for all well-baby visits? Who will see Baby when he's sick? You may be expecting to see this particular doctor at every single well- and sick-baby visit. That's just not the case in many practices, at least as far as sick calls go. You may need to see the doctor on call (who may be someone you don't know).

- ✔ **What are the office hours?** If you work full-time you may want to look for a practice with evening or weekend hours for well-baby checkups. Many practices have a scheduled time where a doctor or nurse answers routine questions that don't require an office visit (such as the recommended dosage of cold medicine for Baby's age and weight, or how to treat diaper rash).

- ✔ **If he's a solo practitioner, who covers his office when he takes vacation?** You want to know that you have a reliable place to take your sick baby when your doctor is out of town.

Tell the doctor if you're concerned or confused about immunizing Baby. Some physicians won't take on a child who isn't going to be immunized. (For more on immunization, see Chapter 18.)

Another important consideration: How convenient is the doctor's office to your home? Driving 20 minutes to see the pediatrician may seem like an adventure to you right now, but the first time you have a sick child on your hands, all you'll want to do is get him in, get him out, and get him home. (Not to mention that if you have more kids in the years to come, dragging two or three sick kids across town to see the doctor becomes even more of a challenge). You can plan on being at the doctor's office plenty over the course of the first year in any event, because your child will have well-baby visits scheduled at 2 weeks or 1 month, 2 months, 4 months, 6 months, 9 months, and 12 months.

Adopting

Although some of the advice in this book centers on a new mom's recovery from childbirth, it isn't meant to exclude adoptive parents. You're taking on the same role as any new parent and facing the same issues during the first year.

In today's open adoptions, birth mothers are sometimes included and/or kept informed of Baby's well-being. This is a good thing for your child: First, the circle of people who adore her is only made larger (and can it ever really be too large?), and secondly, she'll never question where she came from or what kind of medical history she may have.

Bonding sometimes seems to be of particular concern for adoptive parents. But bonding can be a challenge for biological parents, as well. And of course, during this first year, you'll work on achieving that first full night's sleep, on feeding Baby, and on developing her motor and communication skills. One thing is certain: As moms and dads, all of us are in the same boat when it comes to learning about and meeting the basic needs of our kids.

Looking Ahead: Baby's First Year in a Nutshell

You won't believe how much Baby accomplishes during his first year. Almost before your eyes, he transforms from a helpless sleeping and eating machine into an independent, curious toddler who's talking and walking and even telling you "no." Along the way from dependent blob to busy 1-year-old, you can expect Baby to reach the following exciting milestones:

- Baby melts your heart with his **first smile** at about 6 weeks.

- Baby may begin to **sleep through the night** as early as the second month, or after he weighs 10 to 15 pounds.

✔ At about 3 months, not only does he start **cooing** and get his first taste of mobility by **rolling over,** but — much to your relief, no doubt — he's likely to **conquer colic.**

✔ Listen for his first real **belly laugh** to come at about 3 months.

✔ Watch for Baby to start **holding up his head** for short periods of time — and to start **putting everything in his mouth** — during the fourth month.

✔ At 5 months, Baby becomes a little ball of personality, **showing different emotions** throughout the day, such as happiness (by smiling and laughing), anger (by voicing his anger when you remove an object from his reach), and interest (by attempting to mimic your voice).

✔ Late in the sixth month, Baby may start **sitting up by himself** and even **crawling** or **scooting** (or propelling himself across the floor in some other creative manner).

✔ During the seventh month (Chapter 12), Baby's communication skills take off as he begins to **babble.**

✔ He becomes mobile one way or another during the eighth month, whether he's just beginning to **crawl,** or he begins **pulling up** and **cruising** around your family room.

✔ When Baby is around 9 months, he may suddenly start **clinging to a special toy,** blanket, or other security object, as he begins to realize that he isn't actually part of *you.*

✔ His **comprehension of language** blossoms during the tenth month, when he's able to demonstrate an understanding of what you're saying to him.

✔ During the eleventh and twelfth months Baby will **refine the skills** he's already been demonstrating — namely **language** and **locomotion.**

Chapter 2

Smoothing the Transition to Parenthood

During the final stage of pregnancy, reality starts to set it. You can feel that change is in the air, and you may wonder whether you're prepared — emotionally and physically — to deal with it. This chapter gives you advice on how to best prepare for Baby's arrival, what you may experience during your hospital stay, and how to ease into that transformation from pregnant to parent.

Filling Baby's Bedroom (and Your Entire House)

Many moms-to-be experience a *nesting* phase late in pregnancy, during which they can concentrate on little else aside from preparing a home for Baby. And good thing, because you simply will not believe how much stuff a baby needs, not to mention how much he will acquire in the form of gifts over his first few weeks of life. Your home, once a sanctuary for your most beloved material goods, will become Baby's storage locker. Soon enough, baby clothing, diapering supplies, toys, bottles, pacifiers, and props (his swing, stroller, and bassinet) will be the only visible items in your house — and the only things you'll care about, anyway.

Of course, there's a huge difference between useful baby paraphernalia and clutter. This section gives you the skinny on what you really need to have on hand for Baby's homecoming.

Now that you're honing in on your baby shower wish list, make sure that you have some idea of practical versus pretty baby goods. It's fine to register for all of the things you've ever dreamed of giving your baby (a decorative ceramic nightlight, the finest infant-sized shearling slippers, the sterling silver rattle and spoon set), but you don't want to miss out on the things you actually need (like bottles, bibs, and booties).

Stocking up for Baby's arrival

After Baby comes home from the hospital, you need to be ready to rock and roll with supplies and clothing. (In fact, you won't even be able to drive him to your house without an infant car seat, so that should be at the top of your registry list). The following list covers the items you need during your first few days and weeks:

The Big Stuff

- ✔ **Infant (rear-facing) car seat:** Baby needs something sturdy that will last at least through the first couple of years, so don't cut corners on this purchase.

- ✔ **Stroller:** As soon as you're up to it, you want to show Baby off to the neighbors.

- ✔ **Crib:** These vary widely in selection and price, so assess your needs before you buy. If you're planning on having a large family, for example, look for a sturdy crib that can be used again (and again).

- ✔ **Changing table:** Having a designated area for diaper changes makes life easier during those first few weeks. Stock it with all of the supplies you may need (listed in "Supplies" section).

- ✔ **Baby sack or sling:** Slings allow for discreet and instant nursing and constant cuddling. Sacks carry Baby upright on your chest (also allowing for lots of snuggle time).

- ✔ **Swing:** Wind-up swings are cheaper, but you may wake a sleeping infant when it stops. Battery-operated swings allow Baby to rest comfortably and quietly with no disruptions.

- ✔ **Infant seat**: This serves as a safe place for you to put Baby while you're preparing his bottle or folding the laundry.

✔ **Bassinet or co-sleeper**: Most infants need to feed so frequently in the early weeks that it's just more practical to have them in the same bedroom with their parents. A Moses basket–type bassinet is portable, so you can easily move it from room to room during the day. Co-sleepers (cribs with a side that drops down and opens up to the parents' bed) are discussed in Chapter 6.

✔ **Baby bathtub:** After the umbilical cord heals, you can wash Baby in this small tub that fits right into your sink.

Clothing

✔ **One-piece outfits:** You'll choose between *sleepers* (long sleeves, long legs) and *rompers* (short sleeves, short legs), depending on the time of year and/or climate. You need at least eight to ten of these, because babies tend to mess themselves frequently.

✔ **Drawstring nightgowns:** These are easier to manipulate at changing time than clothing with snaps, but they're a bit harder to find in stores these days.

✔ **One-piece undergarments:** Similar to rompers, with short sleeves, no legs, and snaps in the crotch. The one-piece design doesn't bunch up under Baby's clothes, and adds a layer of warmth. Have at least eight of these on hand.

✔ **Mittens:** Some babies are face-scratching champs. These little mitts are designed to cover Baby's hands and protect him from himself.

✔ **Outerwear:** A baby born in Maine in November is going to need a bunting of some sort, a hat, and baby mittens.

✔ **Booties and socks:** Look for foot coverings with fairly strong elastic around the ankles. Babies who kick a lot are often left barefoot while their moms are searching for stray socks.

Supplies

✔ **Changing table supplies:** Stock the table with diapers, a waterproof changing pad, wipes, petroleum jelly (for care of the circumcision), diaper rash ointment, and a garbage can.

✔ **Burp cloths and bibs:** Spare yourself from wearing spit up. Have at least four tiny bibs and/or six burp cloths handy.

✔ **Bottles and formula:** You need four to six 4-ounce bottles during the early months; when Baby starts to eat more, you need four to six 8-ounce bottles. You also need a bottlebrush and a drying rack.

✔ **Breast pump:** After you and Baby have successfully established breastfeeding (around 6 weeks), you can start pumping your milk. Your partner can take over the occasional feeding at that point.

✔ **Breast pads to prevent soaking your clothes:** You'll really come to appreciate these items.

✔ **Diaper bags:** You only use one at a time, but it doesn't hurt to have a backup. These bags are now available in the coolest, hippest fabrics and colors, so you don't have to frump up your cool-parent outfits with a striped vinyl tote.

✔ **Bath supplies:** For sponge bathing Baby, you need baby soap and shampoo, a waterproof pad, cotton balls (for cleaning her eyes), baby nail clippers (or scissors), a comb, a bath thermometer, and a medium-sized bowl for water.

✔ **Pacifiers:** Some babies love 'em, some hate 'em, and some are very particular as to what type of silicone nipple they'll accept. Have several different types on hand if you plan to comfort Baby with a binkie.

✔ **Linens:** You need crib sheets (at least four), a crib quilt or blanket, a bumper pad (protects Baby's head from the side of the crib), receiving blankets (for swaddling, stroller outings, and placing Baby on an otherwise unprotected surface, like the floor), and baby-sized towels and washcloths.

Medicine chest

Losing sight of your furnishings? Hold on — you also need to stock the medicine cabinet with a few must-have items:

✔ **Thermometer:** Ear thermometers are easy to use, but they aren't as accurate as their digital or mercury counterparts. Infants usually have their temps taken rectally, anyway.

✔ **Petroleum jelly:** To help with the temperature taking.

✔ **Nose syringe:** Useful when Baby is congested. (You will actually remove the mucus from her nose, and you'll realize then and there how much you love this child, because you wouldn't do this for just anyone.)

✔ **Cool mist vaporizer:** You may be a fan of hot steam when you're congested, but because those vaporizers can cause severe burns, cool mist is a safer option for Baby's room.

✔ **Medicine syringe and spoon:** For easy, accurate measurement and delivery of medication.

✔ **Bandages, antiseptic, tweezers, anti-itch cream, and diaper rash ointment:** Babies get cuts, slivers, and rashes. Be prepared.

Supplementing the shower goodies

As if the above lists weren't enough, there are some things you may not receive at your shower that you need throughout Baby's first year, such as:

✔ **Clothes, in all sizes:** Sizes you need include infant, 0 to 3 months, 3 to 6 months, 6 to 9 months, and 9 to 12 months. Although it's tempting to purchase everything now, you may want to wait and see how Baby grows. It's not unusual for a big 6-month-old to wear 9- to 12-month clothing.

✔ **Toys:** There are educational toys, amusing toys, and hybrids of each type for every age level. Baby gyms, for example, are a good early toy. They dangle eye-catching toys above Baby's head and encourage development of his hand-eye coordination.

✔ **Bathtub ring:** After Baby is able to sit (or almost), he's ready to move into the real bathtub. These rings are designed to help him sit upright (though you should *never, never* leave him unattended).

✔ **Ring pillows:** Designed to hold Baby during breastfeeding, prop up a smaller baby, and to fit around an older baby's bottom, helping him to sit up.

✔ **Playpen and/or baby gates:** If you wind up with a very active baby, popping him in the playpen may be the only way you'll ever find time to make your lunch. Gates protect Baby from those areas of the house that aren't baby-safe.

✔ **Exercise ring:** Pediatricians generally discourage the use of walkers and jolly jumpers (also called Johnny jumps-ups). There are just too many accidents involved in their use (walkers can easily slip down a flight of stairs with Baby on board, and jolly jumpers can actually flip Baby over on his head). Look for an exercise ring or saucer — Baby can rock and roll to his heart's content, but he can't actually go anywhere.

Taking a bare-bones approach

You're averse, you say, to buying anything before you're sure you need it? Fair enough. Just make sure that before Baby is carried through your front door that you have the following items:

✔ Rear-facing infant car seat

✔ Diapers and changing supplies (listed above)

✔ Clothes suitable for your climate and season

✔ A safe place for Baby to sleep

✔ Bottles and formula, if bottlefeeding

✔ Burp cloths

Packing for the Hospital

You're thinking you don't need all that much for this little trip? After all, you're just going to give birth, and you'll be right home. Rethink this position.

Your labor ultimately determines many of the things you need from home — and unfortunately, there's no way to tell whether yours will be quick and easy or long and arduous. Better to pack too much than to find (too late) that you've forgotten the one thing that would have been a great comfort to you during the delivery.

Don't leave home without:

- ✔ Your insurance card.

- ✔ A digital watch or a watch with a second hand for accurately timing contractions.

- ✔ Change for the vending machines.

  The hospital may want you to pay for TV and phone service in cash. Check with them in advance. If not, change should be all you need, and you're wise to leave big bills and any valuables at home.

- ✔ A list of your loved ones' phone numbers. They'll be waiting to hear the good news!

- ✔ Socks and slippers.

- ✔ A robe to cover yourself up (hospital gowns don't cover your backside very well) in case you want to walk the halls during labor and for walks to and from the nursery afterward. Also pack your slippers for walking the halls.

- ✔ Glasses and contacts.

- ✔ Soap, shampoo, razor, toothbrush, toothpaste, hairbrush, gel, deodorant, hair dryer, and anything else you to make yourself feel fresh. The hospital will supply you with sanitary napkins after delivery.

- ✔ Books, magazines, knitting, crossword puzzles (for the earliest stages of labor and possibly for after delivery, as well).

- ✔ Going-home outfits for you and Baby. Don't pack the jeans you were wearing the week you got pregnant; they probably won't fit for several months. Instead, opt for an outfit for yourself that's comfortable and loose fitting. If it's cold outside, remember that Baby will need to be bundled up on her trip home.

Rethink purchasing and packing a beautiful new nightgown for your hospital stay. You'll be dealing with sanitary napkins again after giving birth, for one thing, and for another, you'll be feeding an infant who won't think twice about spitting up on your new jammies. You can use the hospital gown or an old nightgown from home, but go for comfort over style.

You may also want:

- ✔ Lollipops to prevent a dry mouth. (Hard candies may be all right, but present a choking hazard when you're breathing heavily during labor.)

> ✔ Tennis balls or massage tools for back pain. If you'd like for your husband to use a little lotion during the backrubs, pack that, too.
>
> ✔ Your own washcloth. You may be allowed to hydrate yourself with a moistened washcloth. Do you really want one from the hospital laundry anywhere near your mouth?

Don't forget that you're going to be bringing a new person home with you. You may want to have a packed diaper bag ready to go to the hospital with you, just to make sure all your ducks are in a row. Turn to Chapter 3 for more on what to include in your diaper bag.

Special Delivery! What to Expect After Baby Arrives

This is what you've been waiting nine months for — Baby finally makes her appearance. Nothing can quite prepare you for the experience, and you may be surprised by the flurry of activity that follows your baby's birth. This section touches on what you can realistically expect in the moments and days following Baby's birth.

Wahhh! Baby wants back in!

Why do babies cry when they're born? (This isn't a riddle — there really is a reason.) First off, the cry is an indication that Baby's lungs are working properly. But consider how you'd feel if you were resting happily in a dark, warm, liquid environment and you were suddenly forced out through a tight little tunnel (or through a surgical opening) into a bright, chilly, loud room, where strange people were wiping you down and whisking you from one spot to another, poking and prodding your little body. You'd cry, too.

Testing, testing: How Baby is evaluated after birth

The delivery room nurses spring into action immediately after Baby is born, and you'll hear them talking about Baby's Apgar score, the heel prick, and measurements. What's happening to Baby, and what does it all mean?

The *Apgar score* is an evaluation of Baby's condition taken at one minute after birth, and then again at five minutes. The one-minute score is basically a tool to evaluate how hard the delivery was on Baby. The five-minute score is a better indication of how Baby's adapting to life outside the womb. Newborns who score seven to ten points at five minutes are in good shape; babies who score between four and six points are in fair condition; infants with a score below four are in distress and need lifesaving measures. See Table 1-1 for a complete explanation of Apgar scoring.

Table 1-1	Apgar Score Chart		
Sign	*0 Points*	*1 Point*	*2 Points*
Heart rate	No detectable heartbeat	Slow (under 100)	Above 100
Breathing	No respiration	Slow or irregular breaths	Ample crying
Color	Pale or blue	Blue extremities, pink torso	Pink all over
Reflex irritability	No reaction to stimulation	Facial grimace	Hearty crying
Muscle tone	Limp body	Some flexing of arms and legs	Active movements

Baby's post-birth routine also includes:

- **Measurements:** Baby's length, weight, and head and chest measurements are recorded in the delivery room. The average infant ranges anywhere from 18 to 22 inches; normal weight can range from just-under-7 up to 10 pounds; head circumference averages around 13 centimeters.

- **Vitamin K:** Baby will be given a Vitamin K injection, which promotes blood clotting.

- **Eye drops:** Erythromycin drops are placed in Baby's eyes to prevent gonoccocal or chlamydial infections.

- **PKU test:** Baby's heel is pricked for a blood sample to test for *Phenylketonuria* (or PKU, a metabolic disorder), thyroid disease, and other disorders 48 hours post-delivery. Tests may vary from state to state. Also, expanded testing is available at parents' cost. Your pediatrician will discuss the need for any further testing with you.

- **Blood typing:** Baby's blood type will be tested if Mom has type O or an Rh-negative blood type. Under these circumstances, Mom and Baby may have incompatible blood types, and Baby could develop jaundice and/or anemia.

The umbilical cord blood contains *stem cells* (immune system cells that have the capacity to develop themselves into other types of cells), which have been a hot topic of conversation in the news lately. These cells can be banked (stored) for future treatment of certain cancers, as well as immune and genetic disorders. If you're interested in finding out more about banking stem cells, ask your doctor or even try an Internet search at home. For more information, including a look at the pros and cons of banking your baby's cord blood, check out www.cord-blood.org.

No pictures, please! Mom's experience after the birth

Very few brand-new moms look or feel like a million bucks right after giving birth. And why would they? They've just been through an exhausting and physically demanding experience that may have included highlights like an *episiotomy* (an incision at the base of the vagina that prevents tearing during delivery) or the appearance or worsening of hemorrhoids from all that pushing. Other lingering effects from the birthing process may be bloodshot eyes or broken blood vessels around the eyes (also due to the strain of pushing) and a shaky feeling, due to having used every muscle in your body to get Baby out of the womb. Whether you've had a natural birth or a cesarean section, you're bound to be feeling tired and anxious after delivery.

The aftereffects of giving birth are temporary, but if you're overly sensitive about your image in pictures, delay the family photos for a day or two. When you look back on these pictures, you may want to focus on the bundle of joy in your arms, and not on how exhausted and pained you appear to be.

Don't panic! Baby's less-than-perfect appearance

In many cases, labor is just as hard on Baby as it is on Mom. Some kids seem to pop right out, but others take their sweet time making their debut, which can leave a newborn with a pointy head, smushed facial features, and a generally surprising (even disappointing) appearance in the days after delivery. A baby who has been delivered with the use of a vacuum or forceps may have swelling or bruises on her head.

Good news: Baby's features will realign themselves over the next few weeks, and she'll eventually be the gorgeous little thing you knew she would be.

Immediately after birth, Baby may be covered in a thick, cheesy coating called the *vernix caseosa,* which protected her skin in utero. She'll be wiped down by the nurses in the delivery room.

Baby's skin will be blotchy and her hands and feet may be purple from time to time. This is all due to poor circulation and will improve over the first couple of weeks.

Many new moms are dismayed to realize that their newborns look nothing like the babies on TV or in magazines. Those babies are most likely several months older and have had ample time to overcome the less desirable effects of the birthing process.

Bond. Mom and Baby bond.

Bonding. What is it? Basically, it's the development of a feeling of intimacy between you and your child. You bond with your baby throughout pregnancy, of course, but the bond becomes even more pronounced after birth.

So here you are, just having given birth. Because you've already spent nine months with this child in the womb, you should know what each cry means, what your baby wants when she's moving her head from side to side, looking like she wants to suck on something. You should know how often she's going to sleep, and what to expect from her personality — right?

Not necessarily. Even parents who take to their new roles right away have moments where things aren't going well. And many parents feel completely overwhelmed from the get-go. You may expect to magically turn into Parent Extraordinaire at the moment your child arrives, but that just isn't the case for everyone. Some parents find that they learn about Baby as they go and that their attachment deepens each day.

Give yourself a break here if you're feeling like you've given birth to a stranger. You *have.* You need to give yourself time to get to know this little person.

You can be a great parent even if you never had any interest in dolls as a child, and even if you've never babysat or particularly enjoyed the company of children. Even if you've never had a nurturing bone in your body, things change when you have your own child; the change may not be immediate, but it will definitely happen. (You have a hard time believing someone when they say they would give their own life for their child? Give yourself a couple of months, and you'll wonder how you could have ever felt differently.)

You may not have the slightest idea of how to care for Baby at this point. Thinking about life at home, alone with Baby, terrifies some new parents. So ask for help, and don't be embarrassed. Your nurses see new parents every single day; there isn't a question out there (about babies, anyway) that they haven't already been asked. The nurses want to see you go home happy and somewhat confident about the days to come, so use 'em while you've got 'em.

Many hospitals also have newborn care classes along with the labor/delivery classes (breastfeeding classes too). Take advantage of these opportunities when available. For more tips on bonding with Baby, see Chapter 6.

Rock-a-Bye Baby: The Hospital Nursery

After Baby gets the all-clear from the delivery room doctor, midwife, or nurse practitioner attending the birth, and when you're ready to be moved to a room on the maternity wing, Baby will be rolled off to the nursery, where his every need is met by a staff of trained professionals. (Notice this says Baby's every need — not Mom's every whim. The nursery staff shouldn't be confused with servants.)

Rooming-in

Most hospitals give Mom the choice of whether she wants Baby to sleep in the same room with her or in the nursery. This can be heaven on earth, or a living nightmare. If you had a very long and/or difficult delivery, or if you're just worn out from the experience, you may want to catch a few zzzzs by yourself, especially if Baby is restless. If you're breastfeeding, the nurses are going to bring Baby to you every couple of hours anyway; there's no point in losing more sleep than you have to. Remember, you'll be on call 24 hours a day for the next 18 years. You'll have plenty of time to get to know Baby over that time period.

If you're feeling great and Baby's happy as a little clam, rooming-in can be one of the best experiences you ever have, establishing a bond with your little cutie right off the bat. For more on bonding with your infant, see the section "Bond. Mom and Baby bond." earlier in the chapter.

Relying on help from hospital staff

Although you can safely say that most nurses in this field genuinely love babies, the maternity wing nurse is a very busy individual. He's responsible for assessing and monitoring your health, and for providing you with all of the information you should have about Baby and about your recovery before you leave for home. He's also responsible for assessing and monitoring Baby's health. And because most hospitals adhere to strict budgets, chances are your nurse has other patients, too. That's enough to keep an experienced nurse running from bed to bed for most of the day.

So what can you reasonably expect from the newborn nursing staff — and, just as importantly, what kind of requests are likely to be met with tight smiles or flat-out refusals? Your nurse is there to help you care for your baby and your health. Feel free to call on him in the following situations:

- ✓ **You need time to yourself.** You chose to have Baby room-in, and now you're not getting any sleep? Use that call button. A nurse won't think you're a bad mom for sending Baby to the nursery. Will Baby be coddled there? That really depends on the number of staff available at the time, but even if Baby cries a bit, he'll bear no long-term scars from the experience.

- ✓ **You could use some help with breastfeeding.** You can discuss feeding information with your nurse, and she can give you some tips for easy breast- or bottlefeeding. The lactation specialist may be around during the daylight hours, but at 3 a.m., your nurse can talk you and Baby through latching on.

- ✓ **You're concerned about pain or other health issues.** Your health is a major issue after delivery. Possible complications include infection and hemorrhage. One of your nurse's main concerns is monitoring your recovery, which includes helping you to manage your pain. She's willing to discuss any pain medications your doctor has prescribed and answer any questions you have about your recovery.

- ✓ **You have questions about taking care of Baby.** Nobody becomes an expert immediately after giving birth. Feel free to call on your nurse when you're unsure about anything baby care–related.

  Before you leave for home, your nurse will give you very specific instructions on how to care for Baby, including how to support her neck, how to dress and bathe her, how to keep her safe, and how to keep your own sanity. Listen carefully, and ask as many questions as you can think of.

On the flip side, your nurse won't be happy about personal requests. She won't run down to the gift shop for you. She will expect you to follow the hospital rules, within reason. Sneaking in one extra family member may be something she's willing to tolerate, but inviting the entire clan in at once may be more than she can overlook.

Send relatives to the cafeteria for snacks and drinks — the nurse isn't a waitress and usually has a lot of other things to keep her busy. Most postpartum floors have a refreshment room for patients right on the unit and the staff should be happy to give you and your partner access.

Routine nursery practices

So what goes on in the hospital nursery, anyway? It looks so quiet and peaceful (well, if you can get past the crying babies), but it's really a hopping place.

Baby will have her first complete physical exam by her pediatrician while she's in the nursery. (If you haven't chosen a doctor yet, the pediatrician on call will perform the exam. Tips for finding the right pediatrician are listed in Chapter 1.) There's quite a bit to this, actually, including evaluation of:

- ✔ **Measurements (height, weight, head circumference):** It's normal for an infant's weight to drop several ounces by the time she's discharged. The length measurement may differ from the one done in the delivery room for the simple reason that some babies won't hold still for this.

- ✔ **Heart sounds:** The doc is looking for a normal heart rate and the absence of any heart defects.

- ✔ **Respiration:** A baby's breathing rate is a bit irregular, but a normal infant has 30 to 60 respirations per minute.

- ✔ **The umbilical cord site:** Are there signs of infection?

- ✔ **Palpation of Baby's internal organs:** The doctor will press on Baby's abdomen to feel her organs, making sure none are enlarged.

- ✔ **Extremities, including hips:** The doctor will check for signs of dislocation, which indicates that the top of the thighbone isn't sitting in the hip correctly.

- ✔ **Genitals:** Are they formed correctly? Any signs of birth defects in this area?

- ✔ **Newborn reflexes:** There are quite a few reflexes that doctors check for, all of which are an indication of Baby's neurological health.

Considering circumcision

If your baby is of the male variety and you choose to have him circumcised, you can expect that procedure to be carried out by a physician in the nursery — unless, that is, circumcision is part of a religious ritual for you and you plan to have it done outside the hospital.

Many parents debate the validity of this practice, wondering whether it's necessary or just a barbaric tradition forced upon baby boys in this country. No matter what you decide, someone will tell you that you made the wrong decision. Tell yourself right now that you're the parents, and it's your opinion that counts.

The upside of circumcising your infant:

- ✔ He will look like everyone else, including Dad (if Dad's circumcised, that is), and his friends. Although this may not sound like a valid "pro" to you, it is a common reason parents cite in favor of circumcision.

- ✔ Lowered risk of infections at this time in his life (including urinary tract infections), and lowered risk of certain STDs and cancer of the penis later in life. These benefits arise because it's easier to keep a circumcised penis clean.

- ✔ If he decides that he wants to be circumcised when he's older, the procedure could be far more traumatic for him then. As an infant, of course, he'll have no recollection of the circumcision.

And the downside:

- ✔ Circumcision carries the risk of complications — including hemorrhage and infection, although rare.

- ✔ Although for many years, doctors believed babies didn't feel a thing, studies have shown that babies do feel pain during the procedure. Some physicians use local anesthesia; some hospitals allow the baby to suck on a sugar water soaked pacifier during the procedure to help alleviate pain. The good news is that most babies fall asleep half way through the procedure; after the clamp is on, it stops hurting.

No matter what your decision, discuss circumcision with your pediatrician first. It's a surgical procedure; make an informed decision.

Where's the Milk?

Baby needs to eat. Do you want to breastfeed or bottlefeed? What are the pros and cons of each? Which is simplest? Which is best for Baby? This section provides an overview of choosing between the breast and the bottle, and tips for making each a successful venture.

Deciding between breast and bottle

You'll be making lots of decisions in the days leading up to Baby's arrival; including whether you're going to breastfeed or bottlefeed the little darling.

This is one of those decisions you need to make *before* Baby arrives, because she may be hungry in the delivery room. If you've made the decision to nurse, you'll put Baby to breast as soon as possible in order to stimulate the flow.

Breastfeeding is very popular in some areas of the country and not-so-popular in other regions. If you're leaning toward the bottle because you can't stand the idea of turning your chest into a snack bar, try to have an open mind about the whole thing. Give it a shot. You may be surprised at how easily Baby takes to the breast, and how you really don't mind so much after all.

Breastfeeding pros:

✔ You never have to mix or warm a bottle, which is a great perk when Baby cries at 2 a.m.

✔ It's free.

✔ Very low possibility of allergic reactions.

✔ Studies show that breastfeeding gives Baby a permanent boost to her immune system (she gets a healthy dose of your antibodies every time she nurses).

✔ Breastfed babies are less likely to suffer from constipation and gas.

✔ It really is a sweet way to bond with your child.

Breastfeeding cons:

✔ It may be painful — at first. When your milk comes in, your breasts might feel like hot rocks, and until your nipples are used to Baby's sucking, they may be sore, too.

✔ Risk of nipple and breast infection (mastitis). If Baby is an eager little eater, or isn't latching on the right way, your nipple could develop a crack, which might allow germs from Baby's mouth into your breast.

✔ You're the sole provider of food for your child, which keeps you incredibly busy, particularly during the first few weeks, when Baby feeds at least eight to ten times per day.

✔ You have to watch what you eat. Strong or acidic foods, like garlic or tomatoes, may cause your milk to smell funny, which may lead to Baby's refusal to eat. Caffeine and alcohol also enter the breast milk, and limiting their use is recommended while breastfeeding.

✔ You have to deal with leakage. Investing in some thick, cotton nursing pads and wearing dark tops can help eliminate embarrassing moments.

Though most doctors will tell you that breastfeeding is best for Baby, it's not always possible — for a variety of reasons. If Mom is sick after delivery, for example, she may not be able to nurse. There's also always the possibility of Mom having inverted nipples (which make it extremely difficult for Baby to latch on) or simply not producing enough milk. Not to worry. Baby can get all of the nourishment she needs from a bottle of formula.

Bottlefeeding pros:

- ✔ Feeding your child isn't your sole responsibility. Your partner has no excuse not to get up with Baby once in a while.

- ✔ You can clearly see how much Baby is eating.

- ✔ Bottlefeeders usually sleep through the night sooner than their breast-fed peers do. (More on this in Chapter 8.)

- ✔ Feeding struggles are minimized. You just don't often see a baby who doesn't take easily to bottlefeeding (as opposed to breastfed babies, who sometimes flat-out refuse to feed from their moms).

Bottlefeeding cons:

- ✔ Formula is expensive.

- ✔ Baby doesn't get any of Mom's immunities.

- ✔ Feeding Baby requires planning — you always have to make sure you have a bottle in the diaper bag, and formula in the house.

- ✔ You'll be washing bottles and nipples constantly.

Here comes the milk!

Whether you decided to breastfeed or not, your breast milk comes in around the third day after giving birth. If you are breastfeeding, you'll start nursing as soon as Baby is ready and willing to eat, but until your milk comes in, he'll be receiving *colostrum*, the pre-milk that includes antibodies that are very important to Baby's health.

Your breasts may feel like rocks on the day your milk comes in. They will be engorged with milk. They may be hot. They may hurt. They may be red. They'll begin to leak. And when Baby tries to latch on, you may wince in pain. You may ask yourself why you ever thought that you could do this — and why no one ever told you how painful it was. Mercifully, the pain lasts for only a short time (a day or two).

Keep several bags of frozen veggies in your freezer at home to use as compresses when your breasts feel as though they may explode. Also, try to nurse as often as possible (every 2 hours or so) to alleviate engorgement.

Choosing to bottlefeed won't spare you entirely from the pain of engorged breasts. To ease the pain associated with full breasts, follow the tips for weaning mothers in Chapter 16.

Getting started breastfeeding

A nurse or lactation specialist will be there to help when you first put Baby to breast. *Lactation specialists* are there to answer all of your breastfeeding questions and to make sure that you're comfortable nursing Baby before you're discharged. Even if things are going fairly well, listen to the advice you're given — after you go home, you may have less support in this venture, and you want to feel confident enough with this method of feeding Baby to be able to quiet any anxious relative who pressures you to stick a bottle in Baby's mouth if a nursing session isn't going well.

Ask your nurse or lactation specialist for outside help if you need it. Certain lactation specialists can visit you at home in the days and weeks after delivery to ensure that you and Baby are, indeed, getting the hang of nursing, and to offer advice about how to make things go more smoothly. There are also support groups which offer advice and encouragement for nursing mothers. Your hospital or pediatrician may be able to hook you up with a local group. Your pediatrician can also offer breastfeeding advice and support.

The most important thing for you to remember about breastfeeding is that the more relaxed you are about it, the more likely you are to succeed at it. Although breastfeeding can be difficult for some mothers and babies, that doesn't make it impossible. Breastfeeding sometimes starts off in a less-than-ideal manner — and you shouldn't be discouraged if Baby doesn't take to the breast like a pro. You have plenty of time to work out these kinks, and maintaining a positive outlook is important in these early days.

Getting Baby to latch on can be the biggest hurdle to clear when beginning breastfeeding. Some tips for easing this process:

- ✔ Try to feed Baby as soon as possible after delivery. He's likely to be hungry then, and may work extra-hard to get some nourishment. In the hours and days after delivery, he may be very drowsy and uninterested in putting forth the effort needed to latch on.

- ✔ Cup your breast in your hand and run the nipple on Baby's lips in order to stimulate his *rooting* reflex (which causes him to follow anything touching his mouth).

- ✔ Squeeze a drop of colostrum out of the nipple and have it ready and waiting for him.

- ✔ When he opens his mouth, allow him to latch on to the breast. Don't pull back. Relax as much as possible.

- ✔ Make sure he can breathe comfortably through his nostrils. Signs that he's getting milk include sucking motions, swallowing sounds, a calm baby (who isn't fighting to get food), and a softening of the breast.

What's it really like to breastfeed?

It's strange at first, no doubt about it — just realizing that your body is actually producing nourishment for your child is mind blowing. And it may be a bit uncomfortable in the earliest days, until your nipples get used to the sucking and you get used to having to bare your breasts (though not completely) every couple of hours. After you and Baby settle into it, though, breastfeeding will probably seem perfectly natural and very easy.

Let him nurse as long as he wants; he's learning a brand-new eating technique that doesn't come easy to all infants. You need to burp Baby after he finishes each breast. If he's having trouble emptying one or both sides, try burping him more often.

There are several different breastfeeding positions: The football hold and the cradle positions are among the most popular. The one you use depends on what works best for you and Baby.

For a more complete look at breastfeeding, check out *Breastfeeding For Dummies* by Sharon Perkins and Carol Vannais (Wiley).

Introducing the bottle

What kind of bottle is best for Baby? It really depends on what you're going to be most comfortable with. The standard baby bottle is easy to fill with formula, but is more likely to allow bubbles into Baby's system, which may result in a gassy, wailing, spit-up-spewing child. Bottles with collapsible inserts eliminate most of the bubbles, but take more time to fill and prepare (you have to squeeze the air out of the insert).

Water for mixing Baby's bottle doesn't need to be boiled as long as you have a safe water supply. Also, bottles can be washed in hot soapy water or in the dishwasher — they don't need sterilization.

Bottles with collapsible inserts come with their own nipples, which are supposed to mimic real breasts. Standard bottles also include nipples, but you may have already discovered that a host of different replacement nipples are available. If your child is doing fine with one particular nipple, don't try to force another one on her. If she starts to balk at taking her bottle, though, it may be time to try a new topper to that bottle. There's no hard-and-fast rule as to the nipple-type recommended by nine out of ten babies. You'll have to try several different types until baby stops squirming and starts sucking down her formula.

What kind of formula will you choose? You can ask your pediatrician for a recommendation, but he may very well tell you that all formulas are the same and you should choose what's most convenient for you. Ready-to-feed formulas don't need any mixing; they're like fast food for Baby (albeit much more nutritious than your average drive-through fare). However, they're the most expensive formulas. Liquid concentrate formula is the middle ground; it requires mixing with water, and is less expensive than the ready-to-feeds but more expensive than the powdered formulas, which also require mixing. Powdered mixes go a long way and are the cheapest option per feeding.

When bottlefeeding Baby, make sure her head is higher than the rest of her body. _Don't_ let her lie down flat while she eats or "prop" the bottle on a toy or towel while she eats. Lying flat increases her risk of developing an ear infection; both of these positions ensure that she's also missing out on snuggle time with you, which is an important part of establishing a bond with your child.

Expect your newborn to eat 2 to 4 ounces every two to four hours. She won't respect the fact that you're used to calling it quits for the day at 10 p.m. and sleeping undisturbed for eight hours; she's going to need to eat around the clock. She may eat more during the day and less at night, or vice-versa. Let her establish how much she's going to eat and when.

Tips for mixing formula:

- ✔ Make sure to use a clean bottle. Remember, bottles can be washed in the dishwasher.

- ✔ Use the scoop provided if you're using powdered formula. In any event, follow directions to the letter. Never try to create a super-nutrient-packed formula by adding more formula to less water; likewise, don't dilute the formula with too much water.

- ✔ If you're mixing more than one bottle at a time, store extras in the fridge. There's no need to warm them before feeding Baby.

- ✔ Store open cans of formula in the fridge and use them within 48 hours. Store cans of powder covered, in a cool, dry place, and use within the month.

- ✔ Pour out any bottles that have been sitting at room temperature for two or more hours.

Make sure to burp Baby at least once in the middle of each feeding and immediately after. You'll figure out with time whether she needs more frequent burping. If she slows down her eating while there's still plenty left in the bottle, chances are good she has an air bubble in her tummy. Get your burp cloth handy, and prop her on your shoulder, gently patting her back, or prop her against one hand on your lap while patting her back. For a look at some common burping positions, refer to Figure 2-1.

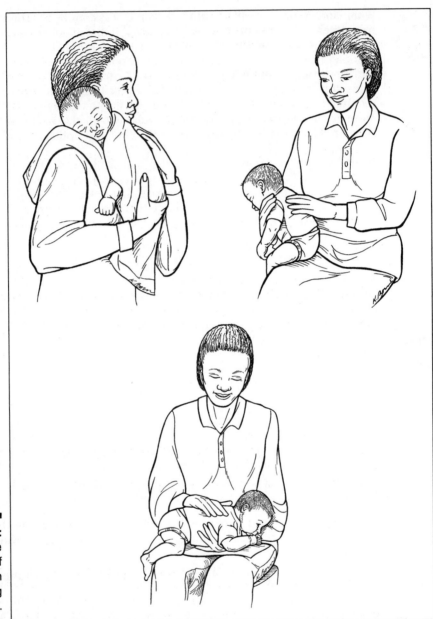

Figure 2-1:
Some
examples of
common
burping
positions.

Feeding a sleepy baby

Baby is tired. He's so very, very tired that he won't even wake up to eat. What do you do?

In the hospital, the nurse will bring Baby to you whenever it's time for him to eat, whether he's awake or not. The nurse will show you some useful tricks for stimulating a little snoozer, including:

- ✔ **Undressing him:** While Baby is warm and comfy cozy in his blankets and jammies, he may not want to be disturbed. This is a good time to change a messy diaper and/or clothes, because this is usually sufficient activity to wake a little sleepyhead. Undressing him down to his diaper may agitate him just enough so that he realizes he *is* hungry, after all.

- ✔ **Tickle, tickle:** Take your finger and run it along the sole of his foot. Or underneath his chin. Or along the sides of his mouth to stimulate his *rooting* (sucking) reflex. This may be enough to bring him out of dreamland long enough for him to eat.

Handling Special Situations

Some parents find themselves facing situations and/or emotions they weren't prepared for. You can do all the reading and research on pregnancy and delivery and still have no idea how you'll fare in certain situations, simply because of the nature of the circumstances. This section gives you tips for coping with postpartum depression, handling two or more babies, and coping with a sick child.

Postpartum depression

Your nurse will almost certainly go over the warning signs of postpartum depression with you before you're discharged. However, because you'll also be receiving so much other information and because you may be too exhausted to remember half of it, I mention it in brief here.

Realize that many, many new moms (some studies suggest the majority of them, in fact) suffer from normal *baby blues* in the first couple of weeks after delivery, which may include bouts of anxiety, general sadness, and mood swings. If you're feeling this way, let it out — talk to your husband, your mom, a friend, your doctor, or Baby's pediatrician. You're not the only woman who has ever felt this way, and no one is going to think any less of you. This is a time of major change in your life — emotionally and physically (your hormones, particularly, may be making you feel unlike yourself) — and that can wreak havoc on your normal coping systems.

Severe postpartum depression tends to have a more gradual onset and lasts for weeks. If you (or your partner) have any of the following symptoms in the weeks after giving birth, call your doctor right away:

✔ Constant crying, perhaps for days on end

✔ Thoughts of harming Baby and/or yourself

✔ Severe fatigue or sleeplessness

✔ No motivation to care for yourself, Baby, or your family

✔ Feeling hopeless and/or helpless

Postpartum depression is real, and it's treatable. There's no shame in asking for help if you need it, so don't try to deal with it by yourself.

Many times blessed: Mom and the multiple birth

If you're a first-time mom giving birth to more than one child, you probably have nothing to compare this experience to — and so much the better for you. Having two or more infants in the house at a time is obviously going to be more time-consuming than bringing home one little guy or girl, but you'll find a way to balance your time and to give each child enough love and attention. You'll have to give it time, but everyone will fall into a schedule eventually, and none of you will be any worse for the wear.

That being said, make sure you have plenty of help lined up for that first month at home. You're going to be juggling babies while you're recovering from giving birth — that's no small task. On top of that, you'll have the logistics to work out (what's the fastest and easiest way to get both twins into their car seats and into the backseat before someone needs to eat?). Having a good support system around you during the early weeks will make your transition much, much easier.

When Baby needs extra special care

Finding out that your child has been born with special health concerns is heartbreaking and terrifying. Fortunately, we're living in an age of medical breakthroughs, and children who are born with special needs are routinely identified and treated earlier than ever before, which means these kids have a better chance at a normal life.

If Baby is identified at birth as having a special health concern, he may be taken to the Neonatal Intensive Care Unit (NICU) for evaluation and treatment. Chapter 18 covers what happens there, and what you can expect.

Gulp! Leaving for Home

After Baby is in your arms, you realize how fragile he really is. His head flops around if you're not holding him correctly, and his little fingers and toes are so tiny, you're afraid you'll break them. Is the hospital staff really going to trust you to take this child home? You're really going to have to dress and diaper him by yourself? Don't they know that you need help?!

Relax. You can do this. In this section, we walk you through some of the first steps. But don't forget to bring your packed diaper bag along. (For more on this, turn to Chapter 3.)

Dressing Baby

When dressing Baby for her departure from the hospital (or any other time, in fact) you need to pick an outfit that's appropriate for the weather. Some moms may advise you to dress Baby similarly to how you're dressed for the day (meaning that if you're wearing shorts, you shouldn't wrap Baby up in flannel). Good rule of thumb, but if you're always sweating (even in the middle of winter), you may not be able to accurately judge how warm or cool Baby is (and because infants can't regulate their body temperature the way adults can, you have to make sure that your child isn't over- or underdressed).

Layers are a good choice for this reason. You can tell if Baby is too warm by feeling for sweat, particularly on the back of her neck. If she's perspiring, remove a layer. If she feels cool to the touch, give her a sweater or a blanket.

When you're dressing Baby, always take special care to see that her neck is being supported. She won't be able to hold her head up consistently on her own until she's about 4 months old.

Try to find clothing for Baby with lots of snaps. The snaps may seem tedious at first, but if you can get Baby's head through a wide shirt hole (surrounded by snaps) without feeling as though you're pulling her through a paper towel tube, you'll both be happier. Make sure you snap up Baby's legs, too, so that her little toes don't get caught if she kicks.

Now boarding . . . Mom and Dad's car

If the idea of dressing Baby for the first time is intimidating, the prospect of taking him for a ride in the car is just insane. (Why do these nurses trust you so much with your child's life? Don't they know you've never done this before?)

It may feel strange when you're actually outside of the hospital with your Baby, ready to roll on home. You may feel like someone from the hospital should really be tagging along, making sure you're being safe enough, giving you pointers for safely transporting your infant from Point A to Point B. (If you're feeling this kind of pressure, this will be the single safest journey you've ever made.)

No hospital will allow you to leave with Baby without first confirming that you have a car seat. It's a law in every state that infants need to be in one, and for good reason. Your arms can't protect your child in the event of an accident. He needs good, sturdy support in the car — at all times.

Car seat installation differs widely, and unfortunately, some reports from police agencies indicate that *most* car seats may be installed incorrectly. You should ideally try to get the seat into your car before Baby is born — just in case there are any major incompatibilities. If you're just not sure whether you've installed it correctly, call your auto club, your local police, your hospital, or your Baby's pediatrician and ask about local car seat inspection sites.

Timing your departure

When Baby is fed and changed, it's time to hit the road. Or, better stated, don't put Baby in his car seat ten minutes before he's supposed to eat, and/or with a loaded diaper. Although some babies sleep through anything while riding in the car, yours may not be one of them. A screaming baby is a major distraction to even the safest driver, so it's in everyone's best interest to take care of Baby's needs before you turn that ignition key.

Arriving home

You pull into your driveway (or parking spot) and realize you've made it from the hospital with Baby in the car, and everyone is safe. Whew!

Now what?

Don't plan on having a house filled with guests when you come home with Baby. Although everyone is chomping at the bit to see the little guy, establish a firm but friendly time limit (such as saying you won't be up for visitors for at least couple days or even a week — and no, your mother is not a *visitor*, so if you want her there to hold your hand, you don't need to explain that to your mother-in-law). You've just been through a major physical ordeal, and you need to give yourself time to rest, even if you're feeling mostly fine and dandy.

You also want to give yourself some time to settle into this brand-new phase of life. Life is no longer all about you and your husband and what the two of you feel like doing at any given moment — it's all about Baby now, and his schedule (which may be irregular for the next few months). It'll take time for you to fall into the groove of caring constantly for another human. That's natural. It will be much easier on you, though, if you aren't also feeling pressured to invite the world over and serve them coffee while they're there.

Chapter 3

Hitting the Road with Baby on Board

*Y*ou already know that staying home and caring for Baby can be stressful. Try taking that show on the road without adequately preparing for it, and you find out what real stress is!

Traveling with your child can be a veritable piece of cake, or it can be a nerve-shattering experience. The secret to not losing your mind? Look at each trip as a learning experience for your *next* venture.

Preparing for the Journey

You want to make sure before you leave your house that you've packed everything you'll need while you're en route. If you're traveling domestically, you can probably purchase almost anything you've forgotten, after you arrive at your destination.

Checklist for traveling with babies:

✔ **The diaper bag:** This bag may be the most important factor in your traveling success. Move the contents of your changing table right into your bag. Here's what you need:

- **Diapers:** Don't underestimate here. Pack plenty of extras.

- **Wipes:** Again, don't skimp here. You need them for diaper changes and for cleaning hands en route. You can buy a portable wipe container at the grocery store.

- **Diaper rash cream:** Sitting in a car seat for long periods could make Baby's bottom red.

- **Bottles, formula, and water:** If you're bottlefeeding, or if you're feeding Baby breast milk from the bottle.

- **Burp cloths:** Pack at least two burp cloths. Napkins won't do the trick if she spews on your lap in the airport.

- **Bibs:** To keep bottlefeeders and solid eaters as clean as possible so that you won't have to change outfits at 30,000 feet.

- **Pacifiers, if Baby uses them:** You want to promote calmness while traveling; if the binkie does the trick, use it.

- **Change of clothing:** Or two, or three. Despite your best efforts at keeping Baby clean, her outfit may start to stink. Also pack Ziploc bags to hold soiled diapers (nobody else wants to smell that in the airplane trash can) and to hold wet or spit-up covered clothes.

- **Snacks, if Baby is old enough:** Keep these simple and safe — nothing sticky, nothing too chunky. Variety helps — include several small bags of different snacks instead of one big bag of Cheerios.

- **Toys:** Bring along some of Baby's favorites, but also have a few brand-new playthings to keep Baby entertained. The quieter these toys are, the happier you'll be over the course of a long trip. (And your fellow travelers will thank you, too.)

✔ **Clothing appropriate for your destination:** Again, don't underestimate here. If you're going to your parents' house, you can do some laundry easily enough; if you're headed to a hotel, however, you want enough clean clothes to last most of the time you're there. No one wants to spend a vacation in a laundromat.

✔ **A small container of laundry soap:** To hand-wash or pretreat stains.

✔ **Stroller:** Most can be checked with the luggage at the airport. If you have a car seat/stroller combination, call your airline to find out whether you can store the stroller component onboard the plane or whether it has to be checked.

✔ **Carrier:** If you're planning on doing a lot of walking and you don't want to lug a stroller along, bring a front-carrier or a backpack (for an older baby *only*).

✔ **Portable crib:** If you're checking into a hotel, call ahead to reserve a crib. If you're going to your sister's house, pack the portable crib.

✔ **Medicines:** You're on vacation and Baby starts cutting her molars in the middle of the night. Do you really want to search for a pharmacy? Pack any pain and cold medication Baby has already been given. If Baby has never had the need for any meds, check with her pediatrician before you leave to discuss the best options and correct dosages.

✔ **A watch set to home time:** Baby doesn't really care what time the clock in a new time zone says — she wants to eat when she's hungry. Having a watch set to *her* time zone helps you to schedule your plans for the day.

✔ **Bring your own car seat:** You can check this on the plane. Car rental companies may not have the most modern, up-to-date (and safety standards) car seats to rent, and they charge you a bundle to use them. Plus, you're more familiar with how to strap your own seat into the car and how to strap the baby safely. It's a hassle, but it's best to bring your own.

Traveling with Baby

Traveling with Baby is full of challenges, and just when you think you have the hang of it, Baby grows and changes — and presents all kinds of new ways to test your parental fortitude.

Planning a successful out-of-town excursion with your infant isn't impossible — in fact, because Baby will be far more active in a relatively short time, this is a golden opportunity to bring your child along without having to chase after her.

When Baby moves past the infant stage, you'll find that travel becomes a bit more of a challenge. For instance, when she cried at 1 month, she either needed milk or a fresh diaper, but when she becomes more observant of the world around her, you have to worry about entertaining her during long trips. If she develops very definite food preferences, you'll be wise to have her favorites close at hand to ward off the munchies (and crabbiness). And if she just can't bear to be in that car seat, you're going to wonder if you can take another trip before Baby's a big kid (and out of the seat for good).

No matter when or where you travel, flexibility is the key to enduring — and actually enjoying — this new phase of travel.

Allotting a whole lotta time

No matter where you're headed with Baby — halfway around the world or to Grandma's house — give yourself plenty of extra time. Babies are unpredictable and totally unconcerned with punctuality. And you, as a somewhat frazzled new parent, are likely to find yourself running through the house at the last minute looking high and low for the blankie Baby just won't leave home without.

Make lists of everything you need for your trip and pack early. Caring for an infant is a labor-intensive, time-consuming job, and you'll find out soon enough that the combination of fatigue and the sheer overload of this new, exciting experience can make a parent forgetful. You may find yourself rifling through the diaper bag during a long car trip, knowing that you meant to pack extra wipes, but finding none.

Baby loves his schedule, so always make sure that Baby's needs are going to be met at about the time he'll expect, or adjust his schedule slightly to work in your favor. Feeding him before you get in line at the airport ticket counter — even though he isn't scheduled to eat for another 30 minutes — will make your life much easier (when you're still standing in line 30 minutes *after* he was supposed to eat). This kind of adjustment takes planning, and planning is difficult when you run into the airport with no time to spare.

Although your mother may put off serving dinner if you're 20 minutes late, the airline is going to be indifferent. They won't hold your flight just because Baby filled his diaper as you were walking out the door. Even if you've never been punctual —perhaps *especially* if you've never been punctual — you need to give yourself some wiggle room when you're traveling with Baby and time is of the essence.

If you're taking a long car trip, plan on making frequent stops to let Baby out of his seat — for comfort reasons, for diaper changes, and for feedings. These extra stops may stretch a five-hour trip into the six-and-a-half hour range. Keeping a positive attitude about the length of a trip with Baby is of the utmost importance. There's really nothing you can do about it — the kid has to eat, he needs a fresh diaper every few hours, and he has to get out of that seat once in a while.

Try not to overplan the trip (by marking exactly where and how often you're going to stop). Babies are unpredictable people. Maybe your little guy will sleep from Point A to Point B. Or maybe he'll start wailing way before your first planned stop.

It's wise for mom to get out and walk around every two hours during a car trip or flight. Prolonged sitting can increase the risk of blood clots in your legs during the postpartum period.

Feeding Baby en route

With all the luggage and lists of last-minute things to do, it may have slipped your mind that you're going to work Baby's normal feeding schedule into your travel plans. If you're breastfeeding, you're about to be faced with a lack of privacy that perhaps you haven't thought about much until now; if Baby takes a bottle, you need to have a plan for keeping the formula flowing while you're en route and out of town.

Breastfeeding

What's more uncomfortable than breastfeeding Baby in an airport terminal?

If you answered "A lot of things," your trip is going to be a breeze. If you answered "Nothing!" you may already be trying to think of another way to feed your child while you're traveling.

Breastfeeding in public is no longer the big deal it was generations ago. You don't have to be overly modest, though, to feel a little strange about nursing in public areas. Unfortunately, when you're traveling, you don't always have a lot of privacy.

Use a baby blanket as a shield. It's light enough so that Baby won't overheat underneath it, and big enough to cover you completely. Or carry Baby in a sling. (Where it's advisable — babies should not be in a sling during a flight. The next section addresses how to safely transport Baby on an airplane.) Chances are, no one will even know when Baby is nursing.

Some airports have a lounge for nursing mothers. This may be located in or near the restroom, and the space often provides a chair and some quiet for a feeding session.

Breastfeeding is (literally) the most natural thing in the world, and if you're feeling fine about nursing Baby whenever, wherever, don't hesitate to do so because you're worried about offending others. (If they're truly bothered by you feeding your child, let *them* find another spot to sit.) It's legal to breast-feed your child in every state (as long as you have a legal right to be on the premises — in other words, as long as you aren't breastfeeding while tres-passing). Ignore (or educate) anyone who tells you otherwise.

Bottlefeeding

Feeding a bottlefed infant on the road takes some planning. It's easiest to pack bottles in your diaper bag filled partway with liquid formula base, and to have distilled water on hand to dilute it, just to be on the safe side: You don't want to use an unfamiliar water source to mix Baby's bottle. As long as there's a safe water supply available, water to mix formula doesn't need to be boiled — and while you're sure of the cleanliness of your home water supply (or the water at Grandma's house), you don't want to take risks with the water in foreign countries, where hygiene standards are not always on par with our own. If you're going camping, or your only water source on a road trip is the rest stops along the way (which aren't always clean and don't always provide potable water), it's best to bring along a jug of distilled water for Baby's formula. That way, there's no question about the safety or cleanli-ness of the water supply.

Well water should never be used in Baby's bottles or for preparing his food, as it may be high in nitrates, which can lead to something called blue baby syndrome. (More details on this in Chapter 10.)

Make sure that you've packed enough formula in case you're delayed somewhere unexpectedly.

Staying safe on airplanes

Jetting off to Paris right after Baby is born? You may want to rethink that plan, because most airlines don't allow infants younger than 7 days old to fly, and some doctors recommend that you keep Baby out of the friendly skies until she's at least 2 or 3 months old. Seems that airplanes are havens for recycled germs, and a tiny infant is not only more susceptible to catching colds (because her immune system is immature), but is also likely to get much sicker than an older baby (and that's the last thing you want when you're out of town).

Children under 2 fly free on domestic flights in the United States, as long as they can sit on a caregiver's lap (who is, of course, sitting in a full-fare seat). We strongly recommend against this practice. It doesn't take a horrifying plane crash to injure a child who isn't in a car seat during a flight — a bumpy ride may be enough. Infants need constant neck support. The fact is, your arms simply aren't strong enough to protect Baby on an airplane in the event of severe turbulence, a rough landing, or an emergency situation. Also, in the event of depressurization, *one* air mask pops down from above your seat. (Enough said.)

Pay the extra fare and get Baby her own seat, if only to give you peace of mind during the trip. Airlines often offer a discount on seats for children under 2, so they're doing their part to keep Baby safe — make sure you do yours.

You may wonder whether it's safe to keep Baby in a front-carrier or a sling during a flight. At least then, she's being held close to your body no matter what, and you're not relying solely on your own strength to protect her. But again, this isn't something we recommend. Some airlines may not permit these carriers during a flight, for one thing, and for another, there's still the issue of Baby's fragile neck. The sling and the carrier just don't offer the same support as a car seat in the most extreme conditions. Why take the chance?

Handling car-seat disputes

The back arches. The wailing begins. Baby's face and entire head turn red from the force of his screaming. The car-seat wars have begun.

No matter how long the trip, avoid the urge to take Baby out of his seat when you're in a moving car or for long periods of time on a flight. He really is safest in his seat, even if he doesn't quite appreciate that fact. Accidents happen quickly and most often without any warning. Your goal may be to quiet and comfort him by removing him from the seat, but when you do that, he's also more exposed to the inherent dangers of travel.

But listening to Baby scream in the car is a safety hazard in itself if you're the one who's driving, and you can be fairly certain that your fellow passengers onboard the plane don't want to hear Baby's screeching for the next three hours.

Do some troubleshooting to begin with:

- ✔ Could he be hungry?
- ✔ Does he need a new diaper?
- ✔ Is it naptime?
- ✔ Is he too warm?
- ✔ Is anything pinching or scratching him? (A tag in his shirt might be driving the poor kid crazy.)

On the other hand, if Baby's just plain miserable because he's confined (unjustly, in his little mind) to his seat, and it's nowhere near his naptime, you'll have to do your best to either distract or soothe him. This is the exact reason you've packed that diaper bag to nearly bursting. Get out the goodies, and keep them coming (slowly — don't overwhelm and/or smother him with surprises; this could annoy him even more). A favorite toy or stuffed animal may do the trick or at least buy you a few minutes of quiet. A snack may make him downright happy. Read one of his favorite baby books, play some finger games, or quietly sing him a favorite lullaby. Baby's ears may pop with the change in altitude. A pacifier or bottle can help to ease this discomfort.

And even if naptime *is* fast approaching, don't be confident that sleep will just overtake your traveling baby. All bets are off when she's not in her own crib *and* in the midst of all sorts of new stimuli, which may cause her to fight sleep. If she appears to be wide awake when she's due for a snooze, rub her little head. Offer her a pacifier. If you're waiting for a flight, hold her, pat her back, rock her back and forth. Even if she doesn't fall asleep, you'll probably quiet her down for a while, and that's better than nothing.

Remain calm — even if you're extremely close to blowing a fuse while Baby is demanding his right to be free of the car seat. Do whatever it takes — take deep breaths, count to ten, concentrate on the scene out your window (or on the tip of your shoe, for that matter) for a minute — but try not to react with anger. Baby isn't old enough to be reasoned with, and he's not screaming to be naughty. He just wants out of that seat — *now*. Raising your voice to him will most likely make the situation worse. Two of the greatest challenges of parenting are summoning patience and understanding when you need it most. Think of this as an opportunity to practice these virtues. (No, *really*.)

Vacation? What Vacation?

Realize before you make your vacation plans that your traveling days have changed forever. Gone are the days when you could sleep until 10 a.m., hit the beach until 4 in the afternoon, nap until early evening, and top the night off with drinks and dancing. Vacationing with babies and kids is pretty much packing up your normal life and moving it to a more scenic locale. The kid runs the show until he's mature enough to accept that he isn't the center of the universe (about the next 20 years).

Schedules, fatigue, and frequent diaper changes are all part of your vacation now. You probably won't be eating in the finest restaurants or toting Baby along to that hot new show. Instead, you'll be eating in whichever restaurant can serve you the fastest (Baby has no interest in watching you eat) and visiting the local zoo.

You may be able to include some of the things you love to do when you travel with Baby, but certain types of trips are of almost no interest to small children. If you're an avid hiker, for example, you may be able to tote Baby along for a relatively short trek in a backpack carrier, but if spending all day sightseeing is your thing, you're probably out of luck. Baby's schedule and dislikes dictate your planning. If she needs a two-hour nap in the afternoon and is in bed at 7 p.m. every evening, you just have to work your daily itinerary around her timetable. Ditto for mealtimes. And if the kid doesn't like to sit still in her stroller, you can forget planning any vacation that involves a lot of walking on your part.

Choose a destination that mirrors Baby's activity level. If she loves to run, make sure you're near a park. If she loves to sit and watch the world go by, tote her around the big city. Don't expect Baby to conform to your expectations of a particular vacation. Mold the activity levels to best suit her needs.

Generally speaking, it's easiest to take babies somewhere you can reasonably create the surroundings and comforts of home. Renting a house or condo is a good choice for this reason. You can still put Baby to bed on time, in her own room, and you won't have to tiptoe around a hotel room for fear of waking her.

Revising your master vacation plan

Vacationing with a small child can feel like more work than it's worth, especially if you're used to taking care of no one but yourself when you travel. Adapting gracefully goes a long way toward helping you enjoy your trips with Baby. For example, when their daughter Abby was an infant, Dr. Gaylord and his wife took her on a camping trip. Abby's colic decided to come along for the ride, but instead of packing it in and returning home, the Gaylords found themselves fashioning a hammock to swing and soothe their little one (thus also sparing other campers from her cries). The family had a successful first outing into the wild, and the memories from that trip are, of course, priceless.

It's hard to imagine — before finding yourself in similar circumstances — that you can accept and adapt to the workload involved with traveling with a child and still be able to enjoy yourself. It's a whole new ballgame, for sure, but the benefits outweigh the drawbacks by far. Every time you take your child on a trip, she's exposed to new situations — and so are you. Essentially, your child is learning about a different environment, while you're learning more about her, about yourself (and what you're capable of dealing with), and about your family dynamic.

Traveling with Baby is, for all of the extra planning and worry, completely worth it. Every vacation is practice for the next one, and an added opportunity to get to know your child better.

A bottlefed baby can be left behind with a trusted caregiver if Mom feels the need to escape on her own (or with her spouse) for a few days. Breastfeeding moms, on the other hand, may spend their entire vacation without Baby pumping breast milk. Either way, when a new mom leaves Baby at home, she's often surprised to realize how much time she spends worrying or thinking about her child.

Keeping Baby Safe Away from Home

Having realistic expectations about vacationing with your child actually means dreaming up anything that could possibly happen while you're away. Is he going to sleep well? Could he possibly get sick? Who will stay in the condo (or hotel) with him while he naps, and who will get a nice, long break? Work out as many details as you can before you leave, including the pre-emptive strikes (packing cold medicine, for example), and you'll have much less to stress over when you arrive at your destination.

Here are some tips for keeping Baby protected while you're out of town with him:

- ✔ **Assess any potential baby hazards the moment you arrive, and be prepared to remedy them.** Bring along a package of plug guards, for example, and put drapery cords up high where Baby can't reach.

- ✔ **Bring sunscreen.** Apply it often and liberally. Babies under 6 months of age should be kept out of the sun entirely.

- ✔ **Watch those waves.** Even if it's a relatively calm day, an unexpected wave can come up on the beach, knocking Baby down and dragging him into the water. Keep Baby out of the ocean, even if you're carrying him. If a wave hits you, you could lose your grip on your child. Stick to the pool, and maintain constant physical contact with him there.

- ✔ **Never leave Baby unattended.** Not in a car, the airport, not in a hotel room, not for a moment. An overheated car can turn into a deathtrap for a child in a matter of just a few minutes, and though rare, abductions do happen to normal people.

- ✔ **Know where the nearest hospital or emergency room is.** In the event of illness or injury, you don't want to lose any time finding help for Baby.

Chapter 4

Returning to Work?

In This Chapter

▶ Making the right decision for you

▶ Getting the best childcare

*W*hile you were pregnant, you may have thought that working after Baby was born would be a piece of cake. After all, you're far more familiar with the parameters of your job than with the parameters of parenting; so going back to work is really no big deal.

Except that you have to find someone qualified and capable to care for your child as well as you would care for her yourself. And you have to leave Baby. Nothing is easy 'bout that.

Looking for good childcare can seem like a crapshoot — after reading this chapter, we hope you will feel it is less of a gamble and more of an informed decision. For a more complete look at hunting down the right sitter or center, read *Choosing Childcare For Dummies* by Ann Douglas (Wiley).

Making the Big Decision

Every mom is a working mom. (And that ain't just lip service.) Some moms, of course, are faced with the decision of whether to work outside of the home. For many, that decision looms toward the end of the second month, when six- and eight-week maternity leaves come to an end. Some new moms have to make the decision even sooner, out of economic need or because they simply don't have the leave time from their jobs.

Realize from the start that each situation has its benefits and its drawbacks. Moms who work in an office building sometimes suffer from the heartbreak of not being with their babies, and moms who stay home sometimes feel as though they're not appreciated by society — or by their families.

Returning to work doesn't have to be an all-or-nothing situation. Maybe easing back into the workplace part-time would work best for you; perhaps taking a leave of absence for six months or a year is an option. You may be able to quit your current job and easily find a new one whenever you're ready to jump back into the workforce. Get creative with your thinking here; resist the temptation to simply follow the same path that your friends have followed when faced with juggling kids and work. Determine what will make you feel best about yourself — as a parent *and* as a person — by asking yourself what you need most. Do you have to be home with Baby in order to feel fulfilled or do you need to have an adult, work-oriented outlet? Happy parents have happy children. It's really that simple.

Every mom eventually comes to the conclusion that she's darned if she does and darned if she doesn't — work, that is. It's best to make this major decision based on what you and your partner feel is best for your family and then ignore the naysayers (and there will always be *someone* who will think you've made the wrong choice). So ignore your in-laws, resist the temptation to listen to your work friends (who want you back at any cost), turn off the TV shows that show working moms balancing everything easily and stay-at-home moms who are miserable, and determine what's going to work best for *you*.

Considering the pros and cons of working away from home

How will returning to your office job affect your tiny infant? Honestly, very little, as long as you find a good caregiver to fill in for you. Baby is pretty adaptable, and far too young to suffer from separation anxiety (something which will kick in closer to the end of the first year). In order to make an informed decision, give some thought to how returning to work may affect *you*.

Here are a few things to consider:

- ✔ **Work stress:** How much will you be expected to do? How many hours per week do you anticipate working? How often will you have to work late?

- ✔ **Baby — and all of his needs:** Are you ready to leave a busy workday and come home to the second shift (feeding, changing, and bathing Baby)? Nursing Baby after you return to work is absolutely possible, but it requires advanced planning on your part. We discuss this in detail later in this chapter.

- **Feeding and clothing the family:** How will you tackle dinner and laundry — the two ever-present (and unending) tasks of working moms everywhere? How willing to pitch in and help out is your partner?

- **General expenses:** Does it make financial sense for you to return to work? Although some moms choose to work because it fulfills them personally, others who are doing it strictly for the money are sometimes surprised to find that they're spending more than they're making when they rejoin the workforce. More on that in the "Divvying up the dividends" section.

Some women are able to return to work without missing a step — from the get-go, everything runs smoothly. Others find that returning is a lot harder than they imagined. Your level of organization and your tolerance for things not running as smoothly as you'd like (at least once in a while) will most likely have some effect on how you come to view life as a working mom.

Divvying up the dividends

If you have the luxury of being able to make ends meet without returning to work, and you have no desire to step foot in your former workplace, your decision is an easy one. However, if you're on the fence about going back to work and you're not quite sure about the money, add up the hidden costs of working outside the home and make sure that you're not going to lose money by going off to work:

- **Wardrobe:** How much do you spend on pantyhose, shoes, and new business outfits over the course of a month?

- **Food:** Do you brown-bag it or do you join your colleagues for frequent lunches on the town? Does your morning commute include a pricey cup of coffee and an expensive pastry?

- **Commuting:** Add up your gas and the wear-and-tear on your car. In some instances, just *having* a second car is a work-related expense (though out in the suburbs, most stay-at-home moms like to have a car at their disposal, anyway).

- **Childcare expenses:** Day care, nanny, sitter — they all cost you.

- **Take-out:** At the end of the day, do you feel the need to order out so that you can spend more time with Baby?

Now, when you crunch these numbers, be honest. Don't tell yourself that you only spend $50 a month on lunches out when in reality you order a $6 pastrami-on-rye sandwich at the deli every day. And although some of these costs are redundant, some of these expenses are likely to be higher than they would be if you were at home. For instance, you *do* need to eat, so it's not as though staying home will totally eliminate your food bill, but remember that by staying home, you could make that same pastrami-on-rye for a fraction of the cost that the deli charges you.

Now, if you do the math and you come out ahead at the end of the month, you're in a good spot — especially if you *want* to go back to your office. Your income could make your life easier all the way around: Hiring a cleaning lady or picking up take-out on your way home from work are ideal ways to make your evenings more relaxed, and to give you more playtime with Baby.

On the other hand, it's tough finding yourself in a pickle where your income is crucial to the family's well-being but you *don't* want to go back to work. Before you make a unilateral decision about quitting your job, you and your partner need to sit down and have a pow-wow about the family finances. A lot of couples find that they really can cut back on their expenses and live on one income (even a rather meager salary). It's not an easy thing to do (especially if you've become accustomed to buying whatever you want, whenever the mood strikes you), but in many cases, it's entirely within the realm of possibility. Check out *Frugal Living For Dummies* by Deborah Taylor-Hough (Wiley) for tips on living within (or even below) your means.

Handling working-mom guilt

Some moms have to go back to work in order to make ends meet or because their job carries the family's medical benefits. But what if you don't have to work — but you know you just can't stay home? What will people say? *Who cares?*

Admitting to yourself that your work makes you happy is *not* a bad thing. A happy mom is what every baby needs, after all.

There's nothing wrong with wanting adult interaction during the day, or with craving the satisfaction you get from your work. Staying home with an infant isn't every mom's idea of heaven. As long as you find a caregiver who can nurture Baby while you're bringing home the bacon, your child will be fine. *Really.*

Some families choose to have Dad stay home instead. What a great opportunity to have a parent at home with the baby when Mom's income potential and health insurance or benefits are better. Don't forget this as an option! More Dads stay home with their kids today than many of us realize. It *is* macho to be a caregiver!

Working breastfeeding into your worklife

Returning to work doesn't mean you must wean Baby from the breast. You *do* need to learn to express your milk in the most efficient way, however, so that you aren't spending every minute of your downtime filling bottles for the next day.

Expressing milk by hand is an option, but it can be messy and very time-consuming. Breast pumps are good options for most breastfeeding moms — though you'll have to determine whether an electric or manual model works best for you. Check with your pharmacy to see whether they rent electric breast pumps. Many do. Look for a double-sided pump that pumps both sides at once — you may feel like a cow at the milking machine, but you'll be done in half the time!

There really isn't a general recommendation concerning which breast pump works best. Every woman is physically different, so the pump that worked wonders for your sister may leave you feeling full and sore — and with nary an ounce in the collection cup.

Be sure to discuss your nursing situation with your boss and co-workers on a need-to-know basis. You need to express milk at work just to keep your supply up, and you need a quiet, private area, free (or almost free) of distractions to ensure a productive pumping session. (So be sure to tell the intern from the mailroom to hold your packages during your lunch break.) You also need access to a refrigerator to store your milk until it's time to go home.

Working from home

Bringing your work right into your home office (even if it *is* technically a dining room) is a growing trend among moms, and for several good reasons:

- No commute
- No wardrobe expense
- You can often set your own schedule
- You can nurse Baby while working
- It's the best of both worlds — accomplishing career goals while not sacrificing time with Baby

Working from home isn't all strawberries and cream, though. It actually has some drawbacks, including:

- **Isolation:** The biggest challenge for many moms who don't work outside of the house is feeling cut off from the world. You have to accept that you won't go to lunch with your co-workers and you won't always be able to bounce ideas off colleagues.

- **Motivation:** You really have to be a self-starter and be disciplined enough to follow through on projects without having a boss to prod you along — all in spite of an extremely demanding "boss" who's still in diapers.

> ✔ **Juggling too many responsibilities:** You just may feel as though you're expected to work, take care of Baby, and keep house *simultaneously.* And you thought your old job was stressful.

Keeping your expectations on the realistic side is an incredibly important part of working side-by-side with Baby. Although you're working your career around him, he's still at center stage. When he's a tiny infant, he's not going to delay any of his needs so that you can work. When he wants to nurse, you'd better be able to feed him. When he needs a nap, you won't be able to run to the post office to overnight a letter across the country.

Having someone to call on in times of work-related emergencies (your boss wants you to come into his office *pronto*) is a sound plan for moms who choose to work from home. If you simply don't have that luxury, try to take each day as it comes and learn from each experience — positive and negative — what you can do to make life run a little more smoothly.

Becoming a full-time mom

Choosing to stay home full time is a major decision, especially if you worked 40 hours a week before Baby came along. You're losing your income, your benefits, and — most importantly to many women — your identity as a career woman. Moving into full-time mom mode results in a whole realignment of how you're seen and judged by others and by yourself.

Staying at home is a luxury that many moms would love to have. Even so, you may find yourself accused of being lazy or putting pressure on your spouse to become the sole supporter of the family. Develop a thick skin and remind yourself that you've made the best decision for yourself and for your family.

A big problem stay-at-home moms face is the equitable division of household duties. Is it fair for a mom who isn't working outside of the home to expect her husband to help out with the baby or the chores when he comes home at night? The answer is yes! Don't expect him to do the laundry, iron, *and* mop the floor, but he should be able to give you a break from Baby at some point, because, after all, you've been working all day, too.

Identify — and *communicate* — your expectations concerning your partner's pitching in around the house. This is brand-new territory for him, too. He may not know that you *want* help at the end of the day. Furthermore, if he's had no prior experience with infants, he may truly believe that you're spending your days napping and gabbing on the phone while Baby sleeps contentedly in his bassinet. Give him the opportunity to spend some time with Baby alone so that he knows that it really is hard work to care for an infant day-in, day-out.

Fitting work into your day

Working from home while caring for a baby presents all kinds of challenges, and figuring out how to accomplish the bazillion things you need to do is one of the biggest. Sticking to a schedule as much as possible can help your days to run smoothly. Run errands first thing in the morning. Schedule playtime during your lunch hour. Plan business calls around Baby's naps.

But realize that your day may not go exactly according to plan (if Baby becomes ill and you end up in the pediatrician's office, for example, instead of finishing up an already-late project), and allow yourself some leeway. Save more time-consuming projects until dad gets home so he can occupy baby and you can focus on work for a couple of hours.

Most importantly, let the less important, less urgent matters go for now. The house may be in need of a good scrub-down, but it's even more critical for your family to find its groove in these infant days.

Finding Childcare

Whether you're thinking about putting Baby in day care, placing her with a private sitter, or bringing a nanny into your home, you've got your work cut out for you. Each choice requires a fair amount of research to ensure that Baby will be left in the most capable hands.

To ease your search:

- ✔ **Know your priorities.** Are you looking for a day care down the street from your workplace, or around the corner from your house? Is cost a major consideration, or is money no object? Do you want your child in a group setting or in a one-on-one situation? Narrowing your choices from the get-go will make your search that much easier.

- ✔ **Do your research.** Ask other parents for recommendations before you do anything else. They'll be eager to tell you about a day care they had a good experience with, and even more eager to tell you what they discovered about lesser day-care situations along the way.

- ✔ **Interview the candidates.** Set up a face-to-face meeting with a prospective caregiver and don't be shy about asking the hard questions.

No matter which direction you're leaning in — finding a day-care center or a nanny — give yourself plenty of time to do your research and to make a decision. Begin your research while you're still pregnant, if possible, so that you're not faced with a time crunch (when you find yourself with a week left on your maternity leave and no arrangements made for Baby!). This one decision will determine your child's comfort level — and, by extension, how well your return to work goes, so *don't rush it.* For a more complete look at this topic, read *Choosing Childcare For Dummies* by Ann Douglas (Wiley).

Checking out day cares

Realize that the most reputable centers often have waiting lists, so the sooner you start investigating day-care options in your area, the better your chance of getting your child into your first choice. Call ahead and make an appointment to tour the facility. Questions you'll want to ask include:

- ✔ **How long has the center been in business?** There's no "right" answer for how long a day care should be in business. Some parents may be more comfortable knowing that the center has been around for a long time, and a center that has been open for years and years may also have the benefit of having built a solid reputation.

- ✔ **Are you licensed?** There is a difference between licensed and unlicensed providers. Check out the rules in your state. If you choose an unlicensed sitter or facility, especially watch caregiver to child ratios.

- ✔ **What kind of training and/or education do the staff members have? Are they infant-CPR certified?** You want to know that your child is being left in capable, experienced hands. Ask how long the employees have been working there, what the center's training policy is, and what the training consists of. (Is training a one-hour thing, or a monthly requirement? The latter is better). Also, there should always be at least one staff member on the premises who is trained in infant and child CPR.

- ✔ **How are staff members screened for employment?** Has the center done a background check for drugs, felonies, child abuse? Have *all* employees (caregivers and maintenance workers alike) been screened?

- ✔ **How do you handle an infant's feeding and sleep schedules?** Infants eat and sleep when they need to eat and sleep. It's unwise to try to foist a rigid schedule on an infant.

- ✔ **Will I have to provide diapers and wipes or are they included in the monthly fee?** Just an extra cost to consider.

- ✔ **Center hours? Weekly fees? Extra fees for late pickup or early drop off? What about their holiday schedule?** You obviously want to find a place that will fit into your work schedule. Keep in mind that good child-care is oftentimes expensive, but that an expensive day care isn't necessarily good. Don't plunk down your money without checking it out. If you're going to be late from time to time, you may be charged for it — ask now so that you aren't left reeling from the bill later. And if you're going to be working on Christmas Eve and the Fourth of July, make sure your day-care provider is going to be working, too.

✔ **What's your sick-baby policy?** Find out what types of symptoms require you to keep you baby at home. If Baby has a runny nose, will she be turned away at the door, or must she kept home only if she's vomiting and/or running a fever of 100 or more? Plus, you may be expected to pay for days when Baby is home sick, so ask about that up front, too.

✔ **What's the caregiver-to-infant ratio?** Centers should generally provide about one caregiver to every three infants — in some instances, four infants to one employee is okay.

In almost every state, a day care is required to be licensed if it has more than 12 kids. However, licensing isn't necessarily a guarantee of excellence, because criteria vary from state to state (some states have much lower standards when it comes to cleanliness, for example). Licensing ensures that a facility has met the bare-bones requirements in areas of health, safety, and childcare training. However, you still need to check centers out for yourself.

What you're looking for in a day care is a good reputation, for one thing. Remember, other parents are only too eager to share their day-care experiences — good or bad. You want to know that this is a fairly stable environment.

If most of the staff is brand-new, the center may have a high turnover rate, which raises two concerns: First, your child may be handed off to someone new every month and never have the opportunity to bond with any one caregiver. Second, why are the employees high-tailing it out of there? There could be any number of reasons, but generally speaking, any business with a high turnover rate has less-than-devoted employees.

Ask what kind of pay is offered at a day care, and/or whether the employees are given vacation and other benefits. Decent-paying jobs with nice perks are more likely to *stay* filled, which means that a caregiver will probably stick around for a while.

Also, take a look around. Is the place clean? Are the *children* clean? Are crying infants being tended to promptly? Do the older kids appear to be having fun — or at least appear content? These are all good signs. Check references and pay an unannounced visit before you make a final decision. And trust your gut instinct. Visit at different times of the day: drop-off, pick-up, nap-time, mealtime, and so on. Know what they're doing throughout the time your baby will be under their care.

Don't settle. If something is telling you that this place isn't right, then move on.

Looking into a home day care

The nice thing about finding someone in the neighborhood who watches children is that you may already know something about this person — and if you don't, you can usually find a friend who does (in fact, a friend may have recommended this place to you in the first place). If you're thinking about using a private day-care setting for your child, make sure to follow the same guidelines we suggest in the earlier section, "Checking out day cares," and also ask the following questions:

✔ **Are there any personal visitors to the home during the day? Who are they?** You want to know that your child is safe and that your babysitter's ex-con son isn't running a less-than-reputable business out of her home (which would mean that his less-than-reputable customers would be around your child all the time). Not that she would be this forthcoming with the information, but if you know about the son and his business, you can check it — and him — out for yourself to make sure all's well on the babysitter front. Try an Internet search to find information about visitors.

✔ **When do you expect to take vacation? What happens when you get sick?** When you depend on one person to watch your child, you have to make concessions — like scheduling your time off around her vacation, or having a backup plan if she comes down with the flu.

✔ **Do you have assistants? How are they screened? How long have they been there?** Again, you're checking on who's going to be around your child. Your babysitter should have done her own background check on any assistants, and should be forthcoming about her methods for doing so.

When you know a person who provides care in her home, you may be more apt to cut corners — to say, for example, "Well, she isn't licensed and she isn't registered with the state, but I trust her, so that's all that matters." (Licensing and registering are two separate actions. A *license* means that a sitter or center has met minimal health and safety regulations; *registering* makes the state aware of the business.) Just be aware that if your state licensing agency is somehow made aware of this *un*licensed, *un*registered facility, they may shut it down immediately — which will leave you in a lurch, big-time. It's a better idea to have all your ducks in a row right from the start and to find someone with a legitimate operation.

Finding a nanny

Searching for someone to come to your home and care for Baby is a luxury that many parents only dream of. Finding the right person can be something of a challenge, however, if you don't know where to begin. Start by asking friends, co-workers, or neighbors if they know anyone in this line of work. One nanny may know of *another* nanny who's between jobs at the moment. Look for postings on public bulletin boards — in coffee shops, cafes, playgrounds, or anywhere college students and nannies may hang out. As your last resort, advertise in the paper — just be forewarned that you may be completely inundated with responses.

Another option for finding a nanny is to contact a local nanny agency. Their services are usually costly, but they prescreen applicants, help you find someone with the qualifications you're looking for, and can also confirm that she is who she claims to be and has the experience she claims to have. (Online nanny agencies provide some of these same services and are generally less expensive.)

What you want to ask a nanny:

- **What's your educational background?** If she's working toward an education or a child psychology degree, for example, you can bet she's not in this solely for the money.

- **Do you have kids of your own? How old are they?** Although a childless nanny can be a wonderful person, a mom who's been in your shoes may be far more sympathetic toward your fussy baby. However, if your nanny isn't planning to bunk with you and has small kids of her own, you may want to know where they are while she's with your baby (in other words, are they going to be at *your* house?), and what she'll do if her own children are sick (will you be left nannyless?).

- **Any previous experience with infants? Why did your last gig as a nanny come to an end?** This is really hard work. You don't want to leave your infant with someone who's never cared for a newborn before. (Sure, she has to learn somewhere, but not on your child.) A good answer to the second question may be along the lines of, "My employers moved," or, "The kids are all grown up now," not, "My boss was too demanding and wanted me to change diapers all day long."

- **Do you have transportation?** You want someone reliable.

- **Do you have another job?** Ditto.

- **Why do you like being a nanny?** Listen for heartfelt responses, like, "I love kids," not, "My parents cut me off without a penny, and I need a job."

- **Do you know infant CPR?** Anyone who takes on a caregiver role should know infant and child CPR.

Babysitting the babysitter: Nanny cams

Nanny cams are selling like hotcakes in some regions. These tiny cameras are hidden in a friendly-looking household object (like a clock, a plant, or a stuffed animal) and provide parents with an opportunity to keep tabs on what's going on between Nanny and Baby while Mom and Dad are at the office. Obviously, an infant can't squeal on a neglectful or abusive caregiver, so these cameras can provide comfort to parents who want an extra measure of security. Two things to consider, though, with the nanny cams: First, in some states, it's legal to secretly record video *only* — clandestine audio recordings are off-limits. And secondly, before you purchase and set-up a secret camera, ask yourself why you're doing it. If you just have to know that your nanny is the saint you think she is, that's one thing. But if you suspect she's not doing her job well or that she's helping herself to your loose change — do you really want her taking care of your baby? Whether your suspicions are confirmed by the tape or not, if there's something you just don't trust about a caregiver, she doesn't belong in your home to begin with.

If you expect her to cook, clean, or run errands, run that by her now. Be prepared to answer her questions regarding pay and vacation.

If you find a candidate who seems like *the one*, have her come to your home for a trial period of a couple of days — just to make sure the arrangement is agreeable to both of you before you're ready to leave her and Baby on their own for the entire day.

Part II
Introducing: Baby!

The 5th Wave   By Rich Tennant

"Let me make a suggestion. Whenever I wash the pickup, I always clean out the truck bed first."

In this part . . .

Coming home with a brand-new baby sets off a verita-ble volcano of emotions in new parents: happiness, fear, excitement, fear. Maybe not all parents are cowering in the corner while Baby coos in her crib, but the realiza-tion that life will never be the same — that *your* basic needs must be put aside in order to care for your newborn — can be overwhelming, as can knowing that you are totally responsible for the care, feeding, and general well-being of another human being.

The first three months can be the most difficult of Baby's entire first year — for you and for her. This section offers a realistic look at what your experience might be like during this time and offers you advice on how to ease into this new phase of life known as parenthood.

Chapter 5

Settling In with Baby

Coming home from the hospital with Baby in tow can be exciting and terrifying all at once. The last time you were sitting in your house, you were just *you*. Now you're a parent. You're completely responsible for this little person.

The first few days at home with your child are like nothing you've ever experienced before, even if you've been around babies your entire life. This time, this experience, this child — they're all yours. These could be the most memorable days of your entire life, or they could end up being days you'd rather forget. Rest assured, you'll make it through your own recovery and your baby's premiere days intact and ready to take on the rest of the first year.

Rolling with the Punches (and Stitches)

Any woman who has given birth must deal with some discomfort afterward. If you were able to watch a video of a real birth before you actually went into labor, then the repairs you've suffered through came as no surprise to you. If, on the other hand, you were expecting a hassle-free delivery and are currently sitting in a sitz bath soothing your episiotomy wound, you may have been a bit shocked to discover the discomforts associated with giving birth.

Post-delivery pain can be magnified by the lack of sleep that many new mothers must endure. If you went through a long labor and delivery, or your child was born in the middle of the night, chances are you missed out on at least one night of sleep. You may wonder how you can ever catch up when your baby needs to nurse so frequently.

You will feel better soon — and you *will* sleep again. This section offers you tips on how to make it through these days with your new baby when all you want is for someone to baby *you*.

Coping with new levels of fatigue

Maybe you expected the nurses to feed your child and were surprised when they brought her to you every three hours — couldn't they see how tired you were? Of course they could. But part of their job is to make sure you know how to feed and care for your child before you head home, and they have a relatively short time in which to teach you everything you need to know about Baby.

Now that you've been discharged, you're finding that Baby isn't sleeping like the nurses said she would — she's been up all day and all night, and you're more tired than you ever dreamed you'd be. You don't even recognize the person looking back at you from the mirror — she looks old and pale and plain worn out. How will you ever recover from childbirth if you can't sleep for more than an hour at a crack?

Many babies hardly cry in the hospital and only eat every four hours. This won't continue at home! Babies wake up, discover they're starving, and want to nurse about every two hours until your milk comes in. Usually this happens the first night you're home sleeping in your own bed again. Be ready!

Although the first days home from the hospital with Baby can be the longest, hardest days of your life, they're not an indication of how the rest of Baby's first year will be. If your newborn isn't sleeping 20 hours a day, her immature nervous system may be keeping her awake; this will probably pass. And no matter what you've heard from other mothers, newborns don't come home from the hospital ready and willing to sleep through the night. They need to eat — often — so don't lose heart if you feel as though you've done nothing but nurse this child since she was born. It's completely normal, and incredibly time-consuming.

The best advice for tired moms during this time is simple: Rest when your baby is sleeping or quiet. If she's content to lie in her bassinet alone, don't feel as though you have to hold her. She's okay. Don't push yourself to fold her little outfits or to restock the changing table when she finally closes her eyes for an afternoon snooze. Seize the opportunity to pull the shades and snuggle under a nice warm blanket all by yourself.

If Baby wakes and cries every time you put her down, go ahead and hold her while you rest. If you're ready to nod off, though, place her in her bassinet or infant seat. Even if she's unhappy, she's safe, and you can (hopefully) sneak in a couple of minutes of rest by yourself.

Holding Baby while both of you rest is fine in these early days, when you both need to get some rest at any cost. Just keep in mind that in a month or so, she needs to start learning to be alone in her bassinet or baby seat. She needs to learn how to comfort herself, or you could be dealing with sleep issues for years to come.

Go to the extreme when you're on a quest for rest. Turn off the phone. Put a sign on your front door telling visitors to come back later. Put your dog in his crate or send him to your mother-in-law's house. Let the rest of the household chores go. Soon enough, real life will be in full effect again. These first days with Baby aren't your average, run-of-the-mill days. You need to take care of yourself now so that you'll have the strength to tend to your child's needs.

Babying your body

You've passed a small human being through your loins or through an incision in your abdomen. (Yeah, ouch.) Recovering from childbirth requires effort on your part — the effort to allow yourself to just sit back and heal. Before you laugh at what seems to be the simplest advice ever given, ask yourself this: When was the last time you let the housework and/or your office work completely go — while you were in the house with full access to cleaning supplies and your computer? A lot of women simply don't know *how* to rest; even when they legitimately use a sick day, they're catching up on projects around the house or on work that has to be done by the end of the week. For the first ten days to two weeks after giving birth, your *one* job is to take care of your baby.

No matter how smoothly your vaginal delivery goes, you're going to be sore afterward. Whether you have stitches or not, keep your weight off your bottom for the next week or ten days — sit on your side, lie down, or use a donut pillow. If ice helps to lessen your discomfort, use it. Having a sore and engorged vaginal region at this point is normal — but being in extreme pain a week after delivery isn't. A simple change in your physical position (from upright to sideways or horizontal) can help to ease the pain.

Although women give birth every day and have been doing so for millions of years, and even though you've heard stories of how your great-great-grandmother gave birth in a field and went right back to planting potatoes — *giving birth is a big deal.* Your body has been through an ordeal (albeit a *good* ordeal). This is true whether you've gone through a natural childbirth or a C-section.

Acknowledge that you're human and that you do need time to recuperate and regain your strength. You'll bounce back faster in the weeks to come if you take care of yourself now.

Caring for an episiotomy

You no doubt received instructions for caring for your episiotomy while you were in the hospital. If those instructions have somehow slipped your mind (little wonder with your fatigue and all of the information you're trying to remember concerning Baby), here's the lowdown on how to take care of it:

- ✔ Change your sanitary pads often and make sure they're secure. You don't need a pad slipping back and forth, irritating the wound.
- ✔ Don't touch the wound.
- ✔ Use the squirt bottle you were given in the hospital to cleanse the area.
- ✔ Practice your usual hygiene when using the bathroom, being extra gentle.
- ✔ To help soothe the area, try sitting in a warm sitz bath (with just enough water to cover the affected area). If you were given anesthetic cream or spray in the hospital, go ahead and use it. Witch hazel pads can also ease the pain.
- ✔ Be alert for signs of infection: a bad smell; intense, constant pain that only gets worse as the days go by; or fever.

Tending to your body after a cesarean delivery

If you had a C-section, you'll be feeling sore for at least a couple of weeks. Your stitches will most likely be removed within the week after you give birth, but remember, you've been through surgery — it's a full six to eight week recovery window you're looking at.

Here are some tips to help your healing process:

- ✔ Don't lift anything heavier than Baby.
- ✔ Don't be surprised if your incision is numb for several weeks. This is normal after any surgery.
- ✔ Try to keep Baby off the incision site.
- ✔ No vacuuming or sex for six weeks. (Bummer for your partner — on both counts.)
- ✔ Watch for signs of infection: A foul smell; worsening pain and inflammation at the incision site; or fever.
- ✔ *Don't* try to tough it out — if you're in pain, take the medication your doctor has approved. Expect the pain to be the worst during the first week after delivery.

Get up and move as much as you can — but don't overdo it. This is good advice for any woman who has just given birth. You want to get your circulation going, but you also need plenty of rest. Take time to assess how you're feeling throughout the day — if you're worn out, *sit down*. And keep an eye on your *lochia,* the bleeding and vaginal discharge that follows childbirth, caused by the separation of the placenta from the uterine wall. During the first post-delivery week, it may be a lot like your normal menstrual flow, or it may initially be heavier than your average period. Lochia can last anywhere from a couple of weeks to more than a month, though it becomes lighter in color and flow as the weeks go on, changing from red to pink to a yellowish discharge before drying up completely. Make sure you've got plenty of sanitary pads in the house. Tampons are banned for six weeks after delivery, because using them could cause a uterine infection.

If bright red, heavy bleeding continues after the first week, if the flow becomes very heavy (soaking through a pad in an hours' time), if the flow and color lighten and then revert back to heavy bleeding, or if you're passing large clots (anything larger than a quarter is the rule of thumb), *call your doctor without delay!* These may be signs of hemorrhage — but may also simply be an indication that you're doing too much physically. Also be alert for signs of infection, which include fever and a foul-smelling discharge.

Accepting help

Maybe you have no trouble accepting offers of help. You don't mind if your mother spends the entire day in your house feeding your pets, cooking, and cleaning. Your mother-in-law is more than welcome to do your grocery shopping. Why, you even let your brother-in-law change the light bulb in the bathroom yesterday. You're lucky to have so much help, and you're going to have a splendid recovery period — as long as you remember that you do have to get up off the couch every now and then in order to keep your circulation surging.

Or maybe you have a very difficult time allowing friends and family into your home for the sheer purpose of taking care of you. You hate being pampered, and as for the cooking and the cleaning — you want it done a certain way, so you'd rather do it yourself. What's wrong with that?

Well, normally, nothing's wrong with having such a can-do attitude. If you're having an easy time with Baby and you're feeling up to making your own lunch every day, go ahead. Just make sure that you're not doing too much — you *do* need time to just sit and rest and care for Baby without worrying about the dishes in the sink or the dirt on the kitchen floor.

A woman who's bouncing back from childbirth shouldn't be tackling the heavy-duty household chores during her first week home — like hauling laundry up and down the basement stairs, or even dusting the house from top to bottom, which may not *seem* like especially hard work, but really does take a toll on the body. There is a slight chance of hemorrhage during this recovery period, so it's essential that you allow your body to heal.

Think of it this way: If you were recovering from a bout with the flu, you'd remember how weak your body was at the peak of the illness, and you'd let yourself recuperate. You may not *feel* particularly weak when you're recovering from childbirth — and that's good. You *want* to feel well. The danger here is that when new moms feel great, they sometimes take on too much, too soon (mopping the floor four days after giving birth, or running errands on the fifth day), and end up feeling completely worn out. Just keep in mind that your body is healing from the inside; you need to conserve energy to heal more quickly.

If you can let the deep-down cleaning go for now, great. But if you can't — if the dirt on the floor is going to drive you crazy — let your mom help. Or look the other way while your mother-in-law does a lousy job of sweeping. Your focus should be on you and your baby right now. The dirt will still be there in a couple of weeks — you can do away with it then.

Defending your right to solitude

After giving birth, you're faced with physical and emotional feelings you've never experienced. You're elated. You're nervous. You're more exhausted than you've ever been. Your breasts are starting to hurt. You're sore. Oh, and you're hormonal, which is causing you to experience the extremes of your emotions (some of which are in reaction to your physical state) in roughly 15-minute intervals. (All right. It's probably not that bad. But maybe it's close.) The last thing you want is a house filled with relatives offering to feed and comfort you.

Go ahead and send good Samaritans away right now. There aren't many instances in a person's life where it's completely acceptable to say, "This is all about me, and if I'm hurting someone's feelings, that's too darn bad." But now is one of those times. We're not advising that you should be *mean* to people who are only trying to be kind. But you have to look out for yourself at this point, and if you can't get any rest with your three aunts and four cousins milling around your bedroom and setting up Baby's crib (which she won't be sleeping in for a couple of months, anyway), speak up now or suffer the consequences of a meltdown later.

Keep in mind that no matter how much you crave solitude right now, you don't want to send *everyone* away. A well-chosen nursemaid/assistant can even be your voice for you, turning visitors away at the door by saying, "She and the baby are sleeping right now. I'll tell her you dropped by." Keep someone around for the first week just in case you're feeling weak or ill.

Realize that you can't be alone forever, and that some relatives just *have* to come in and take a peek at the baby. Your mother-in-law, for example, can't be kept at bay for more than a day or two after you've returned home. So let her in — but don't be afraid to make it very clear that you aren't up for a long visit just yet. You can deal with the fallout later, if there is any, or better yet, let your spouse handle it. And if mama-in-law wants to hold the baby while you get some sleep — weigh the benefits (you *will* be able to rest) against any negatives (will she insist on taking over your entire recovery?). Chances are, she's just ga-ga over her new grandchild, and she means no harm.

Nourishing the Newborn

Whether you're breastfeeding Baby or offering her a bottle, you want to be sure that she's getting enough to eat. Should you feed her when she cries? Should you wake her every few hours? Will feeding her more make her sleep longer? These are common and sometimes confusing issues for first-time parents — and even for parents who have been through this before.

Whether you're bottlefeeding or breastfeeding, most doctors advise parents to feed Baby on demand — which means when Baby shows signs of being hungry (crying, rooting around with her mouth).

Time to nurse . . . again?!

During Baby's first few days and weeks, you can start to feel as though all you ever do is unbutton your shirt and whip out your breasts. You finish feeding Baby, and 90 minutes later, she's hungry again!

Don't worry. Nursing your child won't always be so time-consuming. For one thing, during Baby's first days at home, you're both still getting the hang of breastfeeding. Baby is learning to latch on and suck, and you're dealing with the pain of "breaking in" your nipples and discovering which position works best for you and your child. Baby may not be eating all that much at this point, especially if she tends to doze off every time you feed her. On top of everything else, her little stomach can't hold much at this age anyway.

When the two of you work out all of these little kinks, her nursing sessions will go much more smoothly and more quickly. For now, realize that frustration is something that a lot of new breastfeeding mothers experience and that the vast majority of babies eventually whittle down their nursing sessions considerably.

Some nursing moms worry that because Baby is eating so often, it may be an indication that she's not getting enough milk. For now, you can be sure that she's getting enough to eat if:

- ✔ She has six to eight wet diapers a day.
- ✔ The urine is pale — not dark yellow. Dark-colored urine is actually a sign of dehydration and may mean that she isn't getting enough milk.
- ✔ She has several seedy-looking bowel movements every day.
- ✔ You can hear her swallowing during her feedings.
- ✔ She appears calm and relaxed after nursing.
- ✔ Your breasts may also feel empty or soft after a feeding session.
- ✔ You may be able to see milk in Baby's mouth.

If Baby seems content after she nurses, and she's going through diapers like mad, she's doing fine.

Most doctors recommend waking a sleepy newborn to feed at least every three to four hours during the day. Baby should be fitting in a total of 8 to 12 breastfeedings over the course of 24 hours. Not only does she need the nourishment, but it's also necessary for her to feed often to establish your breast milk (the more she nurses, the more you make in order to meet her demands). Keep in mind that some newborns nurse every couple of hours during the day and then sleep for a longer stretch during the night. That's okay, to a point. She shouldn't (and won't) sleep for eight hours at a crack right now — she needs to eat.

The breastfeeding mother is Baby's only source of nutrition in the early weeks. Don't start introducing supplemental bottles until Baby has clearly mastered the art of breastfeeding. Silicone nipples can sometimes lead to *nipple confusion* in a newborn. Because latching onto the breast is much more involved than sucking from a bottle (each requires its own method of successfully working the mouth and the tongue, as well as different swallowing techniques), offering Baby a real nipple in the morning and an artificial nipple in the afternoon can leave him feeling as though he has no idea what to do with either one. Best to stick to one method for now. Hold off on giving Baby a bottle until he's about 6 weeks old. At that point, you can be sure that he's settled into nursing and a plastic nipple shouldn't throw him into a tizzy.

If you're nursing and things are going well, consider yourself lucky — many babies have a hard time getting the hang of breastfeeding.

Bottlefed babies

Bottlefed newborns usually eat 1 to 3 ounces of formula at a single feeding and tend to need to eat every two to three hours. After she reaches 10 pounds, Baby will probably be ready for more — your pediatrician will advise you in this matter as Baby grows. For now, let Baby determine how much and how often she eats. Don't try to feed her when she's clearly lost interest in the bottle, and never prop a newborn with a bottle in her mouth (by placing the bottle on a pillow or stuffed animal in Baby's bassinet, for example, so that you don't have to hold her while she eats).

You don't need to use boiled or distilled water to prepare Baby's bottle, nor do you need to even warm it. (In fact, if you can get Baby to drink cold and/or room temperature formula, you make your life a heck of a lot easier — especially in the middle of the night, when you can just grab a bottle from the fridge.) If Baby seems to prefer warm formula, however, consider purchasing a bottle warmer. You can also run the bottle under warm water or stick it in a pot of hot (but not boiling) water.

Never use the microwave to warm a bottle, because the liquid may end up with "hot spots" that could burn Baby.

Burp Baby at least midway through the bottle, and sooner than that if she seems to be slowing down. Some kids do well with one good burp; some need to burp several times. Some babies hardly produce any spit-up; some spit up *a lot*. Your doctor will evaluate Baby's progress at the first check-up. Even if your child is a champion spitter, as long as he's growing, he's okay.

If Baby's spit-up shoots halfway across the room, or if it's dark (yellow, green, or brown), consult your pediatrician at once. This isn't normal spit-up and could indicate the presence of gastrointestinal problems.

And with intake comes output: Baby's diaper

Breastfed infants fill their diapers frequently — some of them have a bowel movement every time they nurse, and some very tiny infants can produce huge amounts of poop. Expect these stools to be yellow and seedy-looking and to smell foul. Bottlefed infants tend to have fewer, better-formed bowel movements.

Getting Dad in on the act

Breastfed babies rely on Mom and only Mom for feedings, which means Dad is left out. He may feel like he's out of the picture for more than just feedings. Although bottlefed babies can be fed by anyone (and even breastfed babies can take a few bottles after they're about 6 weeks old), Dad still may need some encouragement to step in and start learning the fatherly arts.

Too often, Dads are relegated to the background, not really expected or allowed to do much of anything. Because Mom is the primary caregiver in many instances, she takes complete control of feedings, diaper changes, and comforting sessions. Dad either sits back and smiles, knowing that he's off the hook, or stands by frustrated,

wanting to do more but feeling inept because — well, he can't learn how to care for Baby if Mom has taken complete charge.

Get Dad in on the Baby game. He really is capable of helping, and the more he's allowed to do, the more he'll do of his own accord — because he feels like he's part of this whole experience, and not like he's watching from the sidelines. In the end, a dad who has been feeding, burping, and changing Baby from the beginning (or, in the case of the breastfed newborn, a dad who has been diapering and rocking his baby from day one) is going to feel like he's really part of this child's life. And that's good for the entire family.

Change Baby as soon as she's finished eating (even if she's fallen asleep) so that she doesn't develop a rash, signs of which include red, raw-looking skin anywhere in the diaper area. Use a diaper ointment to help quell these flare-ups.

Call your pediatrician if the rash turns to meaty-looking welts in the folds of Baby's skin (signs of a yeast infection — possible even in boys), if the rash is brown or crusty (signs of impetigo, which is contagious), or if it spreads to other parts of Baby's body. Your doctor may prescribe an ointment to help clear the rash.

Boys can sometimes get a diaper rash on the penis, which usually clears up in a few days. If it doesn't go away on its own, if it gets worse, or if it's interfering with Baby's ability to urinate, call your pediatrician.

Yes, You Have to Look: Umbilical Cord and Circumcision Care

Although they aren't beautiful, taking care of the umbilical cord and circumcision are easy tasks. Time heals all wounds, right? That holds true here, as well. You need to provide a minimum amount of care to these areas for about ten days to two weeks while keeping a sharp eye out for infection.

Caring for the cord

Until the umbilical cord falls off, you do have to look at it — but unlike parents of days gone by, you probably won't have to clean it. The old medical advice had parents dipping a swab into rubbing alcohol and cleaning around the base of the cord at every diaper change. Today, doctors think that the alcohol does very little to hasten the cord's departure, and many advise parents to just leave it alone.

Even when it's hanging on by its last little thread, don't ever try to pull the cord off! Let nature take its course — it will fall off all by itself.

With the disposal of the alcohol swabbing of the umbilical cord area, the risk for infection increases slightly. Watch for:

- Redness or swelling around the base
- Discharge (yellow or white pus, or anything that smells foul)
- Bleeding

If you aren't using diapers with a cutout for the umbilical area, simply fold Baby's diaper down in front until the cord has been replaced by a cute little belly button. (And keep in mind that a little bit of bleeding is normal when the cord finally comes off.)

Tending the circumcision

Caring for the circumcision is fairly easy. The worst part of the experience is having to look at your little boy's sore genitalia. Use petroleum jelly around the circumcised area (so that it doesn't stick to the diaper) and *leave it alone!* When the glans (the circumcised area) no longer appears red and moist, discontinue the use of the petroleum jelly.

It's normal for the penis to appear irritated or to have white or yellow spots during the healing process. However, it shouldn't be bleeding, it shouldn't continue to swell and appear increasingly irritated, and you shouldn't see any foul-smelling pus. Call your pediatrician if these symptoms of infection occur.

Baby should be creating wet diapers throughout the day. If he has gone more than six hours without urinating, call your pediatrician.

Yellow-Bellied Babies: Jaundice

Jaundice comes in two different types: The type of jaundice that requires phototherapy is usually diagnosed and treated shortly after birth, and because you and Baby are already home, you may think that he successfully dodged this condition.

The truth is, a lot of otherwise healthy infants develop a slight case of jaundice after they've been discharged from the hospital. It can be a bit disconcerting for a parent to realize that the whites of Baby's eyes have gone yellow — and so have his cheeks!

More than half of all healthy infants have a bout with jaundice. It usually peaks on the second or third day after delivery and resolves itself within a week to ten days. Usually, no treatment is required.

If Baby becomes very yellow and appears ill, call your pediatrician immediately. Additional symptoms can include diminished sucking, seeming too weak to cry, not waking for his feedings, not regularly wetting or passing stool, and listless newborn reflexes. These are signs of a more serious form of jaundice that needs to be evaluated without delay. It may be treatable at home with something called a bili blanket, which will be placed on Baby for most of the day. (The more it's used, the sooner the jaundice will clear up.) If Baby is jaundiced but doesn't need the bili blanket, place her in a sunny location in the house and make sure to feed her frequently — this should help in clearing up the yellow tint.

Chapter 6

The First Month: Getting to Know You

In This Chapter

▶ Baby's first checkup

▶ Bathing Baby

▶ Establishing a bond after you get home

▶ Identifying common birthmarks

▶ Encouraging good sleeping habits

▶ Feeding issues

▶ Crying and colic

▶ Outings with a newborn

---

*B*efore you know it, this little person who can't seem to stay awake for more than an hour at a time will be rolling across your living room floor and giggling herself silly. The first month is a really precious time with an infant precisely because it goes so fast. The entire first year is full of firsts for you and for Baby, and they start now: The first checkup, the first real bath, the first time since your wild college days that you've been up all night. (Somehow, bone-crushing fatigue seemed a lot more fun back then.)

Real parenting includes moments of unbelievable pride and joy — along with moments of frustration and fatigue. These are your first steps on a long, long journey, and the lessons you learn now (about yourself and about your child) will be with you long after Baby is out of diapers.

Checking In with Baby

You're going to make a new friend this year — your pediatrician. Baby will be in for six well-baby visits (and possibly a sick visit or two, as well). Hopefully, you've found a doctor you feel comfortable talking to, because your pediatrician is your best source of information as far as your child's health is concerned. (If you're still up in the air about Baby's doctor, Chapter 1 offers some advice for finding a good match.) The 1-month milestones are also listed in this section.

Baby's first checkup

Suddenly you, like your parents before you, are the parent hovering nearby while the doctor checks out your little guy — and you feel all the things your parents felt: You're just so darn proud of this child, and so eager to have the doctor tell you that he's healthy and on the right track.

Taking Baby in for his first checkup is like clearing a hurdle — you and your partner took him home, you took care of him by yourselves, and here you're presenting him back to the pediatrician's staff, fine and dandy. The doctor will attest to the fact that you've done a marvelous job during these first couple of weeks.

Expect this checkup, which will take place anywhere from two to four weeks after delivery, to include a regular examination, including baby's height and weight, and head and chest circumferences. Your doctor will give baby a good once-over, checking his nose, ears, eyes, and mouth. In each case, he's looking for any irregularities. It's not uncommon, for example, for an infant to develop a clogged tear duct. The doctor is also checking to make sure that everything is working as it should. An abnormal fluid level in Baby's ears, for example, can affect his hearing. Doc will pull out the stethoscope and listen for a normal heartbeat and good lung sounds. Baby's internal organs will be palpated to check for any irregularities. His spine will be examined, to make sure it's straight and intact.

Baby was born with several newborn reflexes, which are indicators of his neurological well-being. Your pediatrician assesses the reflexes during this check up and lets you know how Baby's doing.

Baby's *fontanels* are also assessed. These are the soft spot membranes on his skull that allowed his head to change shape and come through the birth canal. The larger, anterior fontanel is on top of the head; it starts to close by the time Baby is about 6 months old (and will completely close by the middle of the second year). You may see this soft spot vibrating to Baby's heartbeat or bulging upward when Baby cries, which, while disturbing, is completely normal. The smaller, posterior fontanel is in the middle of the back of Baby's head and will close by the end of the third month.

In addition, Baby's thyroid is examined, and the doctor checks for swollen lymph nodes in the neck, groin, and armpits. He checks the umbilical site for signs of infection or hernia (the latter will also be ruled out in the groin area). Baby's genital region is examined to make sure there are no signs of abnormalities. Any birthmarks that were present in the hospital are also assessed; any new spots (birthmarks can also appear in the months after birth) are identified.

Immunizations aren't usually given during the first office exam. This is a visit for getting to know your doctor, and for your doctor to get to know you and Baby.

Write down questions as they occur to you at home, and when the doctor turns to you and asks how things are going, toss those questions his way. Just remember, he's heard it all; he's seen just about everything; and he isn't going to think you're a ninny for not knowing what that strange red mark on Baby's arm is. For more on this, see "Identifying Baby's Beauty Marks" later in the chapter.

You can expect the doctor to ask you about Baby's sleep and eating patterns, his bowel movements, and how the adjustment at home is going. Be honest. If parenting thus far has exceeded every expectation you had, tell him that. Pediatricians love to hear good news from the home front.

During the first pediatrician visit, you'll be handed a health record booklet, which you'll tote back and forth to the doctor's office in order to record Baby's growth, immunizations (see Chapter 18), and feeding information.

Milestones this month

From birth through the first month, Baby's development is slow but steady.

These are only guidelines as to what most babies are doing at this age. Your pediatrician is your best source of information regarding your own child.

Here are a few milestones to look for:

- ✔ Having lost weight after delivery, Baby returns to her birth weight by the time she's 2 weeks old.

- ✔ Her length increases about 1½ inches this month.

- ✔ She gains about ½ ounce to 1 ounce a day, which translates into almost 2 pounds.

- ✔ Baby has virtually no neck strength at this point. Her head lolls back and forth or side to side without constant support.

- ✔ Baby's movements are random and jerky. Her limbs are flexed, and she's easily startled.

- ✔ She grabs onto a finger and holds it.
- ✔ Her *rooting* reflex is still strong and she sucks on something placed in her mouth. She also follows an object placed near her mouth with her mouth.
- ✔ Expect her to sleep at least 16 hours a day (but not consecutively).

- ✔ Baby is very nearsighted at this point. She can only clearly see things that are 8 to 12 inches from her face. She also lacks the ability to track objects with her eyes.
- ✔ The umbilical cord falls off ten days to two weeks after delivery.
- ✔ Baby loves faces and will stare at you for long periods of time (as long as you're close enough for her to see you).
- ✔ Baby has an affinity for female voices, perhaps because she's grown so used to the sound of her mother's voice while in the womb.

Charting height and weight

When Baby is born, and with every well-child visit (into his school-aged years), he'll be weighed and measured. Those measurements will then be graphed onto a standardized height and weight chart, and your doctor will tell you where Baby's growth falls, percentile-wise. For a look at growth charts go to www.cdc.gov/growthcharts.

Now, growth isn't a pass-fail thing. If Baby measures in the 50th percentile for height and weight, it doesn't mean that he's not thriving. It simply indicates that about 50 percent of infants his age are somewhat larger and heavier than he is, and about 50 percent are smaller and lighter. And of course, there are all sorts of variations in between — Baby could measure in the 95th percentile for height and the 50th percentile for weight, which simply means he's a long, thin infant.

Parents sometimes worry if Baby consistently measures on the lower end of these charts. But remember, an infant who measures in the 30th percentile for height every single time he's in the doctor's office is showing a definite pattern of growth — he's a bit smaller than his peers, but he's holding his own. The percentile isn't the important thing, its how your baby grows over time. We chart height and weight to track overall growth trends and usually only get worried if a baby is falling off a height or weight curve he was on previously. Generally speaking, a sudden, drastic drop in height- or weight-growth may be a worrisome sign of Baby's not thriving. Your doctor will take note of any radical changes as she charts Baby's progress at each checkup.

Charting the breastfed babe

Do breastfed babies and their bottlefed pals grow at the same rate? Recent studies show that there is a difference: Breastfed infants tend to gain weight faster than bottlefed babies during the first three months of life, and bottle-fed infants tend to be heavier than breast-feeding infants during the second half of the first year. This isn't a worrisome occurrence, as long as Baby is growing consistently. One area of concern may pop up if a breastfeeding mother is feeling pressured to supplement Baby's meals or to put him on solids too early because the child seems smaller than other infants. Talk to your pediatrician if you're concerned about Baby's growth progress. If there's no problem, he'll assure you of this in no uncertain terms; if Baby legitimately needs more nourishment, he'll be able to give you advice on that angle, as well.

The numbers on the growth chart are indicative of where Baby is now and where he's likely to stay, size-wise. Other areas your pediatrician will take a look at when evaluating Baby's growth include:

- ✔ **The size of Baby's parents.** A 5-foot parent is more likely than a taller person to have a child who is on the lower end of the height chart.
- ✔ **Baby's general health and happiness.** Is he eating, sleeping, alert when awake? Does he cry constantly? (If so, he may not be getting enough to eat.)
- ✔ **Baby's development.** Is he hitting those milestones when he should?

The fact is, babies come in different sizes, from teeny to extra-large. As long as your child seems to be eating well, and her growth patterns are consistent, there's no need for concern, no matter where she falls on the charts.

Height and weight charts have undergone a revision in the past few years. The current charts were revised in 2000; the old charts are from the 1970s, when breastfeeding was less in vogue, infants were regularly given whole milk, and babies were started on solids earlier than they are today — hence, babies tended to be larger and heavier during the first year. If you're referring to a chart on your own, check its publication date. Also feel free to ask your doctor's office whether they're using the latest charts.

Rub a Dub Dub, Using the Tub

After Baby's umbilical cord falls off and the circumcision heals, you're ready to move your child from sponge bathing to a real, live mini-tub. (If you didn't get one of these at your baby shower, buy one. They're cheap, and they're the easiest way to safely bathe a small baby.) The tub sits right in your kitchen sink. You can also put it in your bathtub, in which case you only fill the small tub with water, leaving the big tub empty.

Putting Baby in the tub for the first time can be daunting, but it's worth the effort. A real bath may stimulate or soothe your child — and in either case, it may tire her right out, which may be good news for you! And after you get the hang of it, bathing your infant in a tub of water will probably seem easier than trying to both wash her and keep her warm during a sponge bath. In fact, a baby who routinely cries during sponge bathing may surprise you by settling right into her lukewarm bathtub. And another bonus is that Baby won't be as slippery in the tub as she is when you try to sponge bathe her!

Believe it or not, you'll be a bathtime pro in no time. Initially, though, you may need anywhere from 20 to 30 minutes just to get all of your supplies ready, fill the tub, and wash, dry, and dress Baby.

Never, never leave Baby alone in the tub, not even for a few seconds. Take the phone off the hook, put your pets in their crates, and don't answer the door until bathtime is over. In the event of a real emergency, where you have to respond to someone or something, take Baby out of the tub.

Giving Baby a good wash

Choose the least hectic time of your day and take your time. Here's what you do:

1. **Gather all of your supplies and place them near the tub.**

   You need soap, a baby washcloth, shampoo, and a cup to rinse Baby's head. Place these items in easy reach of your dominant hand, and open or loosen the caps before you put Baby in the tub.

2. **Make sure the tub is safely secured on the sink.** It shouldn't wobble or tip.

3. **Fill the tub only halfway (slightly more for a large infant) with luke-warm water.**

   Baby doesn't need to be fully submerged, but you will need enough water to rinse the soap off and so that she isn't freezing. Test the temperature with the inside of your wrist to make sure it's not too hot for Baby's sensitive skin.

4. **Run the cold water (turning the spout away from the tub) until the faucet feels cool.**

   This ensures Baby won't grab a hot faucet; also, any water that drips on Baby will be cold.

5. Ease Baby into the tub.

Keep a constant hand on Baby so that she feels secure. Move her close to the side of the tub if she seems frightened. Sing to her, talk to her, play with her little toes, but keep it on the quiet side for now. You want this to be fun time for her, but you don't want to overstimulate her — at least not until *she* decides that bathtime is playtime.

6. Wash her with baby soap and a washcloth.

Wash her neck, her cheeks, behind her ears, her body, her back. Save her diaper area for last so that you aren't wiping her face with a dirty washcloth. If Baby decides to urinate in the water, you probably won't even know about it, unless you have a boy. It happens. Change the water and continue the bath.

If she has diaper rash, use plain water (without soap) for her bath. If you need to wash off diaper rash ointment, rub it softly with a washcloth.

7. Wash her hair with baby shampoo.

Rinse her head slowly and carefully with a cup of lukewarm or cooler water. Baby-safe shampoo and plain water won't harm Baby's eyes, but if you don't like the idea of her having soap in her eyes, just take extra care to shield her face from the water while you rinse. Hold a hand right at her hairline to redirect any wayward bubbles.

8. Dry her off, diaper, and dress her.

Comb her hair with a baby comb; clip her nails with the baby clippers. Use lotion if Baby's skin is dry, but avoid the use of powder, because it can be harmful to Baby if inhaled.

Now that you've done the work, enjoy the benefits: Take a deep, long sniff of Baby's clean head. *There's* that perfect infant smell!

Cradle cap

You may notice that your child has a thick, scaly substance on her head that just won't come off when you rub it with a washcloth. The substance is probably *cradle cap* — a rash caused by a hormonal reaction. Normally, we all shed our dried skin cells. Baby's sebaceous glands are emitting an oily matter that's causing the old skin cells on his head to stick there.

Cradle cap is unpleasant to look at, but is common in infants. It's not harmful to your child, nor is it contagious.

Dandruff shampoo may be helpful in eliminating cradle cap; use it one or two times a week, making sure to guard Baby's eyes from the suds, because these shampoos are not tear-free. You can also try rubbing some mineral oil into the scales *before* you begin Baby's bath. Let it sit for a few minutes before using Baby's comb to loosen the scales. If this doesn't work, let the oil sit for a longer period of time before using the comb again. Baby's hair will be greasy afterward and will need a thorough cleansing.

If the rash appears to be red and itchy, call your pediatrician. He may prescribe a special cream to alleviate any discomfort. Sometimes, cradle cap is so thick that mineral oil doesn't do much to loosen it. Call your doctor's office for a recommendation in this case, as well. Certain shampoos may help, but they're not formulated for infants' use. Your doctor may advise you to wait on using these until Baby is older.

Connecting with Baby

Comparing yourself to other new parents can really make you feel rotten. Your brother and sister-in-law just had a baby, and they seem completely at ease, as though they've been doing this parenting thing all their lives. In fact, everyone you know who has a new baby seems to have settled in quite nicely, while you're just waiting for the Parent Fairy to sprinkle you with magic dust and make you feel like a *real* mom (or dad).

Deep down, you know that parenting is a tough new gig to jump into, especially if you've never cared for anything more significant than a houseplant in the past. The first month is a time of major adjustment for you and your partner — as mates and as parents. And if you're on your own, bringing a baby into your home may seem overwhelming. With all of the excitement, anxiety, and loss of sleep, you may not fully acknowledge what's really happening in your life at this point. The best thing you can do is to take a step back and go easy on yourself. Everything will fall into place and seem incredibly natural — it just takes some time.

Beginning to trust yourself as a parent

Baby is a complete stranger when you bring her home from the hospital. She may be a very easy stranger to have in the house, or she may be a bit of a scary stranger, exhibiting signs of a temperamental little personality. Either way, you have to give yourself time to get to know her and her patterns.

You have to give yourself time to adjust to the fact that you're caring for this little stranger 24 hours a day now. Sometimes, you may have to try several tactics before you figure out what Baby really wants. Sometimes, you get things right on the first try, and other times, you feel like you have no business being a parent. Don't fool yourself — being confused is *part* of being a parent.

Beginning to trust yourself where Baby is concerned isn't always an easy task, and it seems to come a lot easier if you have a good support system around cheering you on and showing you the ropes. But cheering section or no, you *can* figure this out. Just realize that there is no such thing as a Super Parent. We're all human, we all have real emotions, and anyone who's ever had an infant with a powerful, long-lasting cry has wanted to join in and shed a few tears.

Preserving your mental health is crucial in these initial days when Baby's schedule is topsy-turvy. Tag-team parenting can be very effective during this time: Catch a nap whenever your partner is available to take Baby for an hour. If your partner isn't available, but your trustworthy friend volunteers to help, accept the offer. A well-rested parent is going to enjoy the Baby experience *way* more than a worn-out parent is.

Waiting — and waiting — to feel the bond

You've had Baby home for a week, and still, you're not feeling like a real parent. You may still be suffering the effects from a rough delivery, and you're also feeling the effects of the hormonal changes that come after delivery. On top of that, your breasts may be incredibly sore if you're nursing. If you're a dad, you may be suffering the effects of surviving on very little sleep, along with trying to keep your partner happy. This isn't an easy time for anyone.

Moms and dads alike may also be feeling disappointed that this hasn't been the perfect experience you were expecting — and you may even be feeling guilty for not being happier. Let go of your perception that every new parent is ecstatic.

Baby blues — feelings of anxiety and sadness — are a fairly common occurrence in the first two postpartum weeks, and they can be enough to make you doubt your abilities as a parent and make the bonding experience difficult. More details on postpartum sadness are included in Chapter 2.

Most pediatricians won't treat mom's depression. Call your OB first. The best thing to do is cry for help, not cry alone.

Although the baby blues are fairly common and somewhat fleeting, postpartum depression is less common but far more serious. If your mood changes from a general sad feeling to one of hopelessness; if you can't sleep or you can't get out of bed; if you can't stop crying; or if you're thinking of hurting yourself or Baby, contact your doctor or Baby's pediatrician at once.

Many parents need time to ease into the loving bond they expected to have right off the bat. Rest assured, the love will come, and it will be as strong as you thought it would be — all in due time.

Identifying Baby's Beauty Marks

When you're pregnant, you picture your baby as a perfect little infant with dimpled cheeks and a rosy complexion. No parent ever includes a birthmark on their fantasy child, and yet . . . they pop up all the time. Many will fade or disappear all together, but some will remain with Baby for a lifetime. We explain some of the most common birthmarks in the following sections.

"Stork bites" or "angel kisses"

These are by far the most common birthmarks; well over half of all babies have one of more of these flat purple, red, or pink splotches. They're commonly seen either on the back of Baby's neck or on his eyelids, on the side of his nose, or on his forehead. The *bites* or *kisses* (also called *salmon patches*) are actually dilated capillaries just underneath the skin. Most will fade by the time Baby is 2 years old (marks on the back of the neck tend to be most persistent). In any event, they're harmless and don't require any intervention. You may notice that they become redder when Baby cries or fills his diaper because the blood vessels fill with blood. This is completely normal and nothing to be alarmed about.

Café au lait spots

Also quite common, these tan or brown patches may appear anywhere on the body, and they may also appear in groups. They could be present at birth, or they may show up during Baby's first couple of years. These don't go away, and may become darker if exposed to the sun. If Baby has more than six café au lait spots, make sure your pediatrician is aware of it; this could be indicative of an underlying medical condition and may need further evaluation.

Mongolian spots

These flat spots of pigment are bluish-black or gray in color and appear most commonly on the lumbar region or the buttocks of dark-skinned children, though they can also show up on the shoulders and legs. Mongolian spots are caused by a group of melanocytes (cells containing melanin) close to the surface of the skin. Statistics show that almost all African American, Asian,

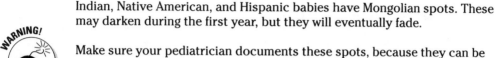

Indian, Native American, and Hispanic babies have Mongolian spots. These may darken during the first year, but they will eventually fade.

Make sure your pediatrician documents these spots, because they can be mistaken for bruises by well-meaning babysitters.

Hemangioma

Hemangiomas are clusters of blood vessels and fall into two types:

✔ **Strawberry hemangioma** may appear as a raised, red area anywhere on Baby's body, either at birth or during the first month. The spot increases in size for six months to one year, and then stops. When Baby is about 1½ years old, the mark will start to shrink, and will eventually fade over a period of years. It will probably disappear completely by the time your child is 10.

✔ **Cavernous hemangioma** involve deeper layers of the skin and vascular system. These are less common than strawberry hemangioma and are usually not present at birth; instead, they start out as flat spots (they may look like a scratch) and increase in size rapidly during the first year. They can be quite large, spongy, and bluish in color — some may resemble a bump or bruise (leaving you to answer the question from complete strangers — over and over again — "What happened to your child?"). Good news, though: Most get smaller by the time your child is in preschool and will probably disappear completely by the time he's in kindergarten.

Hemangioma birthmarks of both kinds can be quite large and disfiguring, especially when they appear on Baby's face. This is sometimes *very* upsetting to parents (because thoughtless people may feel the need to point out your child's birthmark, as though you've somehow overlooked it). Unless the birthmark is interfering with Baby's vital functions (his breathing is obstructed or he can't eat because of a hemangioma on his lip), most dermatologists recommend waiting it out. Removing a hemangioma prematurely can leave a lifelong scar, whereas allowing nature to take its course leaves Baby with almost no visible remnants.

Doctors also get concerned about hemangiomas near the eye and over the spine. Hemangiomas over the spine can be a sign of an underlying abnormality in the spine and need to be brought to the attention of your doctor.

Port-wine stain

Also called nevus flammeus, *port-wine stains* are dark red or purplish flat marks that can appear anywhere on the body. These birthmarks are present at birth, appearing flat and red; they increase in size as Baby grows, and in thickness over time. Port-wine stains can lead to serious emotional distress for parents and children alike. As the child reaches adolescence, laser treatments become an option for fading these birthmarks.

The cause of port-wine stains was unknown until recently; they're thought to be caused by a deficiency in the body's ability to constrict certain blood vessels. Port-wine stains that appear near Baby's eye or on his cheek could also be indicative of other medical conditions, most notably Sturge-Weber Syndrome, in which blood vessels of the eye and brain are also affected. Your pediatrician will evaluate port-wine stains in this area to rule out further complications.

Letting Sleeping Babies Lie

Having a baby in the house makes you stop and consider the most rudimentary needs of human beings. Your day is suddenly focused on a basic need you have probably either taken for granted for years and/or never given much thought to: sleep. And one thing you notice right off the bat is that Baby's internal clock is far different from yours.

How much sleep does she need?

Every baby is different, but generally speaking, newborns sleep 16 to 20 hours a day, mostly in spurts of a couple of hours here and there. Your little one will probably wake to eat, spend some time having her diaper changed, stare at you while you cuddle with her, and then doze off again before too long.

Most children this age don't fall into any kind of sleeping pattern, but some do. If your infant is awake at different times every single day, you're not doing anything wrong. Baby's just doing what her little body is telling her to do: eat and rest. (We should all have it so good.) In addition, she's still working out the little kinks in her nervous system, which is tiring work for an infant. An immature, overactive nervous system can keep a baby awake at the most inopportune times (all night long, for example); when all of her neurons start firing properly (as they will over the next couple of months), her sleep cycle will settle into more of a routine.

Night owls and go-go-go babies

Babies who just don't want to sleep may be at the mercy of their developing nervous systems. Because Baby is easily overstimulated at this age, he may not be able to drop off to sleep by himself. It's all right to rock him and rub his little back in a quiet setting to calm him down, but try to put him in his bassinet or crib while he's still awake. You don't want to establish a pattern of rocking him to sleep every time he dozes off, or he may never learn to comfort himself in those final moments before sleep takes hold.

Night owl babies (infants who are most alert very late at night right into the wee morning hours) have their little clocks mixed up. The theory as to why this happens seems logical enough: In the womb, many infants are lulled to sleep by their mother's movement during the day. These infants begin their kicking and the rolling inside the womb when their moms retire for the evening. This can be fatiguing enough when Mom is still pregnant — when the kicking turns to real-life crying, what's a parent to do?

You can help Baby turn his schedule around by doing the following:

- ✔ **Keep nighttime sacred.** Turn down the lights, keep noise down to a whisper, and all other stimulation to a minimum.

- ✔ **Save the crib for night sleeping.** Put Baby down for his naps in his bassinet out in the living room.

- ✔ **Cut back on his daytime naps.** Keep him busy by putting him under the baby gym, giving him a bath (unless that makes him drowsy), tickling his feet, or singing. Giving him more stimulation during the day may make him *want* to stay awake for longer periods of time.

- ✔ **Don't tiptoe around the house during the day while baby is sleeping.** Let him get used to the daytime noise of the TV, radio, phone, and vacuum. Then when it's quiet at night, he'll sleep more soundly.

Unless he's really crying, avoid the urge to sprint over to Baby when you hear him in his crib or bassinet during the night. Give him a chance to drift off again by himself. By rushing to his side, you could inadvertently encourage his nighttime wakefulness.

Considering sleeping with Baby

For reasons of convenience and closeness, many parents consider sleeping with Baby in the adults' bed. There's a lot of conflicting information about sharing your bed with Baby, and people tend to feel very strongly one way or the other, dismissing any dissenting opinions. There are definite advantages and disadvantages to having Baby in your bed. Take a look at Table 6-1 for a quick run down of both

Table 6-1	Pros and Cons of Sharing a Bed with Baby	
Advantages	**Disadvantages**	
Convenience. It's just easier for a nursing mom to have her infant right next to her in the middle of the night.	There are some very real potential dangers, like suffocation.	
Baby feels safe and may sleep better.	Parents may worry about having Baby in the bed and could actually lose *more* sleep.	
Proponents of bed sharing say that it helps to foster a sense of family between parents and their children.	Bed sharing more often than not leads to a child who needs to sleep with his parents, setting the parents up for years of either sleeping with an older child or bedtime battles over the child sleeping in his own room.	

Weeks and weeks of nighttime feedings take their toll, and you just get to the point where you want a full night's sleep — or anything close to it. But the potential serious risks of sharing a bed seem to outweigh the temporary benefits. Placing your infant in his own bassinet next to your bed is a better option; you'll have him right there, and yet he has a sense of being on his own.

You can also try a crib equipped with a drop-down side that connects to your bed (Figure 6-1), called a *co-sleeper*. This offers you the best of both worlds. Baby is just a reach away, but in his own bed. You'll have the convenience of almost having him right there with you, without the worries involved in sharing the bed with him.

Figure 6-1:
A Baby in a co-sleeper crib is close at hand for nighttime feedings.

Figuring Out Feeding Time

Like sleep, feeding becomes a focus of new parents' lives. You may be surprised by how much time you spend worrying whether Baby is eating enough — or too much. Top that off with some serious concerns about gas and a heart-to-heart about poop, and you can consider yourself fully initiated into new parenthood.

Growing pains

Because pediatricians recommend feeding newborns on demand (that is, when Baby says it's time to eat), new parents are constantly on call, ready and waiting with a bottle or the breast whenever the cries of hunger begin. Baby may not settle into a definite pattern in the first few weeks.

Right around the 3-week mark (and again at 6 weeks and 3 months), all babies (bottle and breastfed) undergo a growth spurt. Your breastfed Baby will start nursing more often, more energetically, and possibly for longer periods of times. Your breasts may start leaking (almost like they did when your milk initially came in) and they may hurt more than usual.

Your body has a remarkable capability to adjust to this demand, and the discomfort you're feeling is only temporary — after Baby has established just how much milk she needs at this point (she's doing this by feeding more and by sucking harder), your breasts will settle into this new phase. Expect her voracious nursing to last a few days, and probably no longer than a week.

Feeding baby too much?

Even small babies can have big appetites. Some parents, especially those of bottlefed infants, who are actually doling out larger amounts of formula to their child (as opposed to breast-feeding moms, who can't see what Baby is eating), start to wonder if they're giving Baby too much to eat. The truth of the matter is that as long as you're letting Baby control the feeding sessions (allowing him to eat whenever he needs to and offering him an adequate amount of formula), he'll cut himself off when he's had enough. This is an automatic part of his programming. You really can't feed him too much, but you can *under*feed him. Remember, his little body has a lot going on right now, and he needs every bit of nourishment he's taking in.

It's important to nurse Baby through a growth spurt so that your milk supply will match her demands. You may be tempted to add a bottle to the feeding schedule in order to give yourself a break during these growth spurts, but doing this is counterproductive. Unless Baby is allowed to feed as often as she needs, your milk supply won't increase to an adequate level, leaving both of you frustrated. In the end, supplementing with a bottle could end up causing you to wean your child sooner than you had planned.

The scoop on poop

Many newborns seem as though they're determined to single-handedly keep the diaper companies in business. An infant may fill his diaper every time he eats, which could be somewhere in the neighborhood of ten times a day for a breastfed babe. This isn't at all unusual. What goes in must come out, after all, and Baby's frequent bowel movements are one way for you to know with certainty that he's getting plenty to eat. (If your nursing Baby is having fewer than five bowel movements per day, he may not be getting enough breast milk.) A breastfed baby's stool may be runny, yellowish, and look like it has little seeds in it. A bottlefed infant has fewer bowel movements (one a day, one every other day, one every third day . . . your child will develop his own pattern) and the stool is usually tan and more solid.

A tiny infant's bowel movement can be surprisingly explosive, so don't be alarmed by the noise (he may even grunt) or the amount of stool in his diaper. Keep a healthy stock of diapers in the house, along with plenty of clean outfits on the changing table.

During the second month, bowel movements tend to become less frequent, though they may remain explosive until Baby starts on solids, at which point his stool will become . . . well, more solid.

Green stools are also normal. Worry about red (blood), black (old blood), or white (possible liver problems) stools.

What a gas!

Babies can be gassy little creatures. Gas can be caused by Baby's swallowing air or possibly by something that a nursing mother has eaten. Some babies pass gas regularly throughout the day, blissfully unaware of it. But sometimes that gas gets stuck in their little tummies or intestines, bubbling up in there, making Baby very uncomfortable.

Painful gas is no laughing matter. Your infant may scream in pain and/or pull her little legs up to her stomach. Your goal, of course, is to soothe her, get that gas out of her, and try to prevent this from happening in the future.

If your bottlefed child suffers from gas regularly, try using a bottle with a collapsible insert. You actually remove all the air from the insert before you feed Baby, so it minimizes the chance of her ingesting a lot of air along with her formula. You can also try changing the nipple on a regular bottle to see whether that helps reduce Baby's gassy spells. The nipple you've been using may be too small, causing Baby to suck air while she's only trying to get some food.

Burp Baby in the middle of her feeding (or two or three times during the feeding if she seems *very* gassy) and after she's completely finished. If you don't get a healthy belch after a minute or two, keep trying. It's important to help her ease the gas out of her system so that it doesn't pop up an hour later and cause her major discomfort.

A breastfeeding mom should keep track of her own diet for a few days and try to eliminate foods that could be irritating to Baby's gastrointestinal system like:

- ✔ Dairy products (milk, cheese, ice cream). Remember, you don't have to drink milk to make milk.

- ✔ Spicy foods (including garlic)

- ✔ Stimulants (like caffeine)

- ✔ Gas-inducing foods (broccoli, beans, or a diet heavy in veggies)

Don't eliminate all of these foods at once, or you'll never know which is the culprit. Instead, isolate and eliminate each group for several days at a time, making sure to note Baby's reaction. If the gas seems to be gone, you can attribute it to whichever food group has most recently been subtracted from your diet.

In spite of your best efforts, Baby may still suffer from an occasional bout with painful gas. There are some positions you can try to soothe her and to break up those bubbles and get that gas out; all of them involve applying firm pressure to her tummy. If doing this causes her more discomfort, stop immediately. Try this:

- ✔ Lay her on her back on a flat surface and press gently on her tummy as you rub it.

- ✔ Hold her up on your shoulder, patting her back, just as if you were burping her during a feeding. You may get a decent belch from her.

✔ Sit in a chair and place her facedown on your leg. Pat her back and bounce her very gently.

✔ Add a little warmth. Fill a hot water bottle with warm water and lay Baby tummy-down on top of it (on a safe surface, like the floor), rubbing her back. (*Caution:* Don't use hot water! You could burn Baby's delicate skin.)

If nothing seems to work and this is a regular occurrence, call your pediatrician for further guidance. He may recommend simethicone drops to break up the gas, but this medicine has very mixed results (it works like a charm for some kids, but doesn't touch the gas in others). He may also want to discuss a change in formula for your bottlefed infant.

Cry Me a River

Every baby cries — some just cry more often and more intensely than others. Your infant, as intelligent as he is, doesn't have the capacity to communicate with you at this point in time except through crying. As Baby gets a bit older, you may be able to discern which cry means what — but right now, there will probably be times when you don't know why the heck this kid is crying. Hang in there. This happens to almost every parent, and it's always confusing, no matter how well prepared you thought you were to care for Baby.

Running down reasons for tears

Hunger is at the top of the list of reasons babies cry. If he's still crying after you've offered him the breast or bottle, run down this checklist to determine whether there's another fairly simple answer to his problem:

✔ Does he need a fresh diaper?

✔ Is he too hot or too cold?

✔ Could he be tired?

✔ Is a tag scratching his neck, or is his toe caught in a snap?

✔ Is he sick? (An infant who has a high fever or is vomiting should be seen by his pediatrician as soon as possible.)

Obviously, you know how to remedy these situations. If nothing jumps up as the obvious cause of Baby's unhappiness, he may be feeling overstimulated, frightened, or just *not right*. Remember, his nervous system isn't fully developed, and things that wouldn't bother an adult (noise, light, a funny smell) can seriously irritate a sensitive little one.

In this case, try some of these comfort measures:

- ✔ **Swaddle him.** Infants love the feeling of being bundled up, safe and secure. Take care not to bundle him too tightly, or this could cause more crying.

- ✔ **Hold him, rock him, move him around.** Motion soothes some criers.

- ✔ **Offer him a pacifier.** Babies need to suck for comfort. Your child may need to suck more often than every few hours at a feeding. Chapter 8 offers a more detailed look at the pros and cons of pacifiers.

It can be incredibly frustrating when nothing soothes a crying infant. Realize that this is also normal, and that it has almost nothing to do with your abilities as a parent. As long as you're looking for the cause and not further over-stimulating him, you're doing everything you can.

If you suspect gas is to blame for your breastfed child's crying, check out the earlier section, "What a gas!" You may also have a child who is more sensitive than the average infant to the world around him. As a result, an entire day's worth of stimulation — light, voices, smells, movement — may result in a volcanic crying explosion in the evening, when Baby has to let it all out. I discuss dealing with sensitive babies in Chapter 8.

When your frustration reaches its apex and Baby is still crying, leave him in his crib for a few minutes while you comfort yourself. All new parents find themselves feeling frazzled from time to time; walking away from the situation for a short time is sometimes the best thing you can do for yourself and for Baby. Take some deep breaths. Do some stretches, if that helps. Call a friend or your mom. Tell yourself that Baby isn't doing this to ruin your day, and that eventually, this will all pass.

Coping with colic

An infant who cries for hours on end at specific times of the day without any obvious cause may have colic, which is an entirely different level of misery — for Baby and for you. Any parent who has dealt with a colicky baby will tell you that it's incredibly difficult, so if you suspect your child's crying is due to something other than hunger or discomfort, you have the sympathies of caregivers around the world.

Colic is loosely defined as crying that lasts for at least two hours, occurs at specific times of the day (often late in the evening), at least three times a week. This pattern usually sets in sometime during the first month. The cause is really unknown. It used to be blamed on Baby's immature digestive system roiling up in gas, and while that theory is still floating around, new theories suggest that colic is due to an infant's immature nervous system and his inability to shut out an irritating environment.

Whatever the cause, colic is harmless to your child, and will usually subside completely on its own by the end of the third month. It's hardest on Baby's caregivers, who listen to the wails every day or every night. There are some tried-and-true tips for quieting the colicky baby, including:

- ✔ **Soothe him with white noise and vibration.** Run the vacuum cleaner or a fan, or buy a white noise machine. Put him near the clothes dryer while it's running. Take him for a long car ride. Let him rest in his swing. The combination of white noise and vibration has been known to put many a colicky child right to sleep.

- ✔ **Tote him around.** Put Baby in a front-carrier or a sling. Sometimes being close to Mom is just what the colicky baby needs.

- ✔ **Give him a pacifier.** Sucking is soothing, especially for a child who's senses are more intense.

- ✔ **Massage him.** Touch is an incredibly soothing force for an infant.

- ✔ **Change the scenery.** Try taking him outside — or giving him a bath. For some reason, some colicky babies sometimes respond to these sudden change-ups. (Hey, if it works, don't question it!)

Most importantly, if someone offers to help with a colicky baby, accept the offer. Listening to the crying on a daily basis can wear out the most patient parent. Go easy on yourself if you find that yourself lying on your own bed crying while Baby is screaming in his crib. The old adage that parenting is the toughest job in the world was likely coined by someone with a colicky baby.

Colic can wreak havoc on your relationship with your mate. Maintain communication about the issue and give each other a break. One person shouldn't deal with a colicky infant all the time — it's not good for that parent, and it's better for Baby to have a well-rested (relatively speaking, of course) caregiver.

Escaping the House with Baby in Tow

Staying home with your baby isn't always the sweet deal other people may think it is. (Like your former co-workers, who truly believe you're sleeping in all day and painting your toenails whenever the mood strikes you.) In fact, spending every waking moment inside your house — no matter what size it is — starts to feel like you're doing hard time, albeit for good reason and with good company.

As long as you're feeling well (with the effects of delivery almost a memory), you can surely take Baby out of the house. Some tips for your first outings:

✔ **Pack the diaper bag with everything you need.** Include plenty of extra diapers, the changing pad, wipes, bottles, and formula for the bottlefed infant, burp cloths, and a pacifier, if your child uses one.

✔ **Don't make any big plans.** There's a lot involved in toting an infant around, including feedings and diaper changes. An errand that took you 30 minutes to complete in your pre-baby days may now take you well over an hour. Be prepared for this.

✔ **Take someone else along on your first outing or two.** You're going to be getting used to an entirely new system of leaving the house and dealing with Baby's needs while you're out and about. Having an assistant the first few times will make your transition to this system much smoother.

✔ **Avoid taking Baby into a house filled with sick people.** A tiny infant's immune system isn't yet equipped to do battle with the cold and flu season. The result is twofold: Baby is more susceptible to catching cold, and is also more prone to becoming very ill from it.

Although you've certainly left the house in the past, doing so with Baby is very different, both from a planning point of view and because your schedule now rotates around Baby's needs. For now, take each moment as it comes and don't have any grand expectations of how things should go. In time — believe it or not — your outings will become a normal part of everyday life. For more information on getting out of the house with Baby, see Chapter 3.

Taking care of yourself

Along with figuring out Baby's wants and needs during this first month, you'll also be figuring out yourself. Parenting takes an extreme amount of fortitude, patience, and sacrifice (the first sacrifice, you've no doubt noticed, is sleep). In order to be ready to take care of your child, you have to take care of yourself. Make sure you're getting enough to eat. Sleep (or at least rest) when Baby does. Accept all offers of help that you can tolerate, and communicate your level of tolerance. (You may not want your mother over all day long, but let her know you'd certainly appreciate her giving you a hand in the evening.)

Above all else, have a realistic outlook. The first few months with Baby require big adjustments across the board, and it takes time for everyone to settle in. Go easy on yourself and on your mate, who's figuring out life with Baby right alongside you.

Allow yourself to take the shortcuts in life that you may have avoided till now: Eat take-out. Clean the house once a week. Let your mother fold your laundry. Maybe fried chicken in a box, a dirty bathroom, and your mother's odd way of folding underwear never made it into the fantasy you developed of the perfect life with Baby, but anything that makes your life easier gives you more energy to care for your child — and that's pretty darn ideal.

Chapter 7

The Second Month: Finding Your Rhythm

In This Chapter

▶ Watching Baby change

▶ Determining whether Baby is going to settle down to a schedule

▶ Adjusting to the breastfed baby's schedule

*B*aby's been very busy, growing and learning new tricks — it's hard to believe she was just a blob a few weeks ago who couldn't smile, coo, or stay awake for very long. The second month is a time of little accomplishments and continued adjustments. Parents who are able to go with the flow may have a slight advantage over parents who live their lives by the clock, simply because most babies aren't quite up to establishing a fixed schedule at this point.

In this chapter, we bring you up to date on what to expect of Baby's new growth and help you deal with Baby's changing activity patterns. Formula-feeding moms may notice that their babies are falling into definite patterns at this point. You know how much Baby is taking at each meal, and feedings are starting to come at more regular times. Breastfeeding moms may not be so lucky; in this chapter we give you some clues on how to deal with a breastfed baby's hectic schedule.

Checking In with Baby

Starting now, the changes come fast and furious. Baby starts to look more like the cutie pie you had imagined while you were pregnant, and he starts to notice his world a bit more. And although you may be content to sit back and watch him grow, you can play an active role in encouraging his development. Don't expect too much, though: He may be ready to roll, but he's not quite ready to run.

In this section, we tell you what to expect from your monthly doctor checkup, give you some tips on how Baby may be changing, and then give you a few clues on how to help her with development skills.

The 2-month checkup

Expect this month's checkup to focus on just about everything. You'll be exhausted, naturally (as much as from the excitement of watching Baby's latest developments as from the 3 a.m. feedings), so prepare yourself with a list of questions and concerns you want to discuss with your pediatrician. You may want to know, for example, whether Baby's explosive bowel movements are normal (yes, they are), or if he can see you from all the way across the room (not yet). Because a baby is an endless source of wonder, there's really no end to the questions that new parents may have. Don't be shy about asking them. Your doctor's your best source of baby-related information!

Keep a small memo pad handy at home for jotting down questions that pop up between visits. Slip it into the diaper bag when you're finished with it, so it won't get lost in the general baby mess in the house.

During this visit, you can expect the following:

- ✔ Baby is weighed and measured (including head and chest circumferences).

- ✔ The doctor takes note of Baby's physical development: Can he lift his head while he's on his stomach? How's that belly button looking? What about the circumcision?

- ✔ The doctor asks about any areas of concern you may have: Is Baby's bottom red and raw? Is this kid a spit-up champion? The doctor will advise you on how to handle anything you're particularly worried about (diaper ointment for that rash) and further assess anything that may cause him concern (he may want to know how far baby spits, for example, to rule out any gastrointestinal problems).

- ✔ Your doctor wants to know how things are going with Baby — feeding, sleeping, bowel movements, bonding, the general state of affairs at home. Be honest. (These first months aren't easy for everyone, and your doctor may have helpful advice that's specific to your situation.)

Immunizations

During the first year, most of Baby's checkups will often include at *least* one immunization shot. These shots come complete with a series of confusing initials that may make you fear you're about to do a geometry problem. Don't worry, we break all this down in Chapter 18 for you, where we tell you exactly what the initials mean and how they protect your child. This month, Baby will be given:

DTaP #1

IPV #1

Hib #1

Ask about the side effects of each, how you can soothe Baby's discomfort, and what sort of reactions warrant a call to the doctor.

Milestones this month

Baby turns the corner from adorable little alien to incredibly cute baby this month — physically and socially. During the second month, Baby will probably do the following:

- ✔ Baby loses the pointy head. The plates in Baby's skull are still quite malleable, and this month, they take on a more normal shape after that trip through the birth canal. The soft spots on the top and at the back of her head *(fontanels)* allow for this realignment of the skull bones.
- ✔ She can lift her head 45 degrees while she's on her tummy.
- ✔ She can follow the movement of an object in front of her by turning her head.
- ✔ Her movements become less jerky, more purposeful.
- ✔ Baby finds her hands, which are an endless source of amusement for some infants (as the month progresses, she may also be able to swing at the toys hanging from a baby gym).
- ✔ She can smile and coo.

Support that neck! Some babies have a good handle on holding their heads up at this age, but most are still pretty wobbly. Real, dependable neck strength won't kick in till about the fourth month. Continue to support Baby's neck and head whenever you pick him up. Allow him to try out his burgeoning neck muscles when you're holding him, but always be prepared to catch a heavy head.

Promoting baby's development

During the second month, baby's strength and hand-eye coordination increase — you can help to develop them faster, though (and no, you don't have to buy him a little baby barbell set or a teeny-weeny eye chart in order to do so).

Allow your little one to spend some time each day on his stomach. Sure, it looks uncomfortable, but it's great way to make him work those muscles. Lift that head! Turn that neck! Find those hands!

Place Baby on a safe, clean surface for his mini-workout — a blanket on the floor will work just fine. Let him try out his muscles for as long as he's content to, or for as long as you can stand to watch him rub his face into the blanket. Even at this age, you can never be sure when the little one will make a surprising movement and propel himself backward, forward, or sideways, which means countertops and sofas aren't good workout areas.

Give your child a baby mirror (available in toy stores) and he'll have ample entertainment during his workout.

Encourage his hand-eye coordination by placing Baby on his back or in an infant seat and holding items of interest in front of or above him. Babies love the contrast of black-and-white objects, and they also love the human face. Before long, Baby will reach out and try to touch someone or something, which is the beginning of his hand-eye coordination. The more opportunities he has to practice this skill, the sooner it'll develop.

Babies aren't able to see in full color until the fourth month, but research has shown that newborns love contrasting, black-and-white patterns. Look for toys with black-and-white swirls, stripes, or checks. Babies are also intrigued by human faces, particularly areas of high contrast, such as your hairline. (So you aren't just imagining that Baby is infatuated with you.)

Sleep, Baby, Sleep (Please!)

Parents of newborns can easily be identified by their drooping eyelids, their pale complexions, and their uncanny ability to compute exactly how many minutes of sleep they've had during the past week. The first sleep-deprived month with Baby takes its toll; by month two, you're seriously starting to question whether your child will ever sleep through the night. The answer is yes — but perhaps not quite yet.

Cutting back on the daytime zzzzzs

If your little one refuses to sleep at night, she may be napping too much during the day. If Baby still has her days and nights mixed up, or if she has simply decided that nighttime is the right time (for eating and cooing), start making a concerted effort to keep her awake more during the day. A sleepy newborn in her first month of life can only handle so much stimulation before she has to conk out; a 2-month-old can take a bit more.

To keep Baby awake and alert for longer periods:

✔ Put her on her stomach for her daily exercise

✔ Show her some cool black-and-white patterned toys

✔ Tickle her tummy and toes

✔ Sing to her

✔ Bring visitors in

Try to keep a 2-month-old night owl awake for at least two hours at a stretch during the day for starters. As she starts to become more alert during your waking hours, add more and more time, in ten-minute increments.

Let Baby sleep when he's had enough! Most babies at this age can't go more than three to four hours without a nap. It's all right to let him get a little cranky — but only for a short time. Get the nap in before he turns into Mr. Miserable. Overstimulated, overtired babies may have a terrible time trying to fall asleep.

Plan some evening activities for the baby who tuckers out at 7 p.m. only to rise three hours later, geared up for the nightlife. Many babies find a pre-bedtime bath very soothing — and exhausting (bonus for you!).

If you address and try to correct each of these potential trouble spots, are you guaranteed to have a baby who sleeps for hours on end during the night? Nope. Each child is different, and what's been helpful for quieting your friend's 2-month-old may only irritate your infant further. Unfortunately, some parents find that no matter what they try, their infant just isn't ready for marathon snoozing. Keep telling yourself that this child will eventually sleep — and so will you.

Supplementing for sounder sleep

Bottlefed newborns tend to sleep for longer stretches during the day and sleep through the night sooner than their breastfed buddies: Formula isn't digested as quickly as mother's milk, so babies on the bottle stay fuller longer. If your breastfed little one is dozing off after his nighttime nursing only to awaken two hours later, squealing for more, chances are good that he's legitimately hungry.

If you've gotten to the point where you just can't take being up constantly during the night, ask you pediatrician about the possibility of adding a supplemental bottle of formula at bedtime. Check out the upcoming section, "Determining whether you need to supplement" for more information.

Breastfeeding Blues

Feeding Baby during the second month isn't the uncertain venture it was when he first arrived on the scene. By now you know what to expect from each session, which is in itself reason to rejoice. When your breast starts spraying milk clear across the room, for example, you hardly bat an eye.

But breastfeeding moms sometimes get discouraged at this time because their babies are often far from being on any sort of schedule, and no one happened to mention this during Lamaze or in the hospital. Your job as a 24-hour diner (Open All Night! Breakfast Served Anytime!) can start to feel like a drag. You start wondering why you aren't putting Baby on some sort of schedule — that's what mothers do, isn't it?

Determining whether you need to supplement

During Baby's checkup, discuss her feeding patterns with the doctor, who will be able to tell by Baby's growth whether she's getting enough to eat. Occasionally, a breastfed Baby doesn't get enough milk — for several reasons (maybe your nipples are inverted, Baby's sucking reflex could be weak, or sometimes milk production is low). This isn't a failure on anyone's part — it's just something that happens from time to time. If Baby's doctor determines that this is the case, he'll probably want you to start giving Baby regular supplements.

If you're not producing enough milk for Baby's growing appetite, take a look at what's going on in your life and see if you can ease up a bit. Moms are often back to work at this point. You may be on the go all day, forgetting to increase your fluid intake; you may not be eating correctly or getting enough rest — all of these are vital to successful nursing or pumping sessions! (Also, continue taking your prenatal vitamins.)

Supplements have other benefits aside from filling Baby's belly. Introducing Baby to the occasional bottle means that Dad can easily take over a nighttime feeding now and then. You can also leave Baby with a sitter for a night out with your hubby, knowing that Baby won't starve before you return.

Don't add supplements to Baby's feeding schedule until your breast milk is well established — usually after six weeks. Introducing Baby to a bottle prior to this time may also cause nipple confusion, because bottlefeeding and breastfeeding require different methods of sucking.

You may be concerned about springing a new feeding system on your infant, but the truth is there's no time like the present. Waiting until he's 4 months old could result in a flat-out refusal from Baby to take to a substitute.

Baby is more likely to ease into taking a supplementary meal with nary a peep if he's good and hungry — but not so hungry that he's screaming for food. If he becomes really upset, he may want the comfort that only you (and your breast) can provide.

Babies may get lazy with the bottle versus the breast. They get instant gratification from the bottle and have to wait for the letdown when breastfeeding. If this is a problem, express a little breast milk before latching the baby on so there is something to taste right away.

What if Baby is starving — but not screeching — and he still won't take the bottle? Let Dad or another caregiver give it a go. Your intelligent, highly sensitive child recognizes your voice, your touch, and your scent, which is likely laden with breast milk. And even if you smell like a daisy, his crying will probably stimulate your milk — and after he catches a whiff of it, he's going to fight for his right to nurse.

Supplementing Baby's meal with formula is fine; adding cereal at this age isn't. Your infant's gastrointestinal system simply can't handle solids yet, so even if you think she's ready . . . she's not.

Feeding more often

If you're determined to stick with breastfeeding, you may need to nurse Baby more often. The more often Baby feeds, the more milk you produce. Alternatively, there is also a feeding system that allows Baby to breastfeed while providing him with supplemental nutrition called the Medela Supplemental Nursing System (SNS). Basically, it works like so: A bottle hangs from the mother's neck. Two long, thin, soft tubes extend from the bottle and are taped to the mother's breasts, so that they are positioned over the areola. As a result, the baby takes the supplemental feeding tubes into his mouth when he latches on to nurse. The sucking is helpful in encouraging milk production, and, most importantly, allows for breastfeeding to continue. For more information on this product, go to `www.healthquest-nf.com/suppnursSys.htm`.

Demanding a schedule

If it turns out that your breastfed baby is getting plenty to eat, then you can just say to him, "Hon, we're going to sit down every three hours for a feeding, and not before then." Right?

Not really. Babies don't just nurse for nutrition. Sucking and cuddling calm Baby's nerves. And most experts advise moms to continue feeding breastfed babies whenever they show signs of hunger (turning their heads to the side, rooting for something to suck on, and finally, crying).

The constant need to breastfeed Baby can be disheartening for the mom who is finding that breastfeeding is a lot more work than she thought it would be, but bear in mind that these early months are by far the most time-consuming as far as nursing Baby goes. If this is your first time at the Mommy Rodeo, breastfeeding can seem overwhelming at this point — especially when you're worn out (and were expecting Baby to be on a normal schedule by now).

You're not a horrible mother if you're feeling tied down to your nursing infant. Many, many new moms feel this way. Take heart in the knowledge that your baby won't need to nurse every two hours for the rest of her life. She'll be on solids in a couple of months, which will curtail her need to breastfeed.

In the meantime, acknowledge that Baby may always nurse erratically, and that it has nothing to do with your inability to put her on a schedule. It's just her nature.

If you really, truly decide that this breastfeeding thing isn't working out, formula is always an option. Tips for bottlefeeding are included in Chapter 2, and tips for making the weaning process easier on yourself are included in Chapter 16.

Seeing things in a new light

When you first start to breastfeed, every session is a huge production. You're still figuring out how to hold Baby, he's learning to latch on, you're concentrating on relaxing so your milk will come in, plus you're exposing your breasts to an audience of relatives (or at least a nurse or lactation specialist). As Baby gets older, it's okay to let go of some of the pageantry of nursing and to find the easiest way to fit feedings into the rest of your busy life.

If nursing still seems like a huge ordeal, try a different position for Baby — or for yourself. Do your reading, prepare your grocery list, or catch up on phone calls and other easy tasks while nursing. On the other hand, if you're feeling exhausted, you need to chuck the chores and relax with Baby while he nurses. Put your feet up and recline in your favorite chair, and you may just find yourself looking forward to the next feeding.

Chapter 8

The Third Month: Rolling Away from Infancy

· ·

In This Chapter

▶ Developments into the third month

▶ Confining Baby safely

▶ Seeing whether Baby is ready for a routine

▶ Looking at a few concerns

· ·

During the third month, Baby continues to develop her little personality. She's morphing from tiny infant to a real baby (*now* she looks like the babies you see in commercials). Depending on how well she's settling in at home, you may be feeling that raising this kid is a breeze or that it's harder than you ever imagined. Either way, you may be wondering how the rest of the first year is going to progress: If Baby is easy to deal with now, are you in for it later, when she starts to walk? And if Baby hasn't slept more than three hours at a time from the day she was born, does this mean that she'll never settle into a routine?

The third month is a transitional time between true infancy and burgeoning, active babyhood. Parents are also transitioning, as they settle into life with Baby, but continue to adapt to the experience.

Checking In with Baby

During the third month, there's usually no well-baby visit scheduled, but if Baby isn't feeling well or if an issue of concern pops up, call your pediatrician for advice or to schedule an office visit. Because Baby is becoming more active and alert this month, questions concerning her development may be coming up on a regular basis. Jot your questions down and keep them in your diaper bag so that you'll have them handy at next month's appointment. Meantime, this section covers what Baby may be up to both physically and socially over the course of this month.

Milestones this month

So, what's Baby up to this month? He's very busy growing, moving, and developing his communication skills. Here are a few changes you can expect to see at this time:

- Baby gains about 1¼ pounds and adds 1 inch to his length.

- Baby starts to gain more neck strength and control. When pulled to sitting position, his neck still lags behind, but noticeably less so than last month.

- He lifts his head and chest when you place him on his tummy. He isn't doing full push-ups yet; he's happy to rest on his forearms.

- He bats and swings at objects in his baby gym. He probably doesn't grasp hold of them just yet, but he's definitely getting closer.

- He can unclench those baby fists; he may be able to hold a rattle or small toy.

- Baby makes small circular movements with his arms.

- Your child starts to discover and explore different parts of his body. (What's this? An ear?)

- He may be able to roll over one way, or at least he's making the effort to do so.

- He makes and maintains eye contact for longer periods of time.

- Baby stays awake (and sleeps) for longer stretches of time.

- He now shows emotions: surprise, fear, anger, happiness. He may also mirror someone else's facial expressions.

- Baby exhibits more interest in the world around him (which may mean he's less interested in nursing or sitting still with his bottle).

- He recognizes voices.

- He attempts deliberate communication by using different cries or by cooing.

- Baby will look at a space where an object used to be, but has no sense of *object permanency* at this point. (In other words, he may notice if something isn't where it should be or where it once was, but he has no idea that the thing is somewhere else now. To him, the object is simply gone.)

Catching Baby's undivided attention

People without kids are sometimes shocked to see relatives talking comfortably with an infant. It just doesn't look natural, and it can seem downright silly. The kid doesn't understand what the heck you're saying, so why say anything, right?

Look more closely, and you can see that Baby loves the attention. She may not be able to answer just yet, but Baby can definitely understand some of your message — the tone of voice you use, for example, is a great indicator of your mood, and the more sing-songy you can make your voice, the more she wants to listen to you.

How can you get Baby to respond to you when you speak? By following some of these tips:

- ✔ **Talk to her.** Keep up a running narration of what's going on: "Now it's time to eat, and then we're going for a walk."

- ✔ **Sing to her.** Even if you're not ready to cut your own CD, Baby won't care. Sing her silly songs, lullabies, or whatever you're into.

- ✔ **Play games with her.** Tickle her little toes and play "This little piggy." Hold her toys where she'll have to reach for them. Blow raspberries on her tummy.

- ✔ **Look at her.** You don't have to stare into her eyes 24 hours a day, but make eye contact while you're talking or singing.

You don't have to use baby talk with your infant — just speak in a soothing tone of voice and give her your undivided attention. You may be pleasantly surprised at Baby's reactions (when she tries to vocalize during part of a favorite song, for example), which can lead to more and more satisfying — and completely natural — interactions between the two of you.

Physically speaking

Babies are a mixed lot. The chubby baby may have thin parents, and the skinny kid may have a heavy family.

But should you worry about a chunky baby — or a very skinny one? Well, as long as your pediatrician isn't worried, you shouldn't be, either. When your pediatrician pulls out the growth chart each month, Baby is put into a growth percentile for height and weight. (Check out www.cdc.gov/growthcharts for more information.)

Kids often change very quickly. As soon as the butterball baby starts crawling, cruising, and walking, he's probably going to slim down considerably (and continue to do so over the next few years, as walking turns to running, climbing, and skateboarding). And instead of being at a disadvantage, the wiry babies often have an *advantage* in the movement department: Because they're thin, it's often easier for them to get up and get going.

Sometimes an under- or oversized child may have an underlying medical condition causing him to lose or gain weight at an unusual rate. Your pediatrician is tuned into these potential problems, and will suggest further testing if he suspects, for example, that baby's thyroid isn't working properly. Otherwise, try not to worry about your child's baby fat (or lack of it).

Keeping Baby Safe and Sound

Baby is becoming more active this month. She's rolling, she's reaching for things, and she's almost ready to do more. Every day is a new opportunity for her to expand her horizons beyond her baby blanket, which means the issue of keeping her safe has just expanded, also.

Baby seat safety

Baby loves her little seat, where she can sit and have a bird's-eye view of you cleaning the kitchen, preparing her bottle, or chatting with Grandma. When she was an infant, placing Baby in her seat on top of the kitchen table was fairly safe — after all, she slept all the time, and when she was awake, she was content to take in her surroundings quietly.

That's changing now, of course. Baby's awake more, for one thing, and for another, she's becoming curious — mostly about herself, and what she can do, but also about her surroundings. Three-month-olds are rollers, kickers, and swatters — and your child may be able to do these things with more force than you realize. If she isn't properly secured in her baby seat, she could accidentally propel herself out of it. This is especially important if you know you've been a little lax at times about strapping her in, figuring she was always sleeping and unable to move about freely in any event.

The seatbelt should be used whenever Baby is in her seat. If unfastened, the strap can become a strangulation hazard if Baby slips down and out of the seat. Figure 8-1 shows you how to strap Baby in securely.

To keep Baby safe in her infant seat:

- ✔ **Secure the strap each and every time you put her in the seat.** Adjust it so that it's tight enough to hold her in place.

- ✔ **Don't place the seat on a raised surface.** At this age, you just never know what Baby will discover she's capable of doing.

- ✔ **Never leave Baby unattended in her seat.** For instance, if you're going to put the laundry away, move her seat upstairs so that you can keep a constant watch on her.

Figure 8-1:
Baby
properly
secured in
infant seat.

Placing her in her seat is sometimes the safest way for you to get some things done around the house (especially if you don't have a playpen or you just hate to put her in there). After all, if you place her on her baby blanket now, she's going to roll right off before long. Just make sure she's not in that seat all day long. She needs the chance to practice her new moves with supervision but without restraints.

Playpen safety

Playpens, portable cribs, and play yards are similar products used for similar purposes. Babies play, sleep, or wait patiently for their caregivers to let them out, depending on the household.

Don't keep Baby in a playpen for long periods of time. Go ahead and put him in while you're preparing dinner or answering the door (at these times, the playpen may be your safest option, in fact, to corral and protect your increasingly active little guy). He isn't going to reach his potential sitting in a playpen, though, and in fact, he may become very bored — very quickly.

Babies at this age are becoming more aware of what's going on around them. If Baby is on his blanket on the floor, he can reach for an object just out of his grasp — and he just may succeed, which will lead to more experimentation. If he tries to reach for something outside the safe confines of his playpen, he fails. No prize for Baby.

No matter what type of playpen you choose — the traditional kind, the portable type, or a more expansive play yard —inspect it thoroughly before you place Baby inside. Make sure you:

✔ **Check all latches and/or hinges to make sure they lock securely in place.** Lean on them a little bit and test their strength. If they don't remain locked, the playpen could collapse, injuring or trapping Baby.

✔ **Always open the playpen completely.** Don't leave a side down because it's easier to get a small baby in and out. Baby could roll into and under that side, becoming trapped or suffocating. See Figure 8-2.

✔ **Keep large stuffed toys, fluffy bedding, or other big items out of the playpen.** For one thing, these items can be used as a ladder to freedom for a little climber. For another, they present a suffocation hazard for smaller babies.

✔ **Only use the mattress that came with the playpen.** It's firm, and it fits snugly in the pen, decreasing the risk of suffocation and possibly decreasing the risk of SIDS. (For more on SIDS, see Chapter 20.)

✔ **Never string toys across the top of the playpen.** The rope you use to string the toys can become a strangulation hazard when Baby decides he's ready to pull up on the side of the pen (and you never know when that may be). The rope can also be a problem if it comes loose from the side of the pen and slips down within Baby's grasp. For the same reason, never tie toys to the side of the playpen.

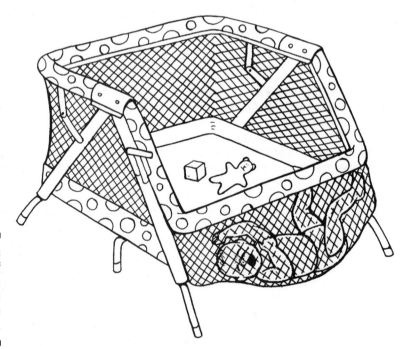

Figure 8-2:
The sides of
a playpen
should
never be
left down.

✔ **Check the sides of the playpen for signs of bites, rips, and other damage.** Teething babies chew on the sides. One piece of foam or plastic from the railing of the playpen presents a choking hazard to Baby. Also look for loose hardware; obviously, the small pieces are a choking hazard, but missing screws can also indicate that something else may be about to come loose.

✔ **Check out the size of the mesh holes before you purchase or borrow an older playpen.** The openings could be wide enough to allow a button from Baby's clothing to get caught in them, which could lead to strangulation. Larger openings may provide a mesh stairway out of the playpen for creative climbers with very agile toes. The openings should be small enough so that you can't get your pinky finger through them.

✔ **If you're using a play yard, be extra safety conscious.** If you move the play yard from place to place — even within the confines of your own home — make sure you thoroughly check the floor for any choking hazards before placing Baby inside. If you're using an older play yard, make sure the slats aren't wide enough for Baby to get his head caught between them.

It is perfectly safe to allow Baby to have his toys in the playpen, by the way, and if he's amusing himself nicely the entire time you're on the phone or writing out bills, don't feel guilty about having some time to yourself. Babies should learn to entertain themselves (some are just better at it than others, as many moms will tell you). It's the *overuse* of the playpens (and infant seats) that could be detrimental to Baby's development.

Setting Your Watch by Baby . . . or Not

By the third month, many babies are starting to do some of the same things at about the same time every day. This may be a great comfort to parents who were starting to wonder whether things in the house would ever settle down to anything approaching normal.

But just as many parents end up with a baby who seems to not have the slightest idea that she's supposed to be falling into a routine. For the parents of a child like this, infancy is a long, unpredictable, and often exhausting journey — one that leaves them wondering what will happen during the second year, and the third. Will this child ever conform to any kind of schedule?

CALL THE DOCTOR

Right on schedule

Co-author Dr. Gaylord sees it all the time: Exhausted parents with their newborns, wondering what the heck they've gotten themselves into. They knew they'd lose some sleep when Baby arrived, but they never expected an infant could wear them out like *this*.

How does Dr. Gaylord comfort and reassure these moms and dads? By letting them know approximately when (during which calendar month) life with Baby will become more enjoyable. Most of the time, his predictions are right on the money: Sometime between the third and fourth month, Baby turns into a little ball of sweetness, even if the first couple of months were rocky.

If your child is just coming into his third month, just watch and see what happens in the next few weeks. You may be very surprised at the way he settles into his little life.

Baby settles into a routine

As the third month progresses, Baby may seem more content with the way her days are going. She's staying awake longer; she's taking naps at the same time each day; she's finding ways to amuse and comfort herself; she's ready to nurse at generally the same time day after day. Her nervous system is settling down now, and her internal clock is starting to kick into high gear. (Yay for you!)

If Baby is settling down, you can safely assume it isn't a fluke. Baby won't be completely upending her schedule next week in favor of a wildly different timetable. You've made it through the hardest part of infancy, at least as far as fatigue goes, if your child seems somewhat settled at this point. Congratulations!

But don't be surprised down the road when Baby starts waking at night or refusing to eat or generally seems cranky. Teething pain will rear its nasty head, perhaps beginning as early as the fourth or fifth months, and Baby's schedule could be thrown for a loop then. (Teething is discussed in more detail in Chapter 10.)

Until then, encourage the schedule. Stick to the schedule. Love the schedule and be thankful for it. The parents of a schedule-adverse baby are envying your life right now (those kids are discussed later in this chapter). It's not always easy, though, to maintain Baby's routine perfectly, particularly if your family is extremely busy. Some tips to keep Baby on track without being a slave to her inner clock:

✔ **Give your sitter complete instructions as to what time Baby usually naps, eats, takes a walk, and so on.** Kids who are in a groove will get cranky if the bottle is slow coming out of the kitchen, or if a sitter decides a nap isn't really necessary.

✔ **Make every effort to squeeze some snooze time in if you're going to be out of the house during Baby's beloved naptime.** If she won't drop off on her own, take her for a spin in the car until she closes those heavy eyes. You may be able to move her from her car seat to her stroller while she sleeps and then continue with your errands.

✔ **Limit off-schedule naps.** If you do miss her naptime entirely, you may be tempted to allow Baby to snooze later in the day. She does need some rest, but allowing her a two-hour nap at dinnertime will only throw her bedtime out of whack (and possibly her morning wake-up time, and her naptime the following day). Curtailing rest time may be painful for both of you, but only allow her a short nap, and put her to bed earlier than usual.

✔ **Feed her when her stomach says it's time.** Feeding time isn't the least bit negotiable, as far as Baby is concerned. Sure, it may be your first day out of the house in weeks, but Baby doesn't really care whether you're enjoying a cup of coffee with your girlfriends. She wants her milk when she wants it.

At this age, babies should only be receiving breast milk or formula. Their digestive systems aren't mature enough to handle solids yet, and studies have suggested that introducing food too early could lead to the development of food allergies and diabetes. (For more information on food allergies, see Chapter 11.)

Whatever you're doing with this child, keep on doing it. She's happy, you're happy, and that's what really counts.

Dealing with an early riser

You feel like you've just fallen asleep, and then you hear it: The cooing. The little "aahs." The kicks in the crib. And then the crying. Baby is ready to start the day. The clock reads 5:15 a.m. Is this some sort of joke?

Is there any way to adjust Baby's schedule, or is this something you just have to resign yourself to?

The answer may lie somewhere in the middle, and it really depends on several factors:

- ✔ **Is Baby going to bed too early?** If he's settling down for the night right after dinnertime, try keeping him up later — but do it slowly, 15 minutes each night until he's going to bed at a time that allows him to sleep in a bit later in the morning.

- ✔ **Can you settle him back down?** Are you resigning yourself to the early morning wakeups too soon, by turning on the lights, for example? Try nursing and rocking Baby in the dark and see what happens. If he settles down, you may be able to slip him back into his crib and grab a few more hours of sleep yourself.

- ✔ **How many naps is Baby taking during the day?** Add up all the little cat-naps, the big naps, and his night sleep time. Although a 3-month-old still needs plenty of sleep, he should be awake for at least ten hours over the course of the day. Lose one of his naps, or cut back on all of them.

- ✔ **Is the room too bright?** Baby may just be sensitive to the morning light. Buy room-darkening blinds.

- ✔ **Is outside noise interfering with Baby's sleep?** Maybe traffic or other noise is waking Baby in the morning. A white-noise machine drowns out outside sounds and may allow Baby to catch a few extra winks in the morning.

- ✔ **Are you rushing to Baby's side?** Give Baby a few minutes to soothe himself before you go into his room. Add a minute or two to this time every morning, and he may eventually decide he's tired of waiting — *really* tired — and fall back to sleep.

Coping with schedule-scoffing babies

Don't blame yourself if your child isn't falling into a predictable pattern just yet. You've probably followed every bit of advice you've been given (feeding Baby on demand, allowing her to fuss but not allowing her to scream in her crib), and this is just the way things have turned out. Not your fault. It's just the way things are. Other parents have been in your position in the past, and are in the same position as you right now — and none of you are less competent than the parents of on-schedule infants

However, a 3-month-old may be ready for you to coax her toward a more regular routine, especially if her naps seem to be willy-nilly all day long, and she wants to nurse the night away. If she seems able to sleep, in other words, she may just need some help in condensing those sleep times into one solid nap and a good nights' rest. To encourage regular sleep and feeding patterns, evaluate what Baby is doing with her day right now:

✔ Is she sleeping too much during the day, or does she refuse to nap at all?

✔ Is there any pattern at all to her feeding times, or are they different every single day?

✔ How does she react when you try to feed her or put her to bed at regular intervals?

Trying to take control of Baby's schedule may feel like an uphill battle, because she's probably going to be very unhappy about it. Naps may be easier to control than feeding times, because frankly, unless she's really insistent on nursing almost constantly (which she shouldn't need at this point), she's probably just hungry at different times every day. On the other hand, you can probably keep her awake a bit longer, stretching the time out in 10 or 15 minute increments each day until you've eliminated a nap, moved her bedtime later, or accomplished whatever it is you're setting out to do.

The baby who never seems to sleep presents a special problem for parents. This child just can't seem to settle down for anything more than a catnap on her mom's shoulder — which is hardly the break Mom's looking for (and after three months of this no-sleep business, Mom needs a break!). Desperate times call for desperate measures. First you need to teach Baby that napping is actually a nice thing for her, so get her to sleep any way you can, even if that means rocking her or taking her in the car for a drive. See how long she'll sleep, and let her wake herself up when it's time. You'll convince yourself — after doubting it for the past couple of months — that this child actually does need to nap, and that she isn't some odd species of infant who runs on batteries.

You can do this until you've established a pattern of when Baby is going to nap. You're developing the habit for her. She'll come to expect it at the same time every day. And that's when you move the nap into her crib. She may fuss at first, or she may take to it like this is what she's been waiting for all along. Don't give up if she cries. Soothe her, but them leave her alone to rest in her crib (unless she's screaming her little lungs out — that's just counterproductive for both of you). This may seem like a lot of work to get Baby to accept that naptime is necessary, but if you can eventually get her to rest on her own every day, it's definitely worth it.

Your goal is to encourage Baby to go to sleep on her own. Avoid falling into a pattern of *always* rocking her to sleep, or else she may never learn to settle down by herself.

Answering Other Concerns at the 3-Month Mark

Now that your child is getting older, you're starting to get an idea of his personality. At the end of the third month, it may be apparent to you that you have a giggly child on your hands — or that your baby doesn't seem to find humor in much of anything (even after colic disappears, as it does at the end of this month). Just as adults have very different personalities, babies do, too, even at this early age. In this section, we delve into concerns parents may have if their child seems too serious. We also let you know that colic should be coming to an end at this point. Pacifiers and thumb sucking are also cause for concern among some parents; we give you the low-down on each and whether either should be outlawed in your home.

"Unhappy" babies: Real or myth?

Just as kids are different physically, they have different personalities. Some babies are downright silly, and others hardly ever crack a smile. If your child falls into the latter group, is it because you're neglecting to do something that would turn him into a laughing machine?

Chances are, no. He's just the way he is. Studies indicate that the "unhappy" or "difficult" baby is just programmed to react to the world differently — often these kids are more observant and sensitive to everything around them, including tastes, smells, and feels (which is why they're often labeled as "unhappy" — a particular blanket is too itchy, or certain foods are simply unpalatable to them). Your serious little one may have suffered from colic, which is a common pattern with these kids. These babies also tend to fall into irregular sleep and feeding patterns, and often resist all attempts to rectify the situation.

The key to dealing with this type of child is to figure out what sets him off and remedy it or prevent it. If Baby cries every time you put socks on his feet, leave his tootsies bare. It could be that his skin is extra-sensitive. If too much noise causes him to have a meltdown, keep the house as calm as possible. You can't force the entire world to conform to his likes and dislikes, of course, but you can create a little peace at home for him — and for you, too.

The end of colic! Hooray!

At the end of the third month, babies who have been howling with colic turn into new little people. Suddenly, they smile. They sleep. Why, they're content! It's like someone flips a switch and hands you the child you dreamed of having — before colic came to call.

Three months of colic can seem like an entire year. You may be shocked — truly shocked — at Baby's new disposition and how much you love being a parent. You've definitely earned this time, so enjoy this new, nice phase with Baby.

Thumb sucking: Okay or no way?

Babies are born with a sucking reflex, which not only comes in handy at feeding time, but also allows them to comfort themselves when they're tired or upset. Should infants be encouraged to suck their thumbs (or fingers), or does this just lead to the heartache of deformed teeth down the line?

Infants who suck on their fingers are doing what comes naturally to them. The major advantage of letting Baby suck on her fingers is that her fingers are always there when she needs them. No pacifier to search for in the car or in the middle of the night, and no wailing while you find it. On the down side, it can be harder to break Baby of this habit, for the same reason — there's a finger, she's kind of bored, and before she realizes it, the finger's in her mouth. Many kids break themselves of this habit later during the first year, and most doctors will advise completely breaking it by the age of 2, as long-term thumb sucking *can* cause misalignment of the permanent teeth. In the meantime, if Baby is content with a thumb or forefinger for comfort at bedtime, let her be.

The pacifier: Godsend or an unnecessary habit?

Now, what about those pacifiers? People (and babies) tend to love them or hate them. If your baby loves his binkie, let him use it. Some infants just need to suck more than others, and long after feeding time is over, such a child is looking for some comfort.

By and large, pediatricians don't object to the use of pacifiers as long as they're not overused. If Baby is using a pacifier occasionally for comfort, that's fine; if he has it in his mouth constantly, because he always wants it or because you're constantly popping it in for him, it may be time to cut back. Saving the pacifier for times when he's tired or agitated instead of using it 'round the clock will make it more effective because it won't be just another fun thing in his life; it will be a tool for calming Baby's nerves.

If you can encourage Baby to comfort himself in some other way (such as sucking on a finger), or if Baby discovers that he doesn't really miss that pacifier after all, taking it from him cold turkey may work. Otherwise, try cutting back on its use little by little until he's not using it at all.

When the pacifier is gone for good, don't keep it around for "emergencies." Allowing Baby to have his treasured pacifier one day and not allowing it the next will only serve to confuse and irritate him.

Of course, the big disadvantage to using a pacifier is that it falls out of Baby's mouth at the most inopportune times. Always have a backup handy when you're leaving the house and when Baby is in his crib. Keep a clean replacement on his dresser so you won't have to crawl under his crib with a flashlight looking for the pacifier he dropped.

Never tie the pacifier to Baby in order to keep it nearby, as doing so is a strangulation hazard.

Tips for using a pacifier:

- ✔ **Buy the right size.** There are small pacifiers for infants younger than 6 months, and larger ones for older infants.

- ✔ **Make sure the plastic guard around the nipple is large enough so that there's no chance of it slipping into Baby's mouth.** The guard should also have airholes.

- ✔ **Wash pacifiers in the dishwasher or sterilize them in boiling water until Baby is 6 months old.** At that point, he's less susceptible to germs.

- ✔ **Try all different nipple varieties until Baby finds one he's happy with.**

- ✔ **Never use the top of a baby bottle as a pacifier.** A voracious sucker could pull the nipple out of the ring and choke on it.

- ✔ **Inspect pacifiers regularly for signs of wear and tear.** Toss and replace them if the nipple is torn or cracked or feels sticky.

Part III
Moving, Shaking, and Growing

The 5th Wave   By Rich Tennant

"The baby's fine, but Karen's still trying to find a comfortable position to breastfeed in."

In this part . . .

In the fourth, fifth, and sixth months, Baby transitions from being your itty-bitty infant into developing a bit of personality. She starts making intentional hand and head movements, gives you her first real laugh, and by the end of the sixth month, might be starting to scoot across your kitchen floor! More advanced communication begins during this time as well, giving you a little insight as to what she *really* thinks about your singing (chances are, she loves it, even if no one else does).

The hardest months are behind you — the fun really starts now! Find out how you can encourage Baby to reach her full potential during this exciting time.

Chapter 9

The Fourth Month: Food!

The first three months are a trial period for parents and Baby alike — you're getting to know each other. You're trying each other on for size, so to speak, and discovering how to work with each other (although *you're* going to be the one making all of the concessions, at least until Baby's a bit older). You're entering into a time of amazing growth and development. By the time three more months have passed, Baby will bear little resemblance to the newborn you brought home not so long ago.

Checking In with Baby

During the fourth month, Baby really starts cracking out of his infant shell by vocalizing and showing an interest in food and activities. He may become a bit more independent and start rolling around on the floor and reaching for toys and other objects of interest. He may also start to take note of the differences among his family members (Mom's the greatest; Dad's the big, strong, one; and Sis is the goofball), who before this point may have seemed like one and the same to Baby's mind. All in all, he's moving toward developing a real personality, which is one of the biggest joys of the first year.

The 4-month checkup

It's business as usual at the 4-month checkup. You can expect your pediatrician to weigh and measure Baby and to assess her progress. There will be a physical exam, of course, during which the doctor will be checking Baby's *fontanels* (soft spots on the head that allow Baby to fit through the birth canal). The *posterior* fontanel (the one on the back of Baby's head) may have closed at this point (which means that the plates in Baby's skull have come together in that area); the one on the top (called the *anterior* fontanel) may actually have increased in size.

While the doctor is assessing the soft spots, he'll also be looking for evenness (which he'll probably call *symmetry*) in Baby's head. You've heard the stories about how your cousin (or friend, or neighbor) has a flat head because his mother never turned him in the crib. You may be surprised to discover that this can really happen because Baby's skull is still so malleable.

If your doctor notices that the back of Baby's head (or one side) is noticeably flat, he'll probably suggest that you observe which side Baby favors in the crib. Although he should be lying flat on his back when you put him in for a nap or for the night, he may naturally turn his head toward the door — or the window, or the mirror on the side of his crib. Make sure he has something to catch his eye on both sides of the crib, or install something interesting that can be moved from side to side, so that Baby is more likely to turn his head once in a while. Most babies' heads start to round out naturally when Baby spends more awake time sitting up.

Make sure Baby is spending time on his tummy while he's awake. Give the back of his head a break while he's out of his crib.

In addition to giving Baby's head the once-over, your pediatrician also checks on Baby's internal organs, including the liver and kidneys (making sure nothing is enlarged), he checks Baby's heart and respiration, and he also checks Baby's groin area (for hernia), and Baby's hips (to rule out hip dysplasia).

Hernias, which are protrusions of the bowel (and usually quite small), can be one of two kinds: An *inguinal* hernia is located in the groin area and usually requires surgical repair to prevent complications. An *umbilical* hernia (located — you guessed it — near the belly button) is a different story. Most will resolve themselves by the time the child goes to school, and don't require any surgical intervention.

If baby has either type of hernia and it seems to be stuck, is painful to the touch, or turns a purplish color, call your pediatrician immediately.

Your doctor will also check for signs of teething, which may include:

- ✔ Drooling
- ✔ Mouthing objects
- ✔ General crankiness
- ✔ Elevated temperature
- ✔ Bumps on the gum

Doctors look for these signs so that they can let you know what's happening. If you know Baby is cutting a tooth, you won't be surprised when he cries in pain and you can't find anything wrong with him. Your pediatrician will give you advice on which pain relievers to use and how much (based on Baby's weight). Just remember that even though Baby may be drooling you a river, the tooth may not come in for another month — or possibly even two.

During the 4-month checkup, your doctor will ask you a host of questions, including:

✔ How is Baby sleeping? How many hours at night? Is he still waking up to eat? How many naps? (Baby should be sleeping about 14 to 17 hours throughout the entire day and night.)

✔ If Baby had colic, is it gone now? For more on colic, see Chapter 6.

✔ What is Baby eating these days? Breast milk? Formula? A combination of the two? Have you started him on cereal?

✔ Are Baby's bowel movements normal? (Before Baby starts on solids, they'll be fairly consistent — yellowish and seedy for breastfed kids; tan and a little more solid for bottle babies)

✔ Is Baby able to roll at least one way? Is he able to push himself up on his arms while he's on his tummy? Is he at least trying to accomplish these things?

✔ Does he reach for things? Can he hold a toy or rattle?

✔ Does Baby appear to see and hear well?

✔ Is he attempting to vocalize? (More on this later in this chapter.)

Of course, the doctor also wants to know how everyone is doing at home, because even though you're starting to feel like a real parent, each month brings its own crop of foreign concepts where Baby is concerned. If you're worried about something, *ask.* (For example, should Baby still be waking up to nurse at this age, or should he be past that?)

Immunizations

This month, Baby continues with her regimen of shots. If the following list makes your eyes cross in confusion, don't worry: We break all this down in Chapter 18 for you, where we tell you exactly what the initials mean and how they protect your child.

Shots given this month may include:

- DTaP #2
- Hib #2
- PCV #2
- IPV #2

Baby may experience pain at the injection sites for a couple of days following the shots. Remember to ask the doctor or nurse about the possible side effects of each immunization and which side effects warrant a call to the office. If you're not sure how much pain reliever Baby should be getting at this age, make sure to ask about that, too.

Milestones this month

The average baby is a busy little person with lots of little milestones to hit by the end of this month. Read on:

- Baby gains about 1 pound this month.
- Baby's neck strength starts to really kick in this month. She holds her head steady when she's on your lap or when you pull her up (very gently, of course) from the floor, although she isn't able to hold her head up for indefinite periods of time just yet. See Figure 9-1.
- Along with neck strength comes head control. In addition to holding her head up nicely now, she can turn it to look at something in another direction.
- She may be able to roll both ways (but should be able to roll at least one way), starting from her tummy.
- She can probably push up onto her hands (lifting her head and chest) while she's on her stomach.
- Baby is able to focus her eyes on objects at this age and hold her gaze. She's also able to follow a person or an object moving across the room with her eyes.
- She reaches for objects, holds them, and puts things in her mouth (she may be teething at this point, though most kids don't start for another month or two).
- Baby is wiggling and kicking now.
- Baby can bear weight on her legs now when you hold her on your lap (she appears to "stand"). Contrary to old wives' tales, this will not make her bow-legged, and will actually strengthen and help straighten her legs.

Figure 9-1:
Baby is able to hold her head steady at about 4 months.

✔ She can probably sit if you prop her up with pillows. (A great use for your C-shaped nursing pillow!)

✔ She may find her hands and feet at this age and just fall in love with them. You'll note that whenever she discovers a new part of her body, she's completely fascinated by it (at least until the thrill wears off and she finds something new).

✔ Baby enjoys interacting with people at this age and may be disappointed when playtime comes to an end (demonstrating her displeasure through frowning, pouting, or crying).

✔ She is also able to communicate fear, pain, and loneliness through crying (with real tears).

✔ Baby shows excitement. She can demonstrate her interest and pleasure at this age. She may be excited about a toy, or because you're tickling her toes, or because she wants some of your food.

✔ She responds to your smile with a smile of her own. And will smile at you to get you to smile at her.

✔ She may react to an angry face by crying.

✔ Babies this age get a big kick out of a game of peekaboo.

✔ Baby is exploring the world through her mouth and will try to put everything in there (or will try to get her mouth _on_ anything and everything).

✔ She attempts to vocalize. She can imitate simple sounds, like "oh" or "ah," and will do so if you initiate the communication. (So for example, stand in front of her and slowly say, "ah," giving her a chance to respond.)

Teaching language

A baby is a blank page, a creature without knowledge, someone who's going to have to learn the relevance of communicating with other people. How does a parent teach this? For starters, let Baby know that we all rely on communication. You can accomplish this simply by talking to her and by making eye contact as you chat, even though she isn't grasping the meaning of your words. During the fourth month, slow your speech down a bit. In addition to telling her what's going on in your day ("We're going for a walk," or "Let's go get Daddy"), give her a chance to show you what she's capable of, communication-wise.

At 4 months, Baby is likely to be making cooing, vowel-like sounds — "oo," "ah," "oh," and "ay" — with some measure of ease. You can help her to develop her language skills by playing an "echo" game with her. Give her a simple sound to throw back at you (you say "oo," she says "oo") and when she does, show her that you're delighted with her efforts. This back-and-forth teaches her that communication requires at least two people, and that she's successfully getting into the game. The first consonant sounds babies make are usually "k," "p," "b," and "d," and this may take a few more months for Baby to master, though you won't cause any harm by trying to teach her now.

Something that helps babies to distinguish the consonant sounds within words is using short, simple phrases, and adding a "y" to the end of words where it's appropriate to do so. For example, say the word "dad" out loud. Now say "daddy." The "d" in the middle of the word becomes much more obvious to the ear when the "dy" ending is added. So a short, simple sentence like, "Let's go get Daddy," contains sounds that are short, crisp, and completely audible to a child, whereas a phrase like, "We've gotta run to the office and pick up your father" has a bit too much going on. Yes, in time, Baby will be able to decode a sentence like this, but the process is a bit easier if the information comes in easy bits and pieces.

Keeping Baby Safe and Sound

Baby is reaching, stretching, rolling, grabbing, and starting to find the most interesting things on the floor. Coupled with his increased mobility comes Baby's ability to actually manipulate small objects with his hands and work them into his mouth — and *everything* goes into the mouth at this age. This becomes a big safety issue: Choking is the number one safety hazard to small children.

Sweeping up the hazards

Offer Baby toys that are safe for him to mouth. These may include teething rings, rattles, or rubber blocks.

Just because a toy is soft doesn't mean it's safe. Always check the label to make sure that a toy is intended for your child's age group. A foam-rubber ball, for example, isn't meant to be chewed on. For one thing, it may have a plastic coating, and chips of the plastic will surely end up in Baby's mouth if he chews on it long enough. For another thing, foam rubber may break into small pieces, which then present a choking hazard.

Another thing to think about: What's actually *on* your floors? Baby will be spending more and more time down there as he works on his rolling, sitting, and crawling skills. His hands will be on that floor, and guess where they're going after that? You know it — in his mouth. Although you don't have to sterilize the floor every single time you put Baby on it (after all, if he's never exposed to any germs, he'll never work up a resistance to them), you should pick up any clumps of dirt or dust bunnies within his reach. Establish a habit of sweeping hard surfaces in the morning and at night to keep any stray dirt out of your child's hands (and mouth).

Make sure that he's on a relatively clean surface and that you're not allowing him to play on a surface that's wet with cleanser. Pretty much all commercial cleansers are unsafe as far as ending up in Baby's mouth goes. Even the "organic" cleansers (like vinegar or baking soda) can make a kid sick.

Continue to check your floors for small pieces of food, buttons, loose change — anything Baby may be able to put into his mouth and choke on. (Even though it may seem unlikely that Baby could pick up a penny, kids really do the darndest things. Anyway, if you see something laying there, how hard is it to pick up?)

Advice on baby-proofing your home (including items that should be kept completely out of Baby's reach) is given in Chapter 20.

Keeping Baby on the table

Of course, now that Baby is kicking and able to move about more intentionally, the changing table becomes even more of a safety issue. Sure, you've been keeping one hand on him at all times, even using the safety strap most of the time. Now it becomes absolutely imperative that you don't take your eyes off this child for even a second while he's being changed. He can roll, wiggle, or kick his way right down to the floor and sustain a serious injury in the process.

If your child is still happy as a little clam on the changing table, content to lay perfectly still, be aware that he is now strong enough to surprise you with a big move to the left, to the right, downward, or upward. Even if you haven't really needed to hold your child down, now's the time to start doing so. Remember, Baby has no concept of heights — and therefore no fear of falling — at this age, so it's up to you to make sure he doesn't learn the hard way about taking a spill. Sooner or later, wiggling at changing times becomes a safety concern for every parent. You want to catch it, so to speak, before you're actually catching Baby on his way down to the floor.

Try distracting an extremely squirmy kid. Because he can hold a toy now, keep a couple of rattles or teething rings on the changing table. These can be special toys, used only at changing time, or they can be his all-time favorites (though you'll have to remember to bring those along with you when you whisk him off for a fresh diaper). If that doesn't work, try talking to him while you're freshening his diaper. Teach him those consonants now. Smile at him. Sing to him. Keep his concentration on you, and chances are he'll forget that he has places to roll to — at least for a moment or two.

In the event that changing time becomes an exercise in torture for both of you (with Baby trying his hardest to roll away and you trying your best to change this child without losing a grip on him), move the show down to the floor. Your diaper bag probably has everything you need for a quick change, so use it as your portable changing table. This won't stop Baby's squirming, but it eliminates the potential for a great big fall.

Expressing Herself

Right around this age, an amazing thing happens to your baby: She starts recognizing herself as an entity separate and apart from the rest of the world. Though this recognition will grow and deepen with time and maturity, the first little seeds are starting to sprout right now. Her desire and ability to communicate is one indication of this; you'll soon see other signs in the ways she chooses to express herself.

The crying game

Say you're having a nice little tickle time with Baby, and suddenly the phone rings. Although obviously nothing could ever come close to being as important as this game the two of you are playing, you're expecting a call from your mother (or from the office), and you're suddenly forced to stop tweaking Baby's toes and focus some of your attention elsewhere. Your child, in all of her intelligence and burgeoning independence, may frown at first, and then she may cry out of frustration. She'll soon realize that crying is one way to bring your focus back to herself.

Baby's ability to capture your attention is something brand-new to her — something she didn't realize was possible just a few weeks ago. This skill is pretty huge in both its communicative and socialization aspects. She'll use it in the future with other skills after she learns them. (Crying? That works. Laughing? That works. Playing quietly when she really wants your attention? Doesn't work.)

Realizing that Baby's frustration can be part of her development

At this age, frustration can start to work its way into Baby's daily activities. She's learning new skills now, with the intent of accomplishing things (in other words, she's *trying* to roll; it's not just a reflexive action). When the intent precedes the skill, she may become frustrated enough to cry — *hard.* Crying may increase when babies are in the process of learning a new trick. This, of course, is usually related to the child's temperament. High-intensity kids (those who appear to be very serious and determined, no matter what they're doing; possibly the same kids who had colic) may become more easily frustrated when a new task isn't going as well as they'd hoped. Easy-going babies may not be as susceptible to frustration, at least at this age.

If you're the parent of a child who seems to be crying more as she's trying again and again to accomplish a new feat of physical strength, what's the best course of action? Should you just hand her that toy she's working so hard to get? Will that make her happy?

Probably not. Allowing the child to work through her frustration is probably the best course of action (within limits). Let her keep inching her way toward that toy, even if she's clearly not happy about it. Give her a tiny push to help her flip over if you must, but let her do most of the work on her own. Kids who are intense enough to get frustrated are also intense enough to *stay* frustrated until the job is done, so to speak. So, for example, you may hand her a pacifier that's just out of her reach — something she's been slowly working her way toward — and she'll continue to act unhappy, or she'll continue to kick and squirm, because she wasn't able to get all of her energy out. A little frustration can be a healthy thing if it helps her work toward her goal.

You know your child best. If she's becoming frustrated working at a new skill, watch her closely. Allow her to keep trying until she's obviously had enough (when healthy frustration has spiraled downward into a crying fit). Pick her up and soothe her then — and repeat the process later. Hand her the toy she was working toward. If the toy helps to quell her anger, great; if it makes no difference to her at this point, put it away. The real point here is that she must learn to do some things on her own, and handing her every toy before she can even *try* to get it only delays the process.

Getting to know you

Babies at this age show a definite preference for their parents, siblings, care-givers — basically anyone they're in regular contact with (though no one really compares to Mom and Dad). They delight in sharing smiles with their loved ones, but may begin to show signs of wariness around people they don't know. This is another sign that Baby is becoming more of a social crea-ture — she's fine while hanging out with certain people, but she may need a minute or two to warm up to others.

These are also the tiny little seeds of stranger anxiety — something that won't truly affect Baby's mood for at least three or four more months. For now, if you notice your child is becoming less comfortable with strangers, give her a short time to adjust to the new person. Chances are, the two of them will become fast friends after Baby gets over her initial wariness.

Planning for First Foods

Pediatricians these days recommend waiting until closer to 6 months to begin Baby on a regimen of varied solids. However, if baby is showing signs of being ready for solid food, most doctors will give you the green light to add some iron-fortified cereal during the fourth month. These are the things to watch out for:

- ✔ Baby can easily hold her head up.
- ✔ She's putting things into her mouth.
- ✔ She shows an interest in what you're eating.

Iron-fortified cereal is the best food to start Baby on for a few reasons:

- ✔ **Baby may not be getting enough iron from Mom's milk.** Breastfed babies need some additional iron by the time they're 4 to 6 months old in order to stave off anemia.
- ✔ **Cereal is a fairly bland substance, and yet it's filling.** So it's well worth your time — and Baby's. Baby's delicate digestive system just isn't ready to handle sugar and/or spice at this age.
- ✔ **Cereal is highly unlikely to cause a food allergy.** It's a good jumping-off point into the world of real food.

You'll be feeding Baby just once a day for now, so cereal is a good bedtime meal, because it may help to keep her from feeling hungry until the morning. If Baby hasn't yet been able to sleep through a night, you just may find that she snoozes away after she's fed cereal before bed. After all, Baby's stomach is getting larger now, big enough to hold enough food to keep the hungries at bay while everyone gets a good night's sleep. Some kids continue to cry for Mom in the middle of the night even after they've established a routine of having cereal before bedtime. These babies are probably not hungry — they're looking for the comfort of a parent to pass the dead of night with.

If your child continues to wake up regularly during the night even after he's been taking cereal well for a few weeks, talk to your pediatrician. He can evaluate your child and may advise you to feed Baby more during the day, precisely because children this age need to start sleeping through the night — for their sake, and for yours. Most doctors recommend maintaining at least four bottle or breastfeeding sessions throughout the day, regardless of Baby's schedule of solids.

It will take you some time to work out your feeding routine after you add solids, but you'll be mixing his cereal with breast milk or formula, so he'll be getting some of those nutrients there, anyway. Because he's settling in for the night, he'll want to top off the meal with his bottle or the breast. You may choose to nurse him, feed him cereal, and then finish nursing. Or you may feed him the cereal and then let him have his bottle or the breast.

Be aware that although she may meet the minimum criteria for eating solids, Baby may not be good to go yet. If you notice that most of the cereal you're putting into her mouth is coming right back out, over and over again, it probably means that she still has an *infant tongue thrusting reflex* going on. (Touch Baby's lips, and her tongue will thrust out of her mouth. This reflex is present at birth and disappears within the first several months.) Scrap plans for the cereal feeding and try again in a few weeks.

Preparing for the feeding

Preparing Baby's first batch of cereal is really very simple. She's not going to eat much at this age, so start by spooning a tablespoon of rice or oat cereal into a bowl (as Baby's appetite grows, you use more cereal). Mix it with breast milk or formula until it's fairly runny. After a week, when you're sure that Baby isn't going to have a negative reaction to the cereal (a rash or diarrhea, for example), you can opt to mix the cereal with a Vitamin C fortified juice (apple or white grape juice, for example), which will help Baby absorb the iron in the cereal. Avoid citrus juices (orange and grapefruit, for example) at this age, because they may be too harsh for Baby's digestive system. After she masters watery cereal, cut back a little on the liquid. And remember: You don't have to warm the cereal in order to make it edible.

In this year of firsts, you just never know what's going to happen, so when you introduce Baby to his first feast of cereal:

- ✔ **Make sure he's hungry.** He's much more likely to give the solids a whirl if it's time to eat — just make sure he hasn't crossed into "I'm so hungry, I'm going to explode" territory. (He should be somewhat at ease when being introduced to *anything* new.) You can nurse him for a short time or allow him a bit of his bottle, but don't let him fill up on liquids.

- ✔ **Use the appropriate utensil.** Don't try to feed him with a teaspoon. They make baby spoons for a reason — they fit into Baby's mouth.

- ✔ **Don't try too much, too soon.** Especially during the first feeding, offer Baby *teeny* little bites of cereal. Let him get used to the texture and the taste. It may seem like a pretty dull meal to you, but remember, putting something in his mouth that he's supposed to swallow — and that *isn't* liquid — is a foreign concept to him. He needs time to perfect his swallowing technique.

- ✔ **Keep the cereal pretty watery at first in order to let the baby get used to the spoon and texture.** Gradually thicken it up as he gets used to the solids.

- ✔ **Use the bib and have a burp cloth nearby to clean up any messes.** And there will be plenty.

When Baby starts eating solids, you'll notice a change in his bowel movements. Where once a breastfed child produced seedy, loose stools, you'll notice a trend toward more solid stool. A bottlefed child's already semi-solid stool will also follow suit, becoming more like real poop. Bowel movements will also decrease in frequency. This is good news for you, because Baby is likely to go through fewer diapers and *less* likely to shoot poop out the side of those leg openings (yes, very gross) after his stool becomes firmer.

Safety hints for feeding solids

Four-month-olds don't belong in highchairs, unless the chair reclines to allow younger children to sit comfortably. Even though your child can hold his head up well at this point, he can't sit up without being propped — and that's not what those highchair safety straps are meant for.

Instead, keep him in his infant seat when introducing cereal. He shouldn't be lying down, obviously, but he should be comfortably (slightly) reclined. Forcing him to sit propped up while he eats will only cause his head to droop and the rest of his body to sag all over the place.

Never feed Baby cereal in a bottle. Baby is likely to be completely reclined when eating from the bottle, which makes the cereal a choking hazard. Also, he's not learning to eat from a spoon, which is something he's going to have to do in the next few months if he ever hopes to conquer vegetables and fruits!

Chapter 10

The Fifth Month: Rocking Baby's World

In This Chapter

▶ Seeing what Baby's up to

▶ Protecting Baby

▶ Adding more to Baby's plate

▶ Teething

The fifth month is a nice, quiet time for Baby to practice what he's already learned and prepare for the next stages of development. His communication skills continue to blossom this month, and for the first time, you may see signs of a little sense of humor (like when he blows a raspberry and smiles, absolutely delighted with himself). Baby may also start to mimic a speaker, adding pitch, tone, and length to his cooing sounds. He's rolling over like a champion by this point, and by the end of the fifth month, some children are starting to get up on their elbows while trying to pull their knees beneath them — they've got wanderlust, all right, and are preparing to explore the world beyond the baby blanket.

In this chapter, we take a look at some safe "exerciser" choices for the increasingly active child and explain why you should avoid walkers and bouncers. We also touch on teething — what to look for, and how to comfort a child who is suddenly mad at the world (but mostly at his gums).

Checking In with Baby

Most pediatricians don't schedule well-baby visits during the fifth month. Baby's next appointment will likely be his 6-month checkup. Of course, this doesn't mean that you won't have questions this month. Questions borne of simple curiosity that aren't really related to something that could actually hurt your child can probably wait until the next office visit (Baby can stick his entire hand in his mouth and you want to know if you should allow him to do this). Questions regarding medical conditions warrant a call to the doctor right away (Baby has diarrhea and a high fever).

Milestones this month

What's Baby up to during the fifth month? He's getting bigger, stronger, and much more personable. Here's what he can do by the end of the month:

- ✔ Baby holds his head up well.

- ✔ He pushes himself up on his arms, raising his chest.

- ✔ He may try to get his knees underneath himself and begin a primal form of crawling by the end of the month.

- ✔ He can grab objects and transfer them from one hand to the other.

- ✔ He's able to put an object in his mouth, which means that you have to be on constant lookout for choking hazards. For information on how to perform the Heimlich maneuver, see Chapter 20.

- ✔ Baby may show signs of displeasure or anger if you take something away from him.

- ✔ He smiles and laughs. You'll love the tickle-me game — Baby will roll with laughter, and so will you!

- ✔ He may be able to sit when propped up or by himself for a second or two. (Most children this age are still pretty floppy.)

- ✔ Baby turns his head in the direction of a speaker.

- ✔ He tries to imitate a speaker by using a singsong voice.

- ✔ Baby loves to blow raspberries.

- ✔ Teething may begin.

- ✔ Baby may love to "stand" on your lap while you hold him.

- ✔ A particularly strong child may be able to pull himself up toward the end of this month and stand while holding onto something or someone.

- ✔ Baby may be able to drink from a cup (or hold his own bottle) and/or feed himself a biscuit.

- ✔ He may begin to babble at this age (and even though he says "Dada" or "Mama," he doesn't attach meaning to his words yet).

Baby's emotions are really beginning to show during this month. He lets you know if he objects to you removing something from his grasp. He shows his delight when he works hard to reach a toy — and finally does it!

Encouraging language development

Though Baby may not be a masterful speaker just yet, he's learning the basic rules surrounding communication — that people *use* speech for a purpose, that people take turns speaking, and that you're happy when he makes the effort to "talk" to you. He enjoys interacting with people and loves to practice his own form of speech. Encourage him to do so by talking to him throughout the day. Keep your words short and simple, giving him the chance to hear the sounds. By 5 months, he may repeat simple consonant sounds back to you at this age: "ma," "ka," "da," "ba," or "ga."

Introducing Baby to books at this age — if you haven't already — is a wonderful way to encourage speech. Picture books focus on simple words and concepts; basically on Baby's first words. Ball. Dog. Cat. Your child may not truly understand at this age that everything has a name, but it's never too early to acquaint him with new sounds and words.

Books for Baby should be short, sweet, and filled with interesting colors and pictures. He's not ready for chapter books or longer stories that may interest older children. Look for books that are made of durable material (cardboard, vinyl — your child may find that chewing on books is as much fun as looking at them), and are chunky enough for Baby to hold easily.

When he's through looking at his picture book, try reading a simple story to him. Reading to him engages him in so many ways — he's looking, he's listening, he's trying to imitate your sounds — his developing brain is getting a real workout from this one simple activity.

Other benefits of reading to Baby from an early age:

✔ It ensures cuddle time for the two of you, which is also an important part of Baby's day.

✔ Reading to Baby may help to increase his vocabulary later in the first year.

✔ Sitting through a story may help to increase Baby's attention span.

✔ Introducing him to the world of books now will make him more likely to embrace the possibility of reading later in life — he'll want to know for himself what those words say!

Encouraging a love for reading in your child now can have positive effects for a lifetime. After Baby can read for himself (years down the road), an entire new world of ideas and imagination opens up for him. For now, *you* can lead him through that door by reading to him. Shoot for at least 15 minutes of reading every day at this age. Even if he isn't willing to sit and listen at first, he may show signs of interest as you continue to make storytime a regular part of the day. Those 15 minutes can come in 5-minute increments if that's what works for your baby.

Keeping Baby Safe and Sound

Baby's at a crossroads this month: She's too small to sit by herself, and yet, she's got the itch to do more on her own. Before you let her loose in an exercise device or highchair she isn't ready for, make sure she's going to be safe. She may seem a little bored or frustrated with her inability to actually move around freely these days — but she isn't going to be amused if she suffers a major injury.

Walkers, bouncers, and saucers

Active children need, well, action. Years ago, parents would pop their children into a walker at this age and then stand back as the babies delighted themselves with their newfound mobility. Children loved being in these seats-on-wheels. Why, they could shuttle themselves all over the house while eating a snack on their tray. Life couldn't get much better, as far as these kids were concerned.

Today, pediatricians discourage the use of walkers. Thousands of children suffer walker-related injuries every year, most caused by walkers slipping down a flight of stairs. Many walkers on the market today are wider than those of years gone by, which may prevent the walker from fitting through a doorway, for example, but the best way to prevent the devastating injuries that can result from an accident in a walker is to keep your child out of it in the first place.

Bouncers, also called "Johnny-jump-ups," are also discouraged by pediatricians. These are the swinglike contraptions that attach to the top of a doorway and dangle down to a seat that's connected by a spring. Baby is able to spin and jump to her heart's delight. The problem with these products is that Baby may also be able to flip herself forward and bang her head on the floor. Jumping exercisers can also cause stress fractures in an infant's legs. Simply put, a baby's legs are not designed to handle this type of activity.

A popular and much safer alternative to these products is the stationery baby ring. Baby is placed into a seat that's much like a walker's. She can spin around, rock, play on the tray that surrounds the saucer-like contraption, but she can't go anywhere. She can't flip herself over and suffer a concussion. She's not going to hurt her developing bones. She's happy as a little lark being held upright, being able to move around, having her toys all around her, and at the same time — she's safe. And that makes Mom and Dad happy, too.

Using the highchair

If Baby can sit fairly well this month, she may be ready to try out her high-chair during her feedings. If your highchair leans back to support the child who is just getting used to the upright seated position, it's best to adjust the seat slowly, letting her get the hang of sitting like a big kid. Using a chair that has only one position — upright — is a little trickier for a novice. Even after she can sit by herself, she won't be able to do it for extended periods of time. You may have to use a towel or pillow for support.

Always use the highchair's safety strap. It doesn't qualify as support for the newly-sitting-up baby, but it does help make sure that she isn't going to slip out of the chair.

If she isn't ready to sit up, don't try to train her by putting her in her high-chair. This is *not* what those straps are designed to do! Continue to feed her in her infant seat until she's able to hold herself up —at least for short peri-ods of time.

Buying (or Preparing) Baby's First Foods

Whether Baby has already had his first taste of cereal or you've held off and plan to add solids now, he'll be ready to move on to vegetables and fruits in the near future. You may wonder whether it's better to buy the prepared baby foods in the grocery store, to go organic, or to make your own.

Going with regular ol' baby food

Many, many parents make their initial foray into the baby food aisle wonder-ing if there's some sort of secret to choosing the right food for their child. Should they go with the most popular brand or with the all-natural food? Which foods should you feed to your child first?

Most doctors recommend starting Baby off on the yellow vegetables (corn, squash, and the like) before moving onto the green ones (beans and peas, for example). Read the labels on commercial baby food jars and avoid foods con-taining high levels of sugar or salt or that use tapioca as filler. Your child only needs the simplest ingredients (like the vegetable itself and some water) to get the nutrition from his meals. Stick with pureed foods during these early feeding months. Baby won't be ready for chunky foods until much later in the first year.

The main perk of using commercial baby foods is that they're extremely convenient. However, if you take the time to break down the cost-per-ounce of many of these prepared fruits and veggies, you find that they're usually more expensive than the vegetables you find in the produce section. If you're looking to pinch pennies, we offer some helpful advice for preparing your own baby food later in this chapter.

Looking for organic options

These days, you can buy prepared organic baby food in the grocery store. Look for a commercially prepared baby food that lists the fruit or vegetable as its first ingredient on the label. A truly organic food won't use sugar or water as its main filler, nor will it use chemical additives or preservatives.

Many parents choose to go organic because they're concerned about the amount of pesticides in their child's food. Because most research on the pesticides contained in food has been focused on what effects, if any, adults may suffer, we don't have a lot of solid evidence (good or bad) about the effects that pesticides may have on a developing child.

Becoming Baby's personal chef

Preparing your own baby food at home is easy as pie (though Baby's not quite ready for your delicious desserts). There are a couple of major benefits to this do-it-yourself approach. First, it's much cheaper to buy an entire squash, for example, and to cook it, puree an entire batch of it, and freeze it for your child than it is to buy that same quantity of squash already prepared by the big baby food companies. Secondly, you have the final word on what goes into Baby when you prepare his food. (You know that you didn't add food coloring or any preservatives.)

Making your own baby food really isn't hard. You need some basic kitchen equipment and fresh fruits and vegetables. Keep in mind that if you plan on purchasing your produce in the supermarket, it could very well contain the same pesticides you may be trying to avoid. Growing your own or purchasing produce at an organic market is a better choice for parents whose main concern is keeping Baby pesticide-free.

To prepare Baby's food at home, you need:

- ✔ **A pot:** For boiling fruits.
- ✔ **Steamer basket:** For steaming veggies.
- ✔ **Blender:** For pureeing foods.

> ✔ **Peeler and corer:** To make removal of skins and cores easier.
>
> ✔ **Storage containers:** You prepare the food in batches and save some for later.

Even if you're not an experienced gourmet cook, making your baby's food is a snap. Here are some tips for making the entire process incredibly easy:

✔ Peel, core, and chop hard fruits (like pears and apples) before simmering them in a pot (filled with just enough water to cover the food, anywhere from 10 to 30 minutes, depending on the type of fruit) to make them soft. Puree and serve or freeze.

✔ Steaming veggies allows them to retain more nutrients than boiling them. Vegetables should be peeled and diced and then placed in a steamer basket or a double boiler. Puree them.

✔ When Baby is ready for meats, poach them before pureeing them.

✔ Softer fruits (like banana and mango) can be mashed and served to Baby without any further preparation.

✔ Don't add salt, butter, or sweetener to Baby's foods — he hasn't had them yet, and he won't miss them.

✔ Store pureed foods in the freezer for several months; in the fridge for three days maximum.

Use ice cube trays to freeze small portions of Baby's food. This method is neat, gives you a small serving size, and enables you to easily blend and mix two different foods together (if Baby really hates peas, for example, you can try mixing them into the sweet potatoes that he just loves). Use plastic wrap to cover the tray and protect the food from freezer burn, or place the frozen cubes in freezer bags. To thaw, leave several cubes in the fridge overnight or use a double boiler.

Steering clear of risky foods

Baby's body is growing and developing at breakneck speed during the first year — inside and out. Because her digestive and immune systems aren't as strong as an older child's, there are some foods that need to be limited in quantity or avoided altogether during the first year.

Don't give Baby any honey at all during the first year, because it may contain Clostridium botulinum, the spores that can cause *botulism,* a form of food poisoning that can make Baby very ill.

Steer clear of stringy vegetables like broccoli, or put them through a baby food strainer before freezing or feeding. The strings are a choking hazard.

You should also limit Baby's intake of nitrates, which, if ingested in large quantities, can lead to *methemoglobinemia,* a serious medical condition that prevents the red blood cells from effectively transporting oxygen throughout the body. Children under 6 months old are most susceptible to this condition, which is sometimes called blue baby syndrome.

Foods that are high in nitrates include leafy vegetables, like:

- ✔ Spinach
- ✔ Kale
- ✔ Collard greens
- ✔ Lettuce
- ✔ Cabbage

The nitrate levels in these foods are high to begin with; the levels rise if the foods have been grown with nitrate fertilizers. Improper storage and preparation of these foods further raises the levels (and allows the nitrates to turn to *nitrites,* which are the agents that damage the red blood cells).

Root vegetables (like carrots, beets, turnips) also contain nitrates, though not at levels as high their leafy counterparts.

If you're preparing these foods at home for Baby, *choose only organic produce and freeze leftovers immediately.* Organic veggies are grown without the use of nitrate fertilizers, thus eliminating a huge risk factor in using these particular foods. Commercial baby foods are also a safe choice; their produce comes from low-nitrate regions (areas where nitrate levels in the soil are low and less likely to seep into the veggies) and their preparation methods don't allow time for the nitrate/nitrite exchange to take place.

Relieving the Torture of Teething

If Baby hasn't shown any signs of teething just yet, it's only a matter of time. Many kids cut their first teeth between 4 to 6 months of age, although it's not uncommon for babies to cut them much earlier — or later. Most often, the bottom central incisors (the two bottom front-and-center teeth) are the first little guys to come in. (The top central incisors will be next.)

Some of the signs of teething include:

- ✔ Crankiness
- ✔ Drooling
- ✔ Rash
- ✔ Desire to chew or bite on *anything*
- ✔ Diarrhea
- ✔ Low-grade fever (below 100)
- ✔ Loss of appetite
- ✔ Difficulty sleeping
- ✔ Cough (due to all that drool)

Now, obviously, these are all symptoms of illness, as well. How can you tell the difference between a tooth that's making your child miserable and a virus?

You can usually tell by taking a peek at Baby's bottom gum. If the gum is red and angry-looking and Baby is showing all the other signs of teething, he's teething, but it's going to be a while yet before any teeth show up: Teeth can take up to two months to break through the gum surface. If the gum has a bluish blister-type sore on it (called a *hematoma*), that's a tooth coming in. Hematomas contain blood. Those bluish things are usually eruption cysts, which contain clear fluid. They pop, and there you have it: a tooth!

Baby is in a very oral stage right now, where he naturally wants to put everything into his mouth, so his chewing on everything in sight is not in itself a reliable indicator of teething.

How can you comfort Baby and make his little mouth feel better? Pain reliever sometimes works wonders (although sometimes it seems to make very little difference to a teething baby). If you're unsure of the dosage that Baby should be receiving, call your pediatrician's office for advice. Oral gels seem to work very well for relieving some kids' teething discomfort. Use the recommended dosage on the container; if Baby doesn't respond to it, discontinue its use. And with either medication, only use it if Baby appears to be uncomfortable (instead of using it to ward off *potential* discomfort).

If used to excess, some of the oral gels can cause methemoglobinemia, a serious medical condition that is also caused by the feeding Baby foods that are high in nitrates. (For more on this, see the section "Steering clear of risky foods," earlier in the chapter.) Gels should not be used more than four times a day. Also, health food store teething tablets contain chemicals you may not want your baby to have, like catnip and belladonna.

Other ways to soothe Baby during a teething spell:

- ✔ **Have some teething rings on hand.** This is what they're made for. Baby may prefer a solid rubber chew toy or a fluid-filled ring. Stick with whatever works. Don't freeze the ring, but keep it in the back of the refrigerator so it's really cold.

- ✔ **Offer Baby cold, soft, bland foods and drinks.**

- ✔ **Baby may enjoy chewing on a teething biscuit or a bagel.**

- ✔ **Give him extra comfort during the day and at sleep times.** All he knows is that something hurts. Mom's love can make the pain a little better.

- ✔ **Wipe the drool from his chin and neck as often as possible.** Change his shirt when necessary. Constant exposure to saliva can cause an irritating rash. If you just can't keep him dry, rub a little bit of petroleum jelly on these areas.

- ✔ **If Baby has diarrhea, make sure to change his diaper often.** The last thing he needs right now is a sore bottom.

If Baby's fever rises above 100 degrees or he seems to be sick, call your doctor to rule out illness. Although the signs of teething can mimic other conditions (like an ear infection), it's always better to err on the side of caution.

Chapter 11

The Sixth Month: Baby on the Move!

*T*he sixth month arrives, and suddenly you realize you're halfway through Baby's first year! Baby heads toward more independence during this time, pushing up on hands and knees, sitting, and possibly — for the very precocious babe — even pulling himself up on the coffee table. Safety becomes more of an issue as you watch your innocent child move toward the stairs (with no inkling of the danger that lies ahead). Some parents may find themselves in a state of anxiety, wondering how all of this happened so fast — Baby was just born, and here he is, squirming on the changing table and rolling away from the spot where you last left him. The changes will come fast and furious during the second half of the first year, so don't blink — you may miss something!

Checking In with Baby

At this age, Baby is becoming more mobile, more sociable, and more responsive at playtime. You may find yourself really enjoying this phase of life, because Baby may become more predictable and generally easier to care for. This is also where he begins to make the change from cute infant to real babyhood — crawling, sitting up, holding his bottle, giggling, and stealing your heart every time he smiles at you.

The 6-month checkup

The 6-month checkup covers a lot of territory. Baby is weighed and measured, as usual, and his growth is plotted on the charts. He's given a physical exam by the doctor, who will probably have a lot of questions about what Baby has been up to this month. The doctor will ask whether Baby is reaching for toys or other objects, whether he tries to get things that are out of his reach, and whether he's rolling both ways, sitting, and pushing up on his hands and knees.

Your doctor will also want to discuss safety issues with you, like installing gates near stairways, and making sure that Baby is strapped into his feeding chair. Make sure that you take the time to write down any pertinent information and to ask any questions that you may have.

Immunizations

Most of Baby's checkups include at *least* one immunization shot. Don't worry, we break all this down in Chapter 18 for you, where we tell you exactly what the initials mean and how they protect your child. This month, Baby will be given:

- ✓ Hib #3
- ✓ DTaP #3
- ✓ PCV #3

He may also receive IPV #3 and/or HBV #3, although these shots can be given anywhere between 6 to 18 months. Pediatricians also recommend a flu shot for children 6 months to 2 years; this is given in two doses in the fall.

Ask the doctor or nurse about the side effects of each shot, and appropriate comfort measures for each. Also make sure to ask which side effects warrant a call to the doctor.

Milestones this month

Baby is a busy little bee this month, both physically and socially. During the sixth month, you'll likely notice the following changes and developments:

- ✓ Expect Baby to gain about 1 pound.
- ✓ He increases in length by about ½ inch.
- ✓ Baby can now hold his head steady.

✔ He can hold and drink from a cup or bottle.

✔ He rolls both ways.

✔ Baby is able to transfer objects from hand to hand.

✔ He may be able to "stand" (support weight on his legs) when you hold him on your lap.

✔ Can probably sit up for a short period of time, supporting himself with his hands.

✔ Baby may begin to push up on his hands and knees or drag himself forward; a few kids perfect the art of crawling this month.

✔ He can feed himself large finger foods (like a baby biscuit).

✔ Baby recognizes the difference between his parents and others; stranger anxiety may begin.

✔ He mimics facial expression and sounds.

✔ Turns his head toward a voice or a sound.

✔ Recognizes and responds to his own name.

✔ Is able to participate in a game of peekaboo.

✔ Begins to babble.

Keep in mind that some kids are slower to reach physical milestones, but may still be well within the range of normal development. Doctors are most concerned with a steady stream of progression — whether or not Baby is working *toward* these milestones. Maybe he can't quite shift a block from his left hand to his right, but does he make an attempt? Is he trying to roll, or does he just lie on his blanket without moving at all?

Some children never really learn to crawl, opting to create their own unique styles of movement instead. This is also quite normal and nothing to worry yourself about.

Stimulating the older baby

So with Baby showing all of this wonderful potential for physical and social growth, how can you encourage his development?

For starters, take a step back and let him try to do some things on his own. Putting the bottle in his mouth just as he's reaching for it only delays the time when he'll actually be able to hold it himself and get it into his mouth. The same goes for his toys: Let Baby struggle a bit to get a toy that's out of his reach. He has quite a sense of achievement when he finally grabs it, and he'll work even harder the next time, realizing that there's a benefit to his efforts.

Speaking of toys, buy him playthings that are age-appropriate. At this age, Baby may take an interest in toys that make noise (something that rattles or jingles when Baby shakes it) or toys that offer some visual interest (bright, primary colors catch Baby's eye now).

The best way to stimulate Baby is by playing with him. Take the time to engage in a game of peekaboo; sing songs and tickle his tummy, giving him a chance to respond.

Reading to Baby at this age seems nonsensical to some folks. (Can he really understand the story? Will he seriously sit through the reading of a book?) Baby's tolerance for listening to a story is as important as choosing the right book. A child who has no interest in sitting still for more than a minute or two isn't going to enjoy storytime right now, and trying to force him into it will only set up a battle of the books between the two of you that isn't necessary. Have some cloth books around for him to look at when he chooses; have a few very brief board books on hand, too. Let him look at the stories when he's in the mood. Soon enough, he'll probably allow you to read one to him — though he may always prefer to be somewhat on the move while you do.

Continue talking to Baby by giving him a play-by-play of the day as it happens. Now that he's starting to babble, slow down on some of the single-syllable words, giving him time to interpret the sounds coming out of your mouth. Six-month-olds are just starting to get the hang of repeating sounds. Give him every opportunity to practice, even if he's only able to copy the inflection of your voice, and in a very short time he'll be forming his first little words.

Keeping Baby Safe and Sound

She's rolling, she's dragging herself all over the floor, she's able to pick things up, and she may even be able to hoist herself up. As Baby becomes more active this month, you need to re-evaluate your safety plan for her. The house needs a good inspection at this point. And every time you go anywhere with Baby, check that she's properly secured in whatever kind of seat she happens to be traveling in (stroller, car seat, grocery cart, and so on). For more on making your home safe for Baby, see Chapter 20.

Now that Baby is becoming more mobile, keep the car seat completely out of her reach unless she's riding in it. Most seats are left in the car for all eternity (or at least until Baby outgrows it), but in some households, the car seat shifts among Mom's, Dad's, and Grandma's vehicles, and is sometimes left in the house when it's between cars. The harness straps, which play a vital role in keeping Baby securely fastened in her car seat, are a strangulation hazard when the seat isn't in use. Don't allow Baby to play in or around the car seat.

Because Baby is so much more portable and interactive at this age, we've included some tips on keeping her safe when you take her for walks and on shopping trips.

Stroller safety

All kids need to be buckled into their strollers, whether they love the ride or hate it. You just never know what kind of hazards may come your way when you're walking Baby down the street or through the park. You could hit a huge bump in the road without even seeing it. You could park him for a moment and the stroller could roll away from you. The stroller itself may have a flaw and fall apart. Kids have been flipped right out of their stroller seats before their moms could even realize and react to what was happening. A seat belt may not prevent injury in every case, but it may help — and it doesn't make matters any worse.

Another reason to buckle Baby into his stroller: The seat belt can be a strangulation hazard when it's not in use. Now that Baby is able to scoot himself around a bit, you just can't take any chances with straps of this sort. Put them to use around his waist and you won't have to worry about them harming him.

Jogger strollers aren't recommended for infants under the age of 6 months. These strollers don't offer Baby the option of reclining or lying down, so really, only older infants who've achieved a good measure of neck strength should be placed in these strollers. Also, because the speed of running (and any bumps along the way) can jolts an infant's neck and spine, many doctors recommend waiting until Baby is 1-year-old before bringing him along on your workout. The same goes for baby bike trailers and baby seats that attach to adult bikes: They're not safe for infants. Baby needs to be able to sit well, control his head movements, and wear a bike helmet — which don't come in infant sizes — before he can ride on or behind your bicycle.

Check your stroller frequently to make sure that all of its parts and mechanisms are working properly and that nothing is rusting or looking ready to fail. As Baby gets older, heavier, and more active in the stroller seat, anything that's ready to break probably will. Children can be seriously injured by faulty strollers, so don't take any chances. Replace a dangerous-looking stroller with something sturdier.

Shopping with Baby

Grocery carts are a common, yet often unconsidered, hazard to infants and older children alike. Every year, kids have accidents in grocery carts.

Carts are fairly prone to tipping. Some stores have carts with wider bases that make tipping a bit less of a hazard, but when an older sibling climbs on the front, back, or side of any grocery cart, that cart may go over. If Baby is in the cart, he's going over, too.

When kids do fall out, it's a long way down onto a hard surface. To eliminate this possibility, an older baby (one who's sitting up) should always be strapped into the seat of a grocery cart. An infant who isn't yet able to sit on his own should be strapped into an infant seat. If you're using your own car seat for this purpose, place it in the basket area of the cart — don't try to balance it on the seat portion up front. Some car seats have been designed for this purpose, but because they're not 100 percent compatible with all grocery carts, there's always the risk of the seat not staying put — which could be disastrous. Many grocery stores offer carts with infant seats bolted on. *Those* seats aren't going anywhere, so use them — and always make sure that you adjust the harness straps to hold Baby in the seat.

Put something heavy in the opposite end of your cart early in the shopping trip to help balance the weight. If baby is the only thing in the cart and you step away to reach for some ice cream, the end-heavy cart can tip over with minimal effort.

Feeding Baby's Changing Appetite

You start to introduce more solids (pureed veggies, for example) into Baby's diet this month. Breast milk and formula are enough to satisfy a small infant's hunger and nutritional needs, but by the middle of the first year, Baby needs more. He's becoming more active, and his body is growing. This includes his stomach, which was just a tiny little pouch when he was born. It can hold more now, which means that Baby can eat more and go longer between feedings (which also means he'll sleep longer at night).

What effect does this have on his already-established schedule? He'll need to nurse less often, or he'll start to take less formula. At this point, continue to allow Baby to set the schedule for breast- and bottlefeeding, just as you did when he was born. He'll make sure he's nursing enough, and he'll drink formula with each meal.

Introducing Baby to the cup now will make weaning him easier in the long run, especially if he's breastfed. Nursing children who are used to drinking from a cup don't need to be weaned to a bottle; they can be weaned directly from the breast to the cup.

Adding solids

Baby has probably had his fair share of cereal at this point. If he hasn't been introduced to vegetables, start easing those into his diet, too, preferably before fruits (Baby is less likely to embrace bland squash and carrots if he's become accustomed to eating sweet peaches and applesauce). Introducing your child to solids is a gradual process. Even if he eats everything you put in his mouth, it takes time to establish a pattern of feeding him every day. Don't rush it. Some days he'll eat solids like a champ; other days, he'll prefer his bottle or the breast. This is normal for all novice feeders.

How will you know when Baby is ready for solids? He should be able to hold his head up well, and he'll probably start showing an interest in what you're eating. Time your initial feedings carefully: Don't try to introduce him to pureed carrots after he's already gorged himself on formula — he won't be interested. Wait until it's mealtime, and allow him to nurse a bit or to have a nip at his bottle before placing him safely in his infant seat (he shouldn't be in the high chair until he can hold himself up well) and presenting him with the good stuff: veggies. Most pediatricians recommend starting with the yellow vegetables (squash, sweet potatoes, corn), because they're fairly bland and packed with nutrients.

At this age, Baby probably can't eat more than half of the smallest jar of food. Because his saliva can break down the remaining food, causing it to become watery and very unappetizing, don't spoon the food directly from the jar. Instead, pour half into a bowl, cap the unused portion, and refrigerate it.

Take it nice and slow, allowing him plenty of time to feel the food in his mouth, to taste it, and swallow it before offering him more. He may resemble a baby bird with his mouth open, waiting for the next bite, or he may decide that he's not wild about this whole set-up. You want him to get acquainted with solids while he's still relatively open to new ideas, but you don't have to make sure that Baby eats the entire portion you've spooned out for him. If he's reluctant to gobble up his veggies, make that spoon behave like a choo-choo train headed for the tunnel or an airplane coming in for a landing in Baby's mouth. Feeding time should be enjoyable, even at this age.

Introduce new foods very slowly — the general rule of thumb is one new food every four to five days — to watch for signs of food allergies. Some parents are so anxious to get into the solids that they disregard this advice, but imagine what a hassle it will be to determine the cause of an allergy if Baby has been given several new foods at once. You have to eliminate all of the new foods and reintroduce them one by one, knowing that Baby is going to react badly to one of them. It's just easier — for you and for Baby — to hold off on introducing each new food until you're sure that the previous new food hasn't affected Baby adversely.

Many doctors recommend introducing veggies to Baby before fruits are brought on board at feeding time. Veggies aren't sweet and they don't taste as good as fruits (or so most children would have us believe, judging by the way they twist their little faces into horrible grimaces upon receiving a spoonful of spinach). Although some parents may argue that children learn to hate their veggies when they're older and they have to finish them in order to have their dessert, it's just a fact that most kids enjoy sweeter-tasting foods, and even a baby will balk at a strange-tasting vegetable — even more so if he's accustomed to eating only peaches and applesauce. So the theory goes that if you introduce him to vegetables first, he accepts them more easily and continues to eat them even after he's gotten a taste of the sweeter side of baby food.

Don't feed Baby real desserts — use fruit as dessert. Babies get introduced to dessert soon enough!

As Baby becomes accustomed to solids, you can add in some finger foods, probably around the end of the seventh or the beginning of the eighth month. We discuss this in more detail in Chapter 12.

When Baby starts eating solids, his bowel movements become less frequent, but more like real poop. They vary in consistency according to what he's been eating: A kid who just loves his sweet potatoes will have orange bowel movements, for example. This will end when he's older and his gastrointestinal system is better able to filter his food.

Food allergies

You need to be on the lookout for allergies as you introduce new foods. Most reactions occur within an hour or two of Baby's ingesting an allergen — but contrary to what you may think, most reactions don't happen the first time Baby eats a food. Allergies tend to develop over time, building up over a *sensitization* period, where the groundwork is basically being laid by the body's immune system for future allergic reactions. (In other words, if Baby has eaten a food three times without any problems, she could still have an allergic reaction the next time she eats that food — which is why it's so important to introduce new foods one at a time and over the course of several days.) The good news is that most children outgrow food allergies by the time they're school-aged.

Watch for the following signs of food allergies:

✔ **Gastrointestinal distress:** Baby seems crampy, bloated, and uncomfortable, or has diarrhea or vomiting.

✔ **Rashes:** Food allergies may result in a facial rash or an itchy mouth. Hives, eczema, and itching are other symptoms of food allergies.

✔ **Cold symptoms in the absence of a cold:** Wheezing, runny nose, or itchy eyes with dark circles underneath them.

✔ **General crankiness:** Unusual crying during the day or at night (especially if Baby is normally a good sleeper) may indicate that she isn't feeling well. If she's been introduced to a new food recently, the food could be the cause.

Many pediatricians recommend holding off on certain foods, because studies have shown allergies may be caused by introducing them too soon, causing the body to prematurely develop antibodies against them. Common food allergens you should avoid feeding your child during the first year include cow's milk, eggs, wheat, strawberries, and soy. Shellfish, and nuts are also common allergens that can cause more serious reactions, like *anaphylactic shock,* which is a severe, sometimes fatal allergic reaction that can include respiratory distress; a swelling of the mouth, throat, or eyes; hives; itching; and a loss of consciousness. If you notice any of these symptoms in your child, call your doctor or get her to the ER without delay.

An allergy to milk is a fairly common occurrence in small children and is different from lactose intolerance, both in its symptoms and its underlying cause. Most kids outgrow milk allergies; lactose intolerance may last a lifetime. Chapter 18 discusses the specifics of these conditions in more detail.

If you suspect that Baby is showing signs of a food allergy, discontinue the food — and then bring it back after a week or ten days. Watch to see whether the same symptoms develop. If they do, food allergies are a probable cause. Talk to your pediatrician about Baby's reaction at her next checkup. If she's showing signs of several food allergies, you may be referred to a specialist.

Giving the cup

Introducing Baby to the cup now can only make your life easier down the road. Remember, eventually you're going to have to wean Baby from the breast or bottle. A breastfed Baby who is comfortable with the cup will never have to use a bottle; introducing a bottlefed Baby to the cup now will make weaning him in the future all that much easier.

Find a cup that Baby can reasonably get his little hands around. If you're using a cup that prevents spills, leave the insert out of the cap for now, so that Baby realizes that there's something in that cup that he wants. (Leaving the insert in requires Baby to suck on the cap to get his drink — and because the cup is completely foreign to him at this point, and completely unlike a bottle or breast, he probably won't quite get it.) Help him to get a drink from it the first time you offer it to him. Don't refuse it to him when he wants to try it himself — just make sure you're not doing this near your brand-new carpet.

If Baby simply won't drink from the cup no matter how you try to cajole him into it, don't lose heart. Put the cup away for now and let him drink from his bottle if he wants to. Try reintroducing the cup in another month or so.

Offer Baby formula or breast milk during his meals. He can also have a little bit of diluted juice during the day. The weaning process is slowly beginning now, but it can take months to complete. Baby will continue to want to nurse before his naps and at bedtime. Weaning is discussed in far more detail in Chapter 16.

Lullaby and Good Night

If you're the parent of a child who still hasn't come to terms with the fact that nighttime is rest time and that he really does need more than a cat nap on your shoulder during the day, you're probably feeling as though you missed some meeting in the hospital where the maternity nurses discussed ways of getting Baby to snooze. Convincing Baby to rest his weary head is a challenge that may drive you both to the sleepy brink of insanity, but some tried-and-true methods may help — or at least prevent you from making things worse, and sometimes, that's the best you can hope for.

At this age, Baby should be taking two decent naps during the day, which may range from one and a half to two hours each. Some kids even consolidate that time frame and take one long power nap. Early risers will need to take a nap sometime mid- to late-morning; later risers can probably forego a morning nap in favor of a longer afternoon rest. Whatever works for you and your household schedule is fine, even if it's very different from the way your friends' babies are doing things.

Baby may also be settling down for a nice, long, uninterrupted, restful night at this point.

Encouraging a schedule

You may have a child who hasn't yet fallen into any sort of discernable nap or bedtime pattern. At this point, your own lack of a daily schedule may be getting to you, as you see and read about parents whose kids sleep and wake like clockwork. *Those* moms are able to plan their days around their kids' naps. You're still playing a guessing game: What time will Baby wake you up tomorrow morning? Will you be able to get your errands done before Baby falls asleep in his car seat? How many times will he have you up in the middle of the night — and will you be so tired tomorrow that you'll spend the day in a fog?

Setting the stage for naps

Some children have trouble settling down in the daytime because they're supersensitive to the environment. It's a myth that all babies can learn to sleep through normal household noise. (Can *you* automatically shut out the light, ignore all the noise, and take a nap?) Plenty of kids can, of course, but there are some who simply need to have a quiet, dark room to settle down in.

If your 6-month-old is still balking at taking a daytime nap, think about making a few adjustments to her room and to the household schedule at naptime:

- **Darken her room.** Install shades, curtains, or blinds and move her crib out of the direct line of sunlight coming through the window.

- **Keep things quiet.** Some babies are light sleepers. Put a fan in her room (on lowest speed) to help take the edges off the loudest noises (like the phone, the dog's barking, horns honking, and so on).

- **Slow things down.** Don't just stick her in her crib according to the clock. Make naptime an event of sorts by establishing certain routines leading up to it. Feed her, change her, read her a story or rock her for a couple of minutes, and then put her in her crib — awake, so that she realizes this is also part of the routine.

- **Allow her to establish her own pattern.** Naptime is sacred — try not to mess with it. After she's down and out, let her sleep. As long as her daytime naps aren't affecting her ability to sleep at night, schedule the rest of the day (outings and errands) around the naps — not vice versa.

Realize that this is a temporary phase in Baby's life. In another year or so, her naps will shift and probably shorten. Encouraging decent napping habits now may have a lasting effect on how well she naps throughout her toddler years.

Creating a bedtime ritual

Establishing a schedule for nighttime, especially if Baby isn't much of a daytime sleeper, should, theoretically, be a snap. (She should be completely exhausted by the time bedtime rolls around if she hasn't slept all day, right?) Unfortunately, this isn't always the case; babies who don't get enough rest during the day can become overtired and overstimulated, which can mean that they have an harder time sleeping at night than their nap-loving peers. This pattern often leads to a vicious, sleepless cycle that repeats itself day-in, day-out.

To encourage a regular bedtime pattern, follow through on what you've done with Baby's naps: Make bedtime an event, every single night. If you find that a bath zones her right out, bathe her. Read to her, rock her, feed her one last time, and put her to bed — again, make sure she's awake so that she realizes that this is something she's expected to do on her own.

If you rock her to sleep at this age, she's not learning to comfort herself before drifting off, and you can guarantee that when she wakes in the middle of the night, she's going to need you to put her back to sleep.

Avoid certain activities in the evening — namely anything that riles Baby up and makes it difficult for her to go to sleep. Don't get Baby wound up with a rousing round of tickling. Put the most stimulating toys away. And don't take her on an outing an hour before you want her in bed. She needs plenty of time to unwind from her long day of exploration and learning.

It can sometimes be very hard for parents to establish a quiet evening ritual, especially if both work all day and look forward to spending the evening with Baby. Just keep in mind that establishing good sleep habits for Baby benefits all of you in the long run, so the sooner you do it, the better.

Nixing nighttime waking

Babies at this age sleep about an average of 11 hours at night — mostly straight through, perhaps stirring once or twice, but without needing Mom or Dad to come in and feed or comfort them. They also usually take two daytime naps of an hour or two each.

This can be heartbreaking news if you're the parent of a child who is still waking and lustily crying two to three times every night. Unlike the baby who wakes and murmurs in the crib only to fall back asleep moments later, your child seems to really be hungry and is unable to go back to sleep without rocking.

Here's the deal: Baby's eating solids now, and by the time he's 6 months old he shouldn't need to eat during the night. If he's waking and crying and latching onto you at 2 a.m. (and again at 3, and then at 4), he's most likely doing so for comfort and company. Breastfed infants seem particularly prone to this behavior, and it's not because they're not getting enough to eat. More likely, it's because they want to snuggle with Mom in the middle of the night. You're his parent, and it's hard to say no when Baby seems so desperate.

Is there such a thing as tough-love for infants? Yes, and it's commonly referred to as letting Baby "cry it out" during the middle of the night. This is exactly what it sounds like: Baby wakes and cries for a parent, only to find that the nighttime feedings and visits are not forthcoming. Baby cries himself back to sleep.

Deciding to let Baby cry it out is a heart-wrenching choice, but it does tend to be very effective — and mercifully short-lived. Many babies cry for a long time the first night (an hour or more), and for a substantially shorter amount of time the second (perhaps as little as 15 minutes); by the third and fourth nights, there's nary a peep out of them. And suddenly, you have a little sleeper.

Making the decision to let Baby cry it out

This is another one of those parenting issues that divides people into two separate and very different camps. Advocates claim that letting Baby cry it out teaches Baby that he must comfort himself, that there's no way of getting around it or doing it halfway, and that he will learn — rather quickly — to put himself back to sleep. Critics of the practice generally frown on leaving a helpless, frightened infant all alone in his crib while he screams.

Where your opinion falls on this topic will probably depend on two things:

✔ Your level of desperation

✔ Your tolerance for hearing Baby cry

Different articles by different experts will give you conflicting advice: One will tell you that allowing Baby to cry will damage his self-esteem for the rest of his life; another will tell you that Baby will be more self-sufficient during his childhood if he learns to comfort himself now. Forget the experts and make your own decision on this one. Only you know the situation in your own home and how sleep deprivation is affecting you, your mate, and your child.

Fact is, unless you've experienced six straight months of almost sleepless nights, you can't appreciate what it's like to be in the position of wanting to let your child cry it out. It's not that you're cruel — it's just that you want to stop this nighttime behavior.

Easing Baby off your nighttime company

Aside from letting baby cry it out (see the preceding section), there are a couple of other methods for breaking Baby's dependence on you little by little:

✔ **Go to Baby when he cries, but don't pick him up.** Instead, keep the lights low and try other means of comforting him, like rubbing his back, singing to him softly, or just standing nearby, slowly cutting back on the amount of time (five minutes the first night, four the second, and so on) you spend with him until eventually he doesn't need you at all.

✔ **Allow Baby to cry for a predetermined amount of time each time he wakes up before you respond to him.** For example, if your child is up three times during the night, you may wait 5 minutes before responding to him the first time, 10 minutes before you respond the second time, and 15 minutes before answering his third call. The next night, you'd start out with a longer time interval the first time he wakes up, and lengthen the others accordingly. This method could take several nights, but if it works, it's less painful than hearing Baby cry for over an hour.

Whether these gentler methods work for you and your child depends largely on Baby's temperament. Waiting several minutes and then going into him anyway isn't going to teach an exceptionally determined child anything except that when he cries long and hard enough, you show up. This could actually make matters worse, because one of two things are apt to happen: You either abandon all hope of sleeping through the night until Baby decides it's time (which could be never), or when you do decide to let him cry it out, it takes longer than it may have originally because now he's convinced he can get you to come running.

Making a difficult process easier

Getting Baby to sleep through the night is likely to be a real challenge, but the following pointers can help:

- ✔ **Make sure he's full.** If you think that Baby is legitimately hungry during the night, talk to your pediatrician. He can take a look at your child's growth pattern to date and determine whether it's possible your child needs more to eat. He may recommend adding more food during the day because Baby needs to sleep at night.

- ✔ **Connect with Baby physically during his waking hours.** Hold him a bit longer, play with him a little more, rock him for few extra minutes before putting him to bed. This may help each of you to let go of those middle-of-the-night meetings.

- ✔ **Help him comfort himself.** Direct Baby to his fingers; sucking is a great comfort to infants, and if he learns to use his own appendages for this purpose during his waking hours, chances are good that he'll continue the practice in the middle of the night. Most finger-suckers break themselves of the habit by the end of the first year.

- ✔ **Stick to your guns.** Try to wean Baby away from your company slowly, but be firm about whichever set of rules you're working with. If you decide to comfort him for two minutes without picking him up, follow through, especially if he continues to cry while you're in the room. Giving into him at that point reinforces the idea that he only has to cry longer and harder to get what he wants, even when it's not the best thing for him. In turn, this only prolongs the nighttime sleep deprivation for both of you.

Baby will still love you in the morning if you let her cry it out. And you'll love her too!

Taking the ba-ba to bed: Baby-bottle mouth

Some babies love to take a bottle (of formula, juice, or breast milk) to bed. It quiets them, it comforts them, and their parents know that their children aren't going to be hungry in the middle of the night. Sounds like a pretty sweet deal, huh?

Well . . . it is, and that's the problem. Sugar can have a detrimental effect on Baby's budding teeth, especially if he goes to bed exposing himself to the sweetness for hours on end.

Baby bottle mouth is tooth decay affecting the front teeth, and can begin in children anywhere from infancy through 2 years. What happens in any instance of tooth decay is that bacteria feeds on whatever food source it can find to break down the tooth *enamel* (the tooth's protective covering). Your child is left with discolored, rotted-out teeth (if they don't fall out or need to be removed) — right there, front and center, for the world to see.

Baby's first teeth set the stage for his future dental and emotional health. He needs his front teeth for biting and chewing. Premature loss of these teeth can lead to speech difficulties. Tooth decay in the early years can also lead to self-esteem issues, when a child is teased about missing or discolored teeth. In addition, the health of his baby teeth lay the groundwork for the condition of his permanent teeth. Depending on the severity of the decay, the child with baby bottle mouth could have a lifelong dental crisis.

Most cases of baby bottle mouth occur when a child is allowed to suck on a bottle for hours on end. There have been instances of nursing babies developing tooth decay, but usually only if they've been allowed to nurse for hours and hours — say, if Mom regularly falls asleep while nursing her child and Baby suckles all night long.

Of course, some sugary drinks are worse than others, and although it's fine to give Baby a bit of juice during the day, she definitely shouldn't be drinking soda. There's no nutritional value to the drink and it's one of the worst things to give a kid, especially one who's developing new teeth. Studies also show that developing a soda habit in early childhood leads to other problems down the road, most notably obesity.

The good news is that baby tooth decay is not an inevitability — in fact, it's easily preventable. Here are some do's and don'ts:

- ✔ Don't put Baby to bed with sugary drinks.

- ✔ Don't substitute a bottle for a pacifier. Babies who need to suck and are allowed to have a bottle throughout the entire day (or night) are extremely prone to tooth decay.

- ✔ Don't give Baby a pacifier dipped in sugar or honey. This is akin to you wiping the sweetener right on her teeth and leaving it there.

- ✔ Don't allow Baby to nurse throughout the night.

- ✔ Do give her plain water if she needs her bottle during her nap or at bedtime.

- ✔ Do wean her from the bottle or from breastfeeding around 12 months.

So when is it time for you to start caring for those little teeth, anyway? As soon as they come in. Baby teeth play a vital role in eating and speech, and are also the foundation for Baby's permanent choppers.

Adequate fluoride intake is very important to the development of teeth. If your water supply doesn't have fluoride in it, your pediatrician will give you a prescription for drops.

As soon as Baby is finished eating, wipe her teeth off with gauze or a soft, clean cloth. This will remove any leftover food and plaque, leaving the bacteria in her mouth little to build cavities with. To encourage good dental hygiene habits that will last a lifetime, you can also buy her a teeny little toothbrush for this purpose.

Adult toothpaste shouldn't be used until your child is 2 years old, and then only sparingly. (If ingested in large quantities, toothpaste can be harmful to your child, so keep it up and out of her reach.) For now, cleaning Baby's teeth with a clean cloth or a toothbrush with water is adequate.

Keep an eye on Baby's teeth and look for the signs of tooth decay, which include discoloration and pitting of the teeth. If you suspect a problem, call your pediatrician. Children generally see the dentist for the first time around the age of 2, but substantial dental problems require earlier intervention.

Part IV
Discovering the World Beyond Mom

The 5th Wave   By Rich Tennant

Get the Huggies, hon—she's reaching for the Diaper icon

In this part . . .

During the seventh to ninth months, Baby becomes more and more curious and mobile — *and* more fun! Of course, parents are presented with new safety issues at this time, and these chapters offer tips on keeping your increasingly active child safe. You may find he's becoming so active he thinks he's too darn busy to eat — or to nurse. Find out how to introduce semi-solids and what to do when Baby loses interest in the breast during these months.

Baby is making an even better effort at real communication during this time and may be able to utter his first little words soon. You can have a huge influence on his speech simply by talking to him. These chapters offer advice on that angle as well. (Listen carefully — he's saying, "The first year is whizzing by, Mom!")

Chapter 12

The Seventh Month: Developmental Delights

*T*he seventh month is a time of major achievements for Baby — in movement, in development, in personality. Although you can hardly count the many changes that Baby's gone through in the first six months, expect at least as many to come during the next six. Not only is Baby continuing to flex his little muscles and show you what he can do physically, he's also starting to use his brain to figure out the world around him. He's not just a pretty little face lying around the house anymore — he's actually putting the pieces of day-to-day life together. For example, he now knows that if he drops something, it doesn't disappear — and someone will probably give it back to him. He's also learning that dropping stuff and getting it back is a pretty fun way to pass some time!

Your child is becoming more independent, more opinionated, and more lovable because of it. He can handle more foods at this point, and he may lose interest in the breast or bottle because he's just so darn busy discovering what he's capable of doing every single day. Language — in the form of babbling — is another significant developmental milestone during this time.

Checking In with Baby

Most pediatricians don't schedule a well-baby visit during the seventh month. And because Baby won't see the doctor again for a checkup until the ninth month, some questions may pop up in the interim, especially because Baby is changing so much. You may just find yourself with the phone in your hand at times, wondering whether you should call or whether the office staff will think you're crazy. (All parents have been in this position at one time or another.) You'll read your baby books, you'll search for information on the Internet, and still, you'll have a nagging feeling that you need to talk to your pediatrician.

So if you have any concerns about Baby's behavior during these months, call the doctor's office and at least speak with the nurse. She may be able to tell you that your child is behaving normally, or she may determine that Baby needs to be seen in the office. Baby is in a stage of major change right now, which may explain why she's crying more these days (it may be due to frustration, as she's trying to accomplish more and having a hard time reaching her goals).

If you're dealing with something that seems to have an underlying medical cause — Baby is crying like crazy for no apparent reason, or she's running a high fever, or something about her behavior or movements just aren't right — call without delay.

Chapter 23 gives you a list of reasons why you would definitely want to call your pediatrician; Chapter 24 provides you with a list of reasons to hold the phone.

Milestones this month

Baby's moving and shaking this month (and bouncing, and creeping, and maybe even standing!). What kind of development will the parent of a kid this age see?

✔ Baby can control his head movements completely and hold his head up indefinitely.

✔ If he hasn't mastered the art of rolling both ways yet, he will probably do so this month.

✔ He may be able to push himself into a seated position from his stomach.

✔ He can sit unsupported.

✔ Baby loves to test out his strength, and may just love to "stand" while you hold him on your lap.

✔ He may be able to pull himself up (see Figure 12-1), and may even be able to stand on his own for a short time. (Smaller, skinny babies seem to master this skill earlier than their larger peers.)

✔ If he's mastered the art of standing while holding onto something, he may even be able to *cruise* around the room ("walking" while holding onto objects).

✔ Baby loves to bounce when in a standing or seated position.

Figure 12-1:
As Baby starts to pull up, take care to remove or block anything he could pull down on himself.

✔ His fine motor skills are coming along nicely: Baby can hold an object with one hand at this age, which leaves the other hand free to explore other objects.

✔ Baby is able to feed himself larger finger foods.

✔ Teething may begin, if it hasn't already.

✔ Baby turns toward the focus of his attention when lying on his stomach or sitting.

✔ He may begin creeping (up on his hands and knees, working toward crawling) or crawling if he hasn't already.

✔ Baby shows signs of preferring Mom over anyone else in the entire world.

✔ Because Baby is becoming more attached to Mom, the first signs of *stranger anxiety* (a definite wariness around new people) are beginning to exhibit themselves, though they probably won't peak for another month or two.

✔ Baby may begin to become attached to a comfort object or two (a result of stranger anxiety and his increasing understanding of object permanence).

✔ Baby loves a good game of peekaboo, "This Little Piggy," or any game that gives him a chance to respond and interact.

✔ He may begin to babble by the end of this month.

✔ Baby now turns his head in your direction when you call him.

No creepy crawlies?

Your child is showing no signs of creeping or crawling at 7 months? Don't lose sleep over it. Although most children gain some sort of major mobility at this age, many don't. The kids in the latter group are content to take the world in from their perch on their baby blanket, and are in no rush to learn how to get from Point A (the family room) to Point B (the kitchen). Some babies never learn to truly crawl at all; they go from dragging themselves along the floor to pulling up to walking, or they may create their own style of crawling (using straight legs instead of bending their knees, for example). As long as Baby is making some sort of attempt to move around and is not just lying listlessly on his blanket day after day, he's probably just taking his time embracing and exploring the joys of locomotion. You'll be chasing after him soon enough and you'll barely remember the days when he stayed where you put him.

Baby should be able to recognize his name at this point, and he should also respond to it. If you call him over and over again and he doesn't respond, make sure to mention this to your pediatrician. Although Baby's lack of response may be due to the fact that he's distracted by a new skill or something happening outside the window, there's a slight chance he may not be hearing you. Your doctor will want to evaluate your child to rule out any hearing problems, signs of which include not only Baby's inability to respond to his name, but also a lack of vocal interaction (if he isn't trying to babble at this point and/or his voice is somewhat monotone).

Building memory

Baby is just beginning to grasp the idea of *object permanence,* which means he knows that when something "disappears," it's really just somewhere else. Prior to this point, when a toy or a person went away, they were gone for good, as far as Baby knew.

At around 7 months, memory starts to increase (though not as we understand it — a child this age may only remember something for a week or two, tops). As memory increases, Baby is able to draw certain conclusions about the constancy of objects in his world, and he begins to expect certain things to happen. For example, if he presses a lever on a toy and it makes a noise or a figure pops up, he's going to play with that toy *knowing* what's going to happen.

Beautiful babble

At this age, Baby moves from acing the vowel sounds ("oo," "oh," "ay") and tries on the consonants for size. The first hard consonant sounds that she will probably master will be "k," "p," "b," and "m," though others (like "d" and "g") will follow soon after. How can you encourage her language skills now? By doing what you've been doing for the past few months: Talk to her slowly, using short words and phrases, giving her a chance to really take in the sounds. At this age, she's listening for the beginnings and endings of the words — a skill called *word segmentation*. She doesn't quite understand the words' meanings, (she probably won't be able to do so for at least two or three more months), but this is a necessary step in that direction. She'll start to mimic your sounds — "ba," "ma," "ka" — and when she does, show her your excitement. Encourage her to try again. This is how she learns what communication is: people responding to one another.

Baby may also start to push *your* buttons at this time, though without any malice. Tossing his toy from the highchair, for example, is his way of seeing what kind of reaction he can elicit from you. (Because he also knows that that toy isn't disappearing off the face of the earth, he can do this without upsetting himself in the process.) If you hand it back to him a couple of times, he'll probably start to think of this as some sort of game. (Clever, isn't he?) Your best bet is to give him a no-nonsense "No" (even though you're secretly proud of his cognitive skills) and employ some sort of diversionary tactic so that this doesn't become a day-in, day-out activity.

Lagging behind: Common concerns

If your child isn't hitting the major milestones on time, should you be concerned? Maybe there's a hidden problem somewhere — physical, neurological, or a combination of the two?

Generally speaking, milestones are just guidelines: They indicate what *most* children can do at a given age. If your child seems to always be a bit behind — but he's making definite strides in the right direction, then there's probably nothing for you to be concerned about. Talk to your pediatrician to rule out any definite problems; chances are, he can put your fears to rest.

Many babies excel in one developmental arena and lag a little behind in others (great mobility but not so much speech for example). This is common and no reason for concern.

However, premature babies may take years to catch up to the development of their full-term peers, for many reasons. Depending on how prematurely your child was born, he may be dealing with quite a few long-term physical problems, or hardly any at all. The child who is suffering from a metabolic disorder, for example, will not grow at a comparable rate to the child whose metabolism is normal. He may also be harder to nourish, which (again) can often mean that the child will be smaller and weaker than his peers. Obviously, this will translate into developmental delays simply because — for example — he may not have the strength to pull himself up, which means he also won't be learning to stand by himself or to walk for some time. Preemies can catch up to their peers in a matter of years, or they may always lag behind. Your pediatrician is your best resource for evaluating your premature child's development.

Keeping Baby Safe and Sound

You're going to want to reassess your baby-proofing plan as your child starts moving about the house with more regularity and purpose.

No matter what you do Baby is going to take her fair share of falls. Just make sure she's not going to fall off your second-story deck or out her bedroom window. No, you can't walk behind her and catch her every single time — and no, you shouldn't even try. She needs to learn that falling isn't failing; it's just part of life.

What kinds of things should be baby-proofed for the increasingly mobile 7-month-old? Basically anything that's within reach, both on the floor and above it. Remember that she's learning to pull up now — which means that she can also pull things down on herself. A tablecloth, a hot cup of coffee, a heavy ornamental bowl filled with potpourri (the contents of which also look and smell like a suitable snack, as far as Baby's concerned) — all of these things need to be out of her reach (and not just for now, but for the next couple of years). If she isn't pulling herself up just yet, she will be soon, so it's not too early to start making these adjustments in your home.

Also remember that Baby's becoming better with her grasp — quicker and more dexterous. Where once she would really have to work at picking up a quarter off the floor, for example, she'll be able to do so with more ease now and in the months to come. Yes, it's always been important to keep small objects out of her reach, but it becomes increasingly important now that she's able to manipulate them so easily.

Hitting the high points of baby-proofing at this age:

✔ **Protect Baby from big falls.** Gate off stairways and open railings. Don't install a pressure gate at the top of a stairway, as it can easily become disengaged by a child leaning or climbing on it.

✔ **Protect Baby from sharp edges.** She's learning to stand, she's pulling up, and she's not looking for hazards when she's on the way down. Cover the edges of the coffee table and the fireplace.

✔ **Look for things she may pull down when she pulls up.** Chairs. Tablecloths. Curtains. Drawers that could pop open and cause a nasty spill backwards. Remove or block these things from Baby's reach or secure them to prevent injuries.

✔ **Keep small objects out of reach.** Coins. Pen caps. Marbles. Hard candies. Button-sized batteries. Buttons. If there's any possibility that Baby could swallow and choke on it, remove it. You can buy "choke tubes" in the baby-accessory aisle, which are plastic tubes representing the size of baby's windpipe. If the object can fit in there, Baby can choke on it. If you can't find one of these commercial tubes, use the cardboard tube from your paper towels as a guideline.

✔ **Lock away household poisons.** Baby's getting more mobile, and faster and better with her grasp. Don't keep potential hazards anywhere Baby will have access to them. (This includes houseplants — many are poisonous. Keep them up and out of Baby's reach.)

It's never too soon to start baby-proofing more and more around the house. These months move quickly, and Baby will be acquiring new skills (like climbing or opening cabinets) before you even realize what she's doing, in some cases. Consider yourself constantly on the offense against Baby's best efforts to find holes in your baby-proofing plan. Get down on all fours and *be* the baby, just for a short time — you may be surprised at what you've overlooked. For more on baby-proofing your house, see Chapter 20.

Fill 'Em Up: Feeding at 7 Months!

By the end of the month, Baby should be accepting solids as part of his daily fare — for a couple of reasons: First, he needs more nutrition at this point than a diet of only breast milk or formula can offer. He's growing, his teeth are starting to come in, and while breast- and bottlefeeding met his every need in the early months, he simply needs a nutritional boost at this point.

Secondly, he's going to *have* to eat solids at some point. It's much easier to start him on "real" food now, when he's more likely to welcome it, than when he's 1 year old and unwilling to try something new. (If Baby hasn't yet started on solids, flip to Chapter 11, where you'll find all the basics for getting this show on the road.)

After Baby has settled into a routine of having solids throughout the day, he may be looking for more. It's not unusual for kids to show a definite interest in what you're eating, by either reaching for your food or doing their best impression of baby birds (sitting with mouths wide open, just waiting for something to fall in). Because Baby's able to pick up large and small objects at this age, it's the perfect time to introduce him to either mashed or finger foods and allow him to feed himself.

As with the introduction of anything new into Baby's life, pick a time when he's most apt to go with the flow of finger foods. Don't hand him a cracker after he's sucked down an entire bottle, but don't wait until he's shaking from hunger, either. He's most likely to accept the idea of eating foreign finger foods when he's in a good mood and ready to fill his little tank.

TIP

If Baby isn't getting the concept of finger foods (picking them up and putting them into his mouth), by all means, help him out by placing a piece of food into his grasp. He'll probably pop it into his mouth before long. If, on the other hand, he seems completely disinterested in the idea of feeding himself, let it go and try again in a week or two. Mealtime should be 100 percent pressure-free, with Baby feeding himself as much — or as little — as he cares to eat. He's his own best regulator in that regard, and when he's ready to feed himself, he'll take over the feeding duties, lickety-split.

Babies do best when introduced to larger finger foods first — teething biscuits, baby pretzels, or something along those lines. As baby's grip becomes more advanced, he'll be able to handle some trickier eats, like:

- ✔ Toasted oat cereal (a perennial favorite)
- ✔ Mashed soft fruits (kiwi, papaya, pear, banana — just make sure any strings from the peel have been removed)
- ✔ Bread (remove the crust)
- ✔ Teeny pieces of meat (chicken or beef, for example, ground or finely chopped)
- ✔ Cooked pasta (*not* spaghetti — twists or wheels are good choices)
- ✔ Vegetables or legumes that are cooked until soft (broccoli, zucchini, potatoes, kidney or green beans, peas, or mashed potatoes)

Before Baby's grasp is fully developed, you can place fresh, mashed fruits and vegetable in a mesh *feeding bag,* available in most baby departments. This bag allows Baby to taste the food and to get small pieces in his mouth while eliminating the risk of choking. (What *will* they think of next?!)

Take special precautions when feeding Baby potentially "stringy" foods, like bananas, oranges, or certain cheeses (meats can also occasionally contain sinewy strings), which can cause gagging or choking.

Can Baby have what *you're* having for dinner? Sure, within reason. You want to keep his foods simple for now, until you know for certain that he doesn't have any food allergies. So although you may be hankering to introduce him to your award-winning Shepard's Pie, hold off on this meal unless he's already been introduced to every single food in the recipe. Otherwise, if he starts to show signs of an allergy, you won't know if it was the carrots, or the beans, or the potatoes. (For more on food allergies, turn to Chapter 11.)

Avoid feeding Baby anything that is very spicy, salty, or sweet. His little digestive system can't handle an overload of these ingredients.

To prevent choking, Baby should only be offered solid foods while he sits upright in his highchair. Also, use the safety straps at all times to prevent any neat little tricks ("Look, ma! I'm standing!") he has up his sleeves.

What kinds of finger foods should be avoided? Anything that's hard or not easily gummed into small pieces (although Baby may have a couple of teeth, he's relying on those gums to break up his food at this age). Baby is not quite ready for:

- ✔ Raisins
- ✔ Nuts
- ✔ Hot dogs (even if they're cut up into small pieces, they're very high in sodium and not the best choice nutritionally speaking)
- ✔ Olives
- ✔ Popcorn
- ✔ Candy (whether it's hard candy or a chunk of chocolate, it's not going to be easily gummed)
- ✔ Hard (uncooked) veggies

Just remember — Baby's got a lot of years ahead of him to sample all the culinary delights in this world. He'll get around to trying that popcorn when he's a bit older. For now, keep his meals soft, simple, and safe.

By the time Baby is about 7 months old, he may be eating:

- ✔ Fruits and veggies twice a day (at lunch and dinner, perhaps)
- ✔ Cereal twice a day (breastfed babies in particular need the extra iron provided by this meal)
- ✔ Formula or breastmilk three to five times over the course of a day

What is Baby getting from these foods? Fruits and veggies are an excellent source of Vitamins A and C. Cereal is iron-fortified. These are essential nutrients for a growing child. (His formula, meanwhile, provides him with protein, and breastmilk continues to provide him with protein and antibodies.)

Wondering about weaning?

When children develop a feeding schedule that's heavy on the solids, moms start wondering how this will affect their nursing or bottlefeeding schedule.

Baby isn't ready to completely abandon the bottle in favor of cow's milk at this point. If introduced in the first year, cow's milk can cause an allergic reaction in Baby. Worse, it can also produce a mild inflammation of the intestine in some babies, which can lead to chronic mild bleeding and iron-deficient anemia.

Formula is still the food of choice for non-nursing mothers, so keep it flowing (or mixing). Although formula intake increases during the first half of the first year, with some kids downing 40 ounces a day by the sixth month, most doctors recommend that your child top off at a maximum of 32 ounces of formula a day after a diet of solids is established. If Baby is drinking more than that, she's not going to be hungry enough to sample the interesting new delicacies (mmm pureed broccoli!) you've prepared for her, and she'll also miss out on their nutrients. For more on introducing food, see Chapters 9 and 10.

Offer Baby a cup at each meal with formula, breast milk, or diluted juice. She can actually be weaned from the bottle to the cup anytime after she masters the art of holding and drinking from a cup. The sooner she knows how to do this, the easier it will be on both of you in the long run. If she's breastfed, teaching her to drink from the cup now will allow you to wean her directly from the breast to the cup when the time comes, without ever having to depend on a bottle as an interim dispenser of liquids.

Vary what you put in the cup. If baby only ever gets juice in the cup, she'll expect sweet stuff to come out of the cup and may reject formula (or later, milk) from the cup.

If you're thinking of weaning Baby from the breast, don't jump the gun. She's becoming more active, she's acquiring new skills, she's tasting new foods — every day brings something different for her. It's only natural that she would let her old habits fall by the wayside a bit in favor of exploring her latest options. She isn't rejecting the breast so much as she's embracing the new world around her, with all of its possibilities. You can allow her to regulate her own intake, offering her the breast after each round of solids, or you can take a measure of control by offering her the breast at different times throughout the day (the downside of which is that you may start to feel as though you do nothing but feed Baby).

Establishing a feeding schedule that includes a healthy dose of solids along with several nursing sessions each day may take some trial and error. Don't worry about what your friends are doing; find out what works best for you and your child and go with it.

Try to stick with a minimum of four breastfeedings daily to ensure proper nutrition. Don't let baby choose food over breastmilk or formula.

Most doctors recommend nursing Baby throughout the first year — but if your child is interested in everything but breastfeeding at this point, you may be thinking that that goal is darn near impossible. It may seem as though nursing means much more to you than it does to your child at this point. Some tips for keeping a distracted kid on the breast:

- **Don't pull her away from playtime to nurse.** She needs a transition time, something (such as allowing her to have some solids first) that signals that she ought to settle down and eat.

- **Limit the cup to mealtimes.** If she's able to crawl around, play with her toys, stand, and bounce, all the while toting a cup of juice or formula around, there's really no need for her to *ever* nurse, is there?

- **Make it fun.** Allow her to bring a toy along while she nurses (unless this causes her to become more distracted), or keep an interesting necklace nearby that you wear only during nursing sessions.

- **Use a different position.** Maybe she wants to nurse while sitting straight up? This change may be so interesting to Baby that she looks forward to nursing again.

- **Offer her the breast more often if you find she's barely nursing — or start pumping.** You have to keep up your milk supply or the weaning decision will be out of your hands.

Rejecting the breast is such a common thing that there's a term for it: a *nursing strike*. Whether you work through the strike or call it quits ultimately comes down to how much nursing means to you.

Gradual weaning — which is simply cutting back on the number of nursing sessions and/or their length — often naturally begins at this age. It doesn't mean that you have to cut Baby off all together. You can nurse her less frequently without weaning her completely.

For more information on how to wean Baby, read Chapter 16.

Eating more, eating less

So how much should a typical 7-month-old be eating each day? As much as he wants to. You really can't overfeed a child this age. His stomach can only hold so much, after all, and he has a wonderful built-in "I'm all full" trigger that tells him when enough is enough. Depending on how active he is, he may come to the highchair starving — or he may not be all that interested in eating. This pattern may vary from day to day. You tell your mother-in-law how your child eats like a lumberjack, and then he refuses anything you offer to him during the course of her lovingly prepared Sunday dinner.

If your child is regularly disinterested in solids at this age, we know of a few ways to lure him into eating a bit more:

- **Make mealtime pleasant.** Let him have plenty of time to sample the new foods on his tray. If he likes to linger over teething biscuits and juice, let him.

- **Time it right.** If your baby tends to get very focused on his activities, he's going to need a few minutes to ease into mealtimes. He may be so busy crawling and playing that he doesn't even realize he's hungry. Start by giving him a cup of water or diluted juice while he's on his blanket, which will signal that lunchtime is fast approaching — and then follow through by putting him in his highchair several minutes later. Establishing this pattern will get him thinking about the act of eating, at least.

- **Demonstrate.** Everyone can picture a parent tasting a bit of the pureed veggies and faking a smile in an effort to coax their child into giving peas a chance. Why are these parents willing to go to such lengths? Because it works — at least in many instances.

- **Offer snacks.** Not every meal has to be structured. Let Baby have some tasty snacks throughout the day (like cereal or crackers), which may whet his appetite for more solids.

Should you be worried if your child isn't into solids at this age? Not really. He will be, eventually. Developmentally, he's probably ready for them — the problem is that he's also developmentally ready to do so many *other* things right now. Food may just be at the bottom of his list of priorities. When should you be concerned?

- **If Baby just won't eat at all.** He may have some underlying illness going on. Ear infections, for example, often manifest themselves in a reluctance to eat because pain radiates down the jaw, making it unpleasant for Baby to chew or suck.

✔ **If Baby refuses all solids, all the time.** He may be so dependent on nursing or the bottle that he isn't at all interested in other foods. Though there is a theory that it's natural for children to nurse exclusively for the first year — a theory that's bolstered by examples of what children do in other countries — it's really in Baby's best interest to start eating other foods now. Remember, children in other countries often don't have other nutritious foods readily available. Sure, they nurse for a long time, but they may also be very limited in their options.

A 7-month-old who was born two months prematurely is 5 months old, developmentally speaking (which means that his digestive system isn't ready for minced chicken and mashed mangoes). At this point, he's ready to get his first taste of solids in the form of strained baby foods. Don't expect him to be able to feed himself at this point. For more on introducing Baby to solids, read Chapter 11. Your doctor is the best source of information where your premature child is concerned, so check with him before starting your child on solids.

Feeding Baby is just matter of finding what works best — for example, does he need to snack during the day, or do snacks prevent him from eating his more nutritious meals? Does he tolerate mealtimes well (can he sit in his highchair long enough to ingest some food without crying?), or does he need to get back to his playtime? The most important thing for you to do is to make the effort. Offer him the food, but don't force it. Baby will eventually fall into a somewhat normal (for him) feeding schedule.

Chapter 13

The Eighth Month: The Cruisin' Kid

*W*hoa! Where's Baby going? He's up, he's steady, he's hanging on — and he's navigating his way through the living room! Though not all kids master the art of *cruising* (walking while hanging on to furniture or walls) by the end of this month, some do!

The eighth month is a busy, busy time, filled with milestones and developments. Parents are often left wondering where their happy-go-lucky, I-love-everybody child has disappeared to and how he was replaced with this shy, timid child. Though it can be hard to watch, stranger anxiety is completely normal — and is a sign of healthy development. By the end of the month, Baby will probably start to show a real preference for certain people and things in his life, whether they're toys (he just loves his stacking blocks), foods (the kid can't get enough mashed banana in his diet), or activities (banging the pots and pans till you're deaf? It's fun!). He may also start to show an interest in — yikes — TV. In this chapter, we go over the possible effects of allowing Baby to get hooked on virtual entertainment at this point in time.

Checking In with Baby

Most pediatricians don't schedule a well-baby visit during the eighth month. Baby will be back in the office next month for a full examination and, if he's missed any shots to date, another round of immunizations.

If Baby falls ill, however, you may need to check in with the doctor anyway. So keep jotting down any questions you may have instead of trying to remember what it was that you wanted to ask as you're walking into your appointment.

Your doctor has less time for chit-chat during a sick call, so don't plan on discussing the nuances of Baby's cruising skills at this time; however, if you're a little concerned that something is amiss and it isn't serious enough by itself to warrant a call to the office, ask about it now.

Milestones this month

Up, up, and away this month — well, almost. Baby may feel as though she has acquired superhuman strength now that she's able to move rather independently. This newfound freedom will take her into new and interesting situations every day, and may result in complete contentedness (because she's able to keep herself busy now) or frustration (as she strives to do so much more).

Here are the milestones Baby is likely to reach by the end of this month:

- ✔ Baby can crawl or otherwise move across the floor (by dragging herself, for example).
- ✔ She sits without support.
- ✔ She has complete head control now. She turns in the direction of a voice or when she hears her name.
- ✔ Baby is able to get into a sitting position from her stomach.
- ✔ She's able to pull herself up.
- ✔ She can stand holding onto something.
- ✔ She may be able to stand briefly by herself.
- ✔ Baby may be able to cruise by holding onto furniture. See Figure 13-1.
- ✔ She's able to hold one object in each hand.
- ✔ She can feed herself.
- ✔ She can "rake" a small object along the floor with her fingers in order to pick it up.
- ✔ Waves bye-bye.
- ✔ Shows a definite preference for particular people, toys, and activities.
- ✔ Expresses her frustration or anger if something is taken away from her.
- ✔ She says "Mama" or "Dada" (without meaning).

Figure 13-1:
Baby may
be able to
cruise at
this age.

- Baby understands the word "no."

- May incorporate "strings" of babbled sounds into her communication.

- Baby will begin to understand the concept of object permanence, if she doesn't already (more on this in Chapter 12).

- Stranger anxiety begins in full force this month. (More on this later in this chapter.)

- Baby begins to understand that certain objects have specific uses. She may start to mimic you by babbling into her toy telephone, for example.

Outfitting the feet?

When Baby starts cruising, you may be tempted to buy the latest high-tech footwear in order to ensure his success on the floor. But shoes are just too bulky for Baby to handle at this point. Instead of offering him support and some sort of podiatric guidance, they're more likely to cause a lot of trips (this is true even after he's learned to walk well). And unless they have rubber treads on the bottom, socks are slippery — even on rugs.

In fact, it's best for Baby to make his first attempts at walking (which cruising is a prelude to) barefoot. He needs to get a good feel for how his bare feet work if he's to master the art of toddling in the next few months. Plus babies' feet have fairly flat arches. Learning to walk barefoot allows the foot to really work out those arches, developing them properly. Walking barefoot also allows the ankles to naturally become stronger over time.

It's fine to have shoes on hand for Baby to wear on special occasions. Just keep in mind that ultra-expensive shoes don't enhance foot development in a baby or a toddler. Look for an inexpensive, lightweight, supportive shoe with a nonskid surface.

TV for babies? No way!

Yes, yes, we know that there are videos available today that are marketed directly to the parents of infants, promising that their babies will become geniuses if they're allowed to sit and watch.

Now check your gut feeling. Chances are, you suspect that watching TV can't really be all that great for a child who should be spending her time exploring and playing by herself. This is what the first few years of life are all about — discovering the world (and not through the magic of television).

You know how easy it is to become completely dependent on the tube for entertainment. Think of all the things that adults miss out on when they have a serious television habit: They're not interacting with their families. They're not fostering any hobbies. They're not educating themselves by reading. They're not using their imaginations to think of anything better to do. Plus, they're getting fat.

The same is true for kids who get hooked on TV, but the results may be even more insidious, because some studies suggest that watching too much TV can actually result in the development of attention deficit disorder and aggressive behavioral problems in older children. At the very least, a child who spends her time in front of the TV isn't spending her time doing what she should be doing — namely, being active in the real world and finding out what she's capable of. TV isn't a necessary part of a baby's life — so avoid starting her on a habit that may be incredibly hard to break years down the line.

Pediatricians don't recommend TV viewing for children younger than 2 years old. At the age of 2, the recommendation is for a child to watch no more than an hour a day of educational programming.

Allowing Baby to watch an occasional show on TV isn't going to irreparably damage her. What it comes down to is whether she watches so much TV that she's going to become dependent on it, unable to amuse herself otherwise, or unable to interact meaningfully with other people. If you know any older children who talk about nothing but their favorite cartoons, then you know what we're talking about here. These kids have nothing else to talk about because their lives revolve around TV shows.

Turning off the tube

Even if you have every intention of keeping your baby TV-free for as long as possible, you may find it hard to keep yourself away from the hypnotic powers of the television. Try the following alternatives:

✔ **Get out of the house.** Join a playgroup. Plan an errand for each day. Go visiting. (Alternatively, have people *in*.) Do *something*. It's good for you and Baby.

✔ **Read.** Now that Baby is old enough to play by herself, at least for a short time, catch up on your own reading. Not only will it expand your mind, it's a good example for Baby. Remember, she's at the age where she's able to mimic your actions. She may become very interested in her own books after watching you read yours.

✔ **Catch up on everything around the house.** Hey, if you're there, you know the work is never done. It's amazing how much you can accomplish when the TV isn't distracting you.

✔ **Take time to play with Baby.** Encourage her new skills. Tickle her. Dance with her. Listen to music together. Read to her. Again, the amount of time you have to spend with your child expands exponentially when there's nothing in the background competing for your attention.

Think of it this way: Baby has this brain that's primed to develop in all kinds of exciting ways. If she gets zoned in on being entertained electronically, certain avenues of her creative development will be stifled.

Avoid the urge to use the TV as an electronic babysitter. An occasional lapse probably won't be harmful to your child, but setting up a habit of all-day TV viewing at this age may lead to a long-term dependency on what will become the love of her life.

So what about those videos that are marketed to newborns and babies? Take a good look at them and decide for yourself whether *you* could be the star of the show, singing the alphabet for Baby in your own home. (Yeah, you *can* do that.)

Encouraging Baby to amuse himself

If you have spent every moment of every day not more than 2 feet from your child, it's time to give him a little more space. He's at the age where he acknowledges that you and he are two separate entities, and he also recognizes the concept of object permanence. (He knows that although you may step out of the room for a minute, you're coming back.)

Although you should certainly strive to interact with Baby, your goal is to find a healthy balance. Baby has to learn to amuse himself at some point. Just as he had to (or still has to) learn to comfort himself at night, he should be able to play by himself now, at least for a short time. He's physically capable of manipulating his age-appropriate toys. He probably has his favorites at this point, and he knows exactly what to expect from them (which is wonderful, because children thrive on repetition).

Don't try to entertain your child *every* minute of the day. Yes, he's the absolute apple of your eye, and yes, you want to play with him and educate him and do what's best for him. It's not in his best interest, though, to think that you are nothing more than his court jester. (Do you want a kid who cries every time you're *not* singing and dancing for his amusement?) So let Baby have some time to himself each day — even if you're sitting nearby (and obviously if you aren't, he should be in a safe environment, like his playpen) — to try to amuse himself with his own toys. Trying to figure what he likes on his own gives him the opportunity to learn a lot about himself — what he finds funny, or what he doesn't care for at all.

Stranger anxiety rears its scary head

Suddenly, Baby has a fearful look on her face when your neighbor — someone she's seen and accepted regularly — approaches. Before you know it, Baby is crying, clinging to you, and won't lift her head from your shoulder. What's going on here?

In the past few months, you've no doubt noticed that Baby has become more interested in interacting with people. You may have felt a surge of pride, thinking that your child is so easy going, so laid-back, so loving toward everyone — why, you could just see her high school yearbook: She had a definite lock on being voted Most Popular. With this latest development, however, you may be concerned that Baby's personality has changed, that she doesn't like people, and worse, if she continues to act this way, people won't like *her!*

You can stop worrying. Your intelligent child is going through a very normal developmental stage — she's experiencing stranger anxiety. Although for several months she truly has enjoyed interacting with other people — no matter who they were — she has just turned a corner, so to speak, and realized that not all people are the same. Or, more to the point, she knows that these people are not her *parents*. She's becoming more selective in whom she chooses to interact with — at least when she's first confronted with someone who isn't Mom or Dad.

The severity of stranger anxiety (which can begin as early as the end of the eight month) varies from child to child, though it does affect almost every baby sooner or later. Some children show a slight reluctance to greet strangers, and some become completely paralyzed with fear. There's nothing wrong with either extreme, and none of this means that you've done anything wrong in your parenting. This is just a normal part of being a baby.

You can help your child through this distressing phase of life by:

- ✔ **Acknowledging her fears as being real.** Although you may think it's crazy for her to be afraid of relatives she's seen many times, it's not crazy to her. Don't force her out of her shell; she needs to know that she's safe with you.

- ✔ **Discussing Baby's stranger anxiety with friends and relatives.** Let them know that Baby is going through a normal stage so that they aren't hurt by her sudden unwillingness to play with — or even look at — them.

- ✔ **Giving her time and space.** When she's entering into a situation with outsiders (or friends are coming into your home), allow Baby to take her time adjusting to the situation. She may want to cling to you the entire time, she may want to play by herself, or she may very well decide that these people are all right after she checks them out from afar. Follow her lead and tell your company to do the same.

- ✔ **Asking visitors not to jump right in and hold or even try to talk to Baby.** Have them just ignore Baby for a while until she's ready to initiate an interaction.

Most kids have resolved their stranger anxiety issues by the time they're 3 years old.

Keeping Baby Safe and Sound

In the eighth month, Baby is more active — which means he will inevitably take a knock to his noggin once or twice. He also may be running into more germs as he gets out and about, exploring his world. Fear not: Bumps and bruises and sniffles and colds are all part of the grand scheme of growing up.

Big steps, big falls

With increased locomotion comes the increased risk for injury to Baby. He'll have lots of falls onto his well-padded bottom, which are rarely cause for any sort of alarm. Though Baby's pride may be hurt, you can be sure that his diaper will save him from any real harm to his backside.

The first time Baby takes a real spill, though, can be an alarming experience for him and for you. Once he's able to pull himself up, and especially after he's off and cruising, there's no telling what can happen, often before you ever have a chance to see it coming. If he smacks his forehead on the coffee table, or he bumps his head on the floor, he may react by screaming in pain. If there's blood or a bump, you may react similarly, as though you actually *feel* his pain.

Stop yourself in your tracks. Reacting to your child's injury by becoming hysterical isn't going to help matters — at all. It won't even make you feel better (which is a justification we moms sometimes use for getting emotional). It will only serve to scare Baby and yourself — perhaps far more than the situation warrants.

When Baby bumps his head, the following steps are your best bet:

- ✔ Go to him. Pick him up and comfort him.

- ✔ Remain calm, even if there's blood.

- ✔ Assess the situation before reacting further. For more information on how to assess a head injury, keep reading.

Chapter 19 covers the treatment of common injuries. What you need to know right now is that babies do get hurt — some more so than others.

Not every bump to the head calls for a trip to the emergency room, but you do need to call the doctor if:

- ✔ **Baby has bumped his head and lost consciousness, even briefly, or if he has sustained a bump to the head and is pale, cranky, vomiting, unable to perform his usual physical activities (crawling, pulling up, and so on), has large or dilated pupils, or has discharge coming from his ears.** Call without delay. These are all signs of a serious head injury.

- ✔ **Baby has cut his head and you can't stop the bleeding.** Head wounds tend to bleed a lot, but a cut that continues to bleed after several attempts at applying direct pressure (ten minutes each try) and/or has jagged edges (which probably won't heal nicely without a stitch or two) warrants a trip to the doctor's office.

- ✔ **Baby has hit his head after a fall from a height (off the couch or counter, for example).** This falls into the category of an *accelerated head injury,* which is more likely to cause serious injury than a simple fall from a standing position.

Now, you may be wondering if it isn't just a better option to pop a little helmet on Baby's head and/or simply hang onto him all the time until he's mastered the art of cruising and walking. The answer is no. He needs to know that taking a tumble now and again is just a normal part of the learning process.

Do what you can to prevent major injuries by gating off stairways and by generally preparing a safe environment where Baby can work on his new skills. But don't hover and don't show him your fear. Seeing a parent fall to pieces after he's taken a relatively minor tumble can send the message to Baby that this walking business is seriously dangerous stuff, which may make him reluctant to try, try again.

Giving up the battle against germs

If Baby has already suffered through a nasty cold, you know how hard it is to stand by and watch as a virus squashes Baby's zest for living. You've made up your mind that you must do everything in your power to keep your child, your home, your car, your spouse, and your entire lives germ-free. It's just part of the job of parenting, you say, and there's just no greater gift that you can give your child.

Put your cleanser down and back away from it — just for a moment. The world is a dirty, germy place. We are all covered in bacteria — our bodies and our mouths are just *loaded* with specimens. We're exposed to germs every single day, mostly without our knowledge, and for the most part, we adapt and survive. Part of that adaptation is being exposed to germs in the first place and building up immunity to them. Simply put, you can't fight the germs if you don't have the strength. You can't *get* the strength if you hide from the fight.

None of this is to say that you should take every illness lightly — just don't think you can *prevent* every illness. When Baby is sick, keep an eye on him for signs of serious complications (fever, listlessness, labored breathing) and call your pediatrician at once if any of these symptoms develop.

Building stronger bacteria?

As antibacterial soaps and cleansers become more widely available, you may think that the world is on its way to becoming germ-free. To the contrary, some studies have suggested that the proliferation of antibacterial soaps, wipes, and cleansers has only encouraged germs to mutate into new forms that are resistant to antibacterial soaps and antibiotics. More research is needed to prove or disprove this theory.

Sterilizing toys for tots

Do toys need to be sterilized if you later find out that Baby's playmate was incubating a contagious illness? If Baby was in proximity to a child with an airborne illness, he's already been exposed. And keep in mind that most viruses can't live on surfaces for a long period of time anyway, so your scrubbing may be for naught. This also goes for toys in the doctor's office. Don't let your baby suck and chew on them, but don't be afraid to let him play.

You need to find a middle ground. Don't let your child play in the cat's litter box, for example, or eat food off the floor, but realize that you can't clean every germ, everywhere. Heck, you can't even *see* the little buggers, so how can you avoid them all?

You *can* take some measures to prevent serious illness, but you needn't spend every waking moment cleansing the world with bleach. A little knowledge and some common sense are all you really need:

- ✔ **Take precautions in the kitchen, particularly when handling raw foods.** Prepare meats and produce separately — using separate areas and separate knives and cutting boards — to prevent the spread of salmonella (from poultry) or *E. coli* (from raw meats). Wash cutting boards and knives thoroughly — either in the dishwasher or in hot, soapy water — after each use.

- ✔ **Use sponges and cloth wipes sparingly for cleaning counters and Baby's highchair tray.** Sponges and wipes create a perfect environment (continually moist) for trapping, spreading, and breeding bacteria (like *E. coli*). Paper towels are a healthier choice for cleaning up spills and wiping down countertops.

- ✔ **Always wash your hands before feeding Baby, after changing his diaper, and whenever the need arises.** This simple act can prevent the spread of many illnesses and bacteria.

Sick baby, well child?

Your child is going to catch colds and other viruses — but each time he does, he's strengthening his immune system, and that's a *good* thing! Studies have shown that kids who aren't in a group daycare setting catch as many illnesses as children who are in daycare — the difference is that the daycare kids are exposed to many germs earlier in life. And the earlier a child is exposed to certain illnesses, the stronger his immune system may be when he goes off to school. He won't be knocked flat by every germ coming down the pike in kindergarten (and there are plenty of them).

In some circumstances, you may have to be more cautious than other parents. If your child has asthma, for example, a common cold can be very serious for him, and you're right to limit his exposure to the outside world during cold and flu season. For an otherwise healthy child, though, being exposed to common illnesses is just a part of normal life. Yes, it's a real drag to have a sick child — but isn't it even _more_ difficult to try to sterilize your entire world?

Bathing in the Big Tub

Now that Baby's getting bigger, you'll probably find that bathing her in the real tub is much easier than dragging out the infant tub, setting up the supplies on the kitchen counter, and taking care of rub-a-dub-dubbing in an area that really was never intended for bathing a child. In this section, we give you some pointers on making the move to the adult tub.

Unless Baby is absolutely filthy (with dried juice in her hair and peas in her ears) at the end of every day, she probably only needs a bath a couple of times a week. However, some parents find that a nightly bath helps to signal the end of the day for reluctant sleepers or helps to calm active children before bedtime. If that's the case in your house, then by all means, make bathtime a soothing nighttime ritual for everyone — followed by a book and some snuggling time. (Your on-the-go child may actually start looking forward to this peaceful conclusion to each day!)

Keeping Baby supported

At this point, Baby should be sitting well unsupported. If she's still a bit wobbly and you're just not comfortable about putting her into the tub without any kind of support, you can use a _bathing ring,_ which attaches to the bottom of your tub with suction cups, and gives Baby the support and security of sitting in an actual seat while she's soaking up the bubbles. (See Figure 13-2.)

Although bathing rings have been around for years and have been used without incident in many households, they are _not_ intended to be a replacement for constant adult supervision while Baby is in the tub. They can flip — forward or backward — if they lose suction, which could send Baby underwater if you're not hanging on to her. Babies have also slipped though the seat portion of the rings. Bottom line: Whether you're using a ring or not, you need to be right next to the tub at all times when Baby is splish-splashing.

Figure 13-2:
Using a bathtub ring requires vigilance on a parent's part.

Considering bathtub safety

Many of the same safety rules that apply to bathing Baby in an infant tub (check out Chapter 6) apply here, with a few additions:

- ✔ **Place a nonslip pad in your tub.**

- ✔ **Never allow Baby to play with the faucet.** She's not coordinated enough to turn it on and off right now, but you don't want to encourage this habit. When she is able to turn on the water, she could inadvertently burn herself.

- ✔ **Buy a cover for the spout.** The spout may have sharp edges, which could cause a painful injury if Baby bumps her head on it.

- ✔ **Don't allow Baby to stand or pull herself up in the tub.** She could slip and hit her head on the side or bottom.

- ✔ **Use baby-safe, liquid soap and shampoo.** Children have choked on the small, sliver-like remnants of bar soap. (Besides, bar soaps are irritating to the eyes.)

- ✔ **Never, ever, ever leave her alone in the tub.** Babies can drown in 1 inch of water in under a minute. Nothing is worth risking your child's safety. If you absolutely must leave the bathroom, take her with you.

- ✔ **Always empty the tub when Baby's bath is finished.** Leaving a tub filled with even a little bit of water could be a hazard for a mobile child.

Baby really only needs 1 or 2 inches of water in the tub at this point. She doesn't need to soak her cares away in a tub filled up to her neck — that's *your* secret escape from the world. She just needs enough water to splash in.

Making tubtime fun

There's no reason bathtime can't be fun, or at least a not-unpleasant experience for the bath-phobic. Try these tactics to keep Baby happy in the tub:

✔ **If she's less than thrilled about the prospect of being in this big, scary, water-filled tank, keep her close to the side.** This could just make her feel secure enough to comply with the bath.

✔ **If she just hates having water dumped on her head, try a bath "hat."** This is basically a foam-rubber ring that goes around Baby's head, keeping the water from running down into her face.

✔ **Wash her hair just before she comes out of the tub.** Shampooing too early can leave her feeling chilled, and may cause her to cut her playtime in the tub short.

✔ **Make sure you have a towel handy and that it's big enough to wrap Baby in.** You want to keep her as warm as possible between tubtime and pajama time.

✔ **Keep a stash of bath toys in the bathroom for easy access when bathtime rolls around.** You don't need to rush out and buy the fanciest, most educational bath-themed toys you can find (though there's certainly no harm in doing so). At this age, kids love simple plastic containers that they can fill with water and dump — over and over again.

Chapter 14

The Ninth Month: Grabbing Your Attention (With Intention)

In This Chapter

▶ Baby's debut as an actor

▶ Finding love in a security object

▶ Comparing children

▶ Dealing with family members who ignore your rules

During the ninth month, your Baby is creeping ever closer to becoming a real little person. He's able to communicate, he's able to move about independently, and he has his likes and dislikes. It's almost easier for you to imagine him as a toddler than to remember what he was like during those first few weeks after he was born (although, thanks to the magic of video, you can replay those days as often as you like — sometimes with a heavy sigh, when you realize how quickly the time has gone, and how quickly it will continue to fly by).

Because he's accomplished so much, and has so much more to tackle, it's easy to fall into the trap of comparing your child to your friends' similarly-aged kids — or to compare him to any older siblings. If you're exposed to children who are about the same age as yours (or if you have older children) what you realize more than anything else during the second half of the first year is that every child is different. They each have their special talents; they each have their own way of doing things. Comparing them to one another isn't fair.

Checking In with Baby

Baby catches up with the doctor this month with a full-fledged well-baby visit, which will cover the basics of measurement and a host of questions about Baby's day. This month, Baby may be hitting some major physical and cognitive milestones, which are listed for you in this section.

The 9-month checkup

Baby's back in the saddle this month, paying the good doctor a visit for a well-baby exam. Baby may be lucky enough to avoid immunization shots this month, although some doctors do give a late HBV at this point. (For the low-down on immunizations, see Chapter 18.) What else will happen during the 9-month checkup?

To begin the visit, Baby has her height and weight measured. Your doctor plots her growth on the charts to make sure she's progressing steadily. She has her head circumference measured. She's examined as usual, with the doctor assessing her overall development and checking for signs of any abnormalities (by palpating her internal organs, listening to her heart and lungs, checking out her hips and spine, and peeking into her ears, eyes, and mouth).

Your pediatrician will have a slew of questions for you, including:

- **How much is Baby eating these days?** If she's bottlefed, the doctor will want to know how many ounces she's taking in each day; if you're breastfeeding, you'll be asked how often and how long she nurses.

- **What types of solids is Baby eating?** Baby should be eating solids by this point. Your doctor wants to know which baby foods and table foods Baby takes in.

- **How long does Baby sleep at night? How many naps during the day, and how long is each nap?** Babies this age sleep an average of 14 hours a day (about 11 hours at night and a total of 3 hours at naptimes). If Baby is sleeping less or still waking at night, your doc may suggest upping her intake of food during the day.

- **What kind of physical activity is Baby capable of?** Does she sit unassisted? Pull herself up? Stand alone? Babble? Enjoy a game of peekaboo? Play with her toys? A list of 9-month milestones is included in this chapter.

In addition, your doctor will want to know about your home. He isn't simply being nosy — he's looking for any potential hazards or situations that may pinpoint trouble on the horizon. He may ask about your baby-proofing measures, for example, and offer you advice on things you may have missed.

The doctor may ask if you rock Baby to sleep each night. Remember that you should ideally put Baby into bed while she's awake so that she can learn to comfort herself. Failing to learn this may mean years of disrupted sleep for her — and for you.

No matter what your doctor asks, answer him honestly. He really does have your child's best interest at heart — and he's an expert. He's seen and heard of situations concerning child development and injuries that may not occur to most laypeople.

Milestones this month

During the ninth month, Baby continues to accomplish new tasks, and he may just discover that he is quite a little thespian. You'll realize that he may not be content to sit in his highchair and eat quietly while you move about the kitchen — he wants all eyes on himself. Children this age suddenly realize that they can garner quite a bit of attention by coughing, letting out squeals of pleasure (or displeasure), and performing "tricks" for their parents. Parents are so amused and delighted at these real attempts at communication that they're only too happy to comply by giving Baby an audience to play to. Here's what else Baby's up to this month:

- Baby crawls well or scoots himself along using his own means of creative movement.

- He may discover that he's able to hoist himself up the stairs — but he probably won't be able come back down.

- Baby is also able to sit well by himself and for an indeterminate amount of time — just like a regular kid. He should be able to work himself into a seated position from his stomach at this age.

- He pulls himself up.

- He may be able to stand without holding onto anything, possibly for a considerable length of time.

- He's able to *cruise* (make his way around the room hanging onto furniture, people, or whatever's available).

- Baby may be able to carefully seat himself when he's finished standing — unlike previous months where he let go of whatever he was hanging onto and simply fell backward.

- He's able to use his *pincer grasp* (thumb and index finger) to pick up very small objects (as opposed to using his thumb and fingers to "rake" objects into the palm of his hand). See Figure 14-1.

  Now that Baby can pick stuff up more easily, you need to be doubly conscious about making sure that small items he can choke on are placed out of his reach.

Figure 14-1:
Baby
masters the
use of the
pincer grasp
during the
ninth month.

✔ Baby learns to command the attention of the masses by intentionally coughing, squealing, or grunting. This is the result of his learning to mimic and repeat the actions he sees going on around him.

✔ Another part of his intentional communication and mimicry is his use of singsong babbling, which is his attempt to sound just like you when he "speaks."

✔ Baby is also quite the cute show-off this month, intentionally doing things (like standing, or giggling, or clapping his hands) for your attention, amusement, and approval.

✔ Baby may point to objects of interest this month.

✔ He looks for objects that have dropped (he understands *object permanence* — that things aren't gone forever just because he can't see them) and may become quite upset if you take something away from him.

✔ He waves hello and goodbye.

✔ He's able to say "Mama" or "Dada," perhaps still without meaning. But some children are beginning to attach meaning to their words at this point. (In addition to naming Mom and Dad, he may also be able to say "ba" for "ball," or "da" for "dog," for example.)

✔ Baby is capable of expressing empathy for others at this age. He may, for example, cry when a nearby playmate breaks into tears.

✔ Stranger anxiety becomes an issue, if it hasn't already. Baby is likely to shy away from anyone who isn't Mom or Dad (or the primary caregiver). More on this in Chapter 13.

✔ Baby may be able to follow simple (one-step) instructions, such as, "Put that down," or "Come to Mommy."

✔ He understands the concept of "no."

✔ He may start to tote a security object around this month. (More on this later in this chapter.)

✔ Children this age begin to develop fears. Prior to this time, your child's brain simply wasn't wired to acknowledge the possibility of danger around him. Baby may start to show a wariness of heights, for example, when he climbs to the top of the stairs and realizes he can't get down without getting hurt.

✔ Baby's memory is also starting to improve at this age. He won't remember for the rest of time the "conversations" the two of you had over lunch while he was a 9-month-old, but he will definitely remember how a story goes (for example, if something exciting happens halfway through his favorite book, you may see his eyes grow wide in anticipation), or how to "sing" along with his favorite songs.

Keeping Baby Safe and Sound

Baby's new moves toward independence may be very exciting for your child — but they can also be a bit unsettling, which may make her want to cling to a security object for comfort. Particularly now that Baby may be crawling up stairs, you need to reassess and upgrade your baby-proofing at this point.

Going up! Baby takes to the stairs

At 9 months old, Baby's no longer satisfied to simply crawl from here to there, pull herself up, stand a while, cruise, and sit back down. Surely there must be something more to do, she's thinking.

And then she spots the stairs. Why, it's so logical, so exciting, so natural — she feels that she *belongs* on those stairs and intends to put her motoring skills to work by climbing them, just the way you and your other family members do. (Remember, at this age, Baby is watching and mimicking your moves.) For some children, crawling up the stairs is just a small trick they quickly add to their already long list of accomplishments; for others, it's like learning to scale the vertical side of a mountain.

Ideally, children this age should be kept off the stairs. Realistically, parents allow kids to climb them. If Baby does nothing but hang on the gate at the bottom of the steps all day long, you may figure that she's ready and that it's best for her to learn to climb those steps the right way. Allow this activity only if you have one hand on her, ready to catch her at every second, and only if you take care to safeguard her from accidental injury.

If Baby has little interest in the stairs, consider yourself lucky. Don't take this as a sign you need to teach her to climb them. Keeping her away from stairs in the first place is the surest way to keep her from taking a roll down them.

Even if Baby becomes a veritable master of the stairs, you *must* continue to gate the stairs at all times. Stairs are just plain dangerous, and Baby should not be allowed independent access to them. Remember, after Baby has navigated those steps, she can disappear out of your sight without your knowing which level of the house to search for her on. She shouldn't be on the steps at all unless you're supervising her and ready to steady her.

Children this age usually don't grasp the concept of coming back down the stairs (something Baby may not manage for at least a couple of months or perhaps not even until she's in the second year). Be aware that if she has not developed any fears — specifically of falling or of heights — she may try to crawl head-first down the steps, which is why you may want to reconsider allowing her access to them until she's old enough to appreciate the inherent dangers of this activity. This is also why it's so important to continue gating off the stairs — just because she can go up without incident doesn't guarantee a safe return trip.

Lovin' that blankie: Security objects

Around this time, you may notice that Baby has a favorite stuffed animal, blanket, or toy that he carries around with him for most of the day. Some children start to develop this loving relationship with a particular object as early as 6 months old, while others never cling to anything special. Baby may play with and talk to his beloved bear, or he may retreat to his super-soft blanket at different times throughout the afternoon. Whatever it is that he's clinging to, it probably goes with him for naps and at bedtime. (Or perhaps these are the *only* times he needs his comfort object.)

Fear not: This new attachment to a security object isn't a result of something you did or didn't do. Attaching himself at the hip to a security object is very normal behavior.

As Baby continues to master new skills, he also begins to recognize that he's not merely an extension of his parents but his own person — able to move more and more independently through the world. At the same time, he's taken a few spills, suffered from a few bumps and bruises, and realized that the world is a big, big place filled with a lot of not-so-nice possibilities — and that his parents aren't always available to comfort his fears. By finding a friendly or soft security object, Baby is looking for a way to comfort himself when he's feeling a bit anxious — which may be almost never, or may be quite often.

Experts actually refer to security objects as *transitional objects* — meaning that whatever Baby is holding onto is merely a temporary stand-in for his parents' comfort and affection. The security object, however, may be a constant presence in Baby's life, whereas Mom — although loving and attentive — isn't able to literally stand right next to the child every moment of the day. Transitional objects also play a part in Baby's developing autonomy — *he* decides how much comfort he needs, and *he* is in control of the object that offers him some peace of mind.

The use of a transitional object actually benefits parents, too. Baby needs to learn to comfort himself. If he's had a difficult time sleeping through the night, the use of a comfort object may help him snooze peacefully. If he cries when you leave him at the babysitter's, allowing him to bring along something that reminds him of home — and of you — may help him quiet down faster.

Some experts believe that children who never find a transitional object to cling to may have a hard time calming themselves. If you have an almost inconsolable little guy who gets very wound up over the course of his day and acts out in frustration or crankiness, offer him a soft blanket or a plush animal while you soothe him. You may see a remarkable change in him, and he may actually start enjoying his naps and quiet times.

If, on the other hand, Baby's attachment to his transitional object is clearly affecting his ability to relate to real people or is preventing him from reaching his developmental milestones, it may be wise to limit the blanket's use to naps and bedtime.

Here's how to keep that blankie or stuffed bear in perspective:

- **Allow Baby his beloved object.** As long as it's not interfering in his normal development, there's no harm in letting him have his stuffed bear nearby.

- **Wash it.** Baby is probably as attached to the smell of his blanket or stuffed animal as he is to the feel of it. Even though he despises the clean smell, it's important to rid the comfort object of all of the germs and bacteria it accumulates while it's dragged along the floor.

It's especially important to wash his blankie or animal after Baby has been sick. You don't want to risk recontaminating him.

✔ **Let him bring it along when possible and when necessary.** The entire point of the security object is to alleviate Baby's anxiety. When he's entering into unfamiliar territory, he's not going to be distracted enough by his new surroundings to forget about his stuffed panda — he's going to need *more* comfort than usual.

✔ **Respect the security object.** The security object is sacred to Baby. Right now, it's second in his life only to you. Don't tease him about it or play hide-and-seek with it.

✔ **Make sure the security object isn't harmful to Baby.** Pacifiers and bottles of water are acceptable as comfort objects, as long as they aren't interfering with Baby's attempts at speech. If Baby is attached to her bottle of juice or formula, however, you need to nip that habit in the bud. Kids who tote bottles filled with sugary drinks around with them during the day or who are allowed to regularly suck on them during naptimes and throughout the night are prone to developing *baby bottle mouth,* or decay of the baby teeth. For more on baby bottle mouth, see Chapter 11.

✔ **Recognize that the object isn't a substitute for you.** His security object only helps him to deal with the fact that he can't constantly cling to you. Continue to offer Baby lots of attention and snuggle time.

✔ **Let Baby decide when he wants his security object.** If he has forgotten all about his stuffed cat and is playing nicely with other toys, don't bring the animal over and say, "Mr. Cat wants to play, too." Let *Baby* decide when he needs comfort — and when he's all right on his own.

✔ **Protect it — or be ready to replace it**. Any parent who has had a child's cherished blanket, stuffed animal, or toy go missing will attest to the fact that it is no fun to search for a stuffed bear in the park after nightfall while your spouse tries unsuccessfully to cajole Baby into going to bed alone. If it's at all possible to have an imposter on hand, by all means, do. Save yourself from witnessing the heartbreak of Baby's first lost love.

Expect Baby to continue to cling to his blankie or teddy bear through at least the second year. By around age 3, the need for security objects dwindles a bit, because your child will be able to emotionally attach himself to people other than you and your partner. In other words, Baby's comfort will come from a variety of sources, and he will become less dependent on receiving consolation and attention *only* from Mom and Dad.

No, you shouldn't feel guilty if your child is in day care and clinging to his blanket — children have been searching for security objects *forever*, and the kids of stay-at-home parents are as prone to needing a little extra comfort as other kids are.

Comparing Kids: The Irresistible Urge to Rank Baby's Development

Comparing children comes as naturally to parents as your child's developmental milestones come to her. Most parents fall into this trap without even realizing it, and most parents believe that their own children are doing things "right" — though occasionally, you may meet a parent who believes that her own mothering skills are so lacking that her child will never catch up to his or her peers (and usually, this is a major exaggeration of the situation).

Why do parents (and grandparents, aunts, uncles, and friends) do this? It may be out of genuine curiosity — first-time parents, in particular, need to seek out and listen to the stories of other first-timers. This can be a great help to parents who are feeling anxious or unsure about the way their child is learning to feed herself, for example (by smashing the food everywhere on her face except into her mouth) — when they hear that someone else's child is doing the same thing, they realize that it's probably normal behavior.

Interacting with parents during a playgroup or another supportive environment where children will inevitably be compared can emphasize the very healthy message that all kids are different — and wonderful — in their own unique ways.

Keeping up with the Joneses' kid

We live in a competitive society. Many moms, at one point or another, have worked outside of the home and have experience with the dog-eat-dog world of business. Many dads go off to the trenches every day to seal huge deals, knowing that aggression is the key to winning. A lot of people live in neighborhoods where they're constantly keeping up with the Joneses. When children come into the picture, parents who are naturally competitive sometimes view their offspring as dominant creatures — at least in relation to the other people's kids.

Of course, there's nothing wrong with thinking your child is the greatest little person to ever walk the planet, as long as you acknowledge that other parents feel the same way about their children — and that *all* of you are correct in your feelings.

When a friend or neighbor has a child who is roughly the same age as yours, your first reaction may be, "How great! Automatic, life-long friends!" That feeling may quickly change to, "How do I get these people out of my life?" as soon as you realize that, at least according to this other parent, your child is not nearly as advanced as hers (look at her child cruise, would you?!), your child has no sense of humor (did you just *see* her child giggling earlier?), and you're using the wrong diapers — and diaper ointment (you're just setting your kid up for a nasty rash — you should really switch to the brands your friend uses for her baby). Oh, and by the way, your child also goes to bed too late and gets up too early, and he should be wearing something on his head at all times during the cold winter months — even indoors — like her daughter does.

Believe it or not, those parents who insist that their child is ahead of the curve and that you're in need of their expert guidance are likely just looking for evidence that they're doing everything correctly. Or maybe these people honestly believe that their child raising is progressing perfectly — which is great. We should all be so happy and confident in our child-rearing skills. Just don't let these competitive parents raise doubts in your mind where there weren't any.

Kids reach physical, social, and cognitive milestones at generally the same ages — but there can be wide variations in these time frames. Some very strong children start pulling up late in the sixth month, while others may not try hoisting their bottoms off the ground until the ninth or tenth months. As long as your pediatrician is satisfied that Baby is progressing normally, you shouldn't let other parents make you feel as though your child is behind in a particular area of development.

Having confidence in yourself

Not only do children develop differently, but parents also *parent* differently. Parents can follow completely different philosophies about raising children — one set of parents may place a high value on rigid scheduling, for example, while another family is working on a much more relaxed timetable — and yet, the children, for the most part, turn out fine. As long as what you're doing works well for you and your household, and your child seems happy, then no one can tell you with absolute authority that your way is wrong.

Recognize "suggestions" for what they are: Another parent's way of determining whether she is doing the right thing for her child. Every time she draws a comparison between what she's doing and what you're doing, it's her way of telling herself that her way is better — and it may be, as far as her own child is concerned. Just remember that she is measuring your methods against her child's personality and specific needs. If her son is exhausted at seven in the evening, then yes, he needs to be in bed at that time. If your daughter fares well until eight-thirty, then that's when she needs to be tucked in. Make sure you're happy with *your* routines; someone else's routine may not fit in your life.

Thankfully, comparisons of this sort are most common among first-time moms and dads and may decrease considerably over the years. As more kids enter into their family picture, you may see a startling mellowing in these folks — because as they juggle their own kids, they realize now that their first-born is not the center of the universe, that they did not, in fact, write the manual on how babies should be raised — and that despite their best efforts, their second-born isn't buying into the scheduling business the way his older sibling did. (Yes, it's all right to smile — just a little, and only to yourself — when this happens.)

Stroller envy: Equating great gear with great parenting

Parents sometimes love to equate spending a lot of money on their child with raising her well. You see it in parks and malls in certain areas of the country: Mothers surreptitiously checking out each other's strollers. Some of them, you see, have spent big bucks on their carriages to ensure that their children will be riding in maximum comfort. They have a certain amount of disdain for mothers who have chosen lesser buggies for their babies. Don't they *care* about their children?

This type of comparison isn't limited to the stroller, of course. Parents choose hand-knitted sweaters instead of fleece pullovers because Baby deserves the best. They purchase the most expensive organic baby foods because they're more concerned with their child's health than most parents (or so they tell themselves — and others). Baby's quilt was imported from a far-flung land, and Baby's teething ring was custom-designed by an orthodontist.

It's enough to make average parents who are trying to make ends meet (especially those who have taken a big cut in income in order to stay home with Baby) feel as though they have no business raising a child. It never even occurred to you to consult with an orthodontist!

Say it out loud: "Spending less money on baby accessories doesn't make me a bad parent." Spending more money on baby accessories doesn't automatically qualify you for Parent of the Year. Spend what you can reasonably afford and stop yourself — and your comparisons between what your baby has and what other babies have — right there.

Having your first child is incredibly exciting, and filling the house with clothes, toys, and decorations for your child can be entertaining beyond belief. But feeling bad because you can't provide your child with the most expensive things is just silly. You may want her to have a round cherrywood canopy crib instead of the plain crib she has now. Sure, it's a beautiful piece of furniture, but it's not going to make your baby any happier than she already is in her less expensive crib. The pricier bed isn't going to help her sleep better; it's not going to ensure that she's a nice child; it's not going to put her at the head of the class later in life. These are just cribs we're talking about — something you'll be forced to put away in a relatively short period of time.

Just about everything Baby has or uses right now will be packed away — or given away — eventually, which is why many parents choose to keep their spending way down. On the other hand, some parents know that they're going to have more children and feel it's wisest to invest in quality items that can be passed down from child to child. Neither way of thinking is wrong — and neither indicates how much or how little a parent cares for a child.

So the next time you're in the children's section of your favorite store and some other mother is sneaking a peek at the make of your stroller, realize that she's the insecure person in this scenario, drawing a parallel between stroller brands and parenting skills. (Ridiculous? You betcha.)

Sibling versus sibling

Maybe this isn't your first time parenting a child. If you have an older child, you'll almost inevitably draw comparisons between him and your baby. Most parents find themselves doing this, although it's not always exactly the healthiest way to look at your children.

Take the children in your baby's playgroup. They differ from one another in:

- ✔ Size
- ✔ Physical appearance
- ✔ Physical development and abilities
- ✔ Language skills
- ✔ Cognitive development and abilities
- ✔ Personality

Guess what? Siblings can have all of these differences, too.

How can that be? If they have the same parents and are raised in the same household by the same set of rules, how could children possibly turn out so differently?

Well, a host of nature versus nurture theories try to explain why some of these differences occur. For instance, boys are often more active and motor-oriented, while girls may grasp language earlier. And personality may be largely affected by birth order, which falls under the nurture label — parents tend to treat their children differently, depending on their birth order:

- **Firstborns** tend to be more responsible and mature than their siblings because parents expect them to be the "big brother" or "big sister."

- **Youngest children** tend to be free spirits and practical jokers. By the time this kid makes his appearance, the rules in the house have sometimes relaxed considerably — and the youngest never has to compete with another baby for attention.

- **Kids in the middle** tend to be mild-mannered rule followers and keepers of the peace. They're caught between domineering older siblings and show-stealing younger ones and find comfort in creating and following routine.

Other traits, like hair color or your child's size, are determined by nature. You may have one son who looks exactly like Mom, another who is the spitting image of Dad, and a third who looks like no one in particular. (Insert your own mailman joke here.) You can't make your tiny son tall or your daughter's black hair blonde. Accept them as they are — because they're beautiful, even if they don't look like anyone else in the family.

Cognitive skills and language development could be dependent on nature or nurture (or maybe both!). Some kids are just wired differently. Speech, in particular, is a milestone that varies widely from child to child, even within the same family. Your older child was saying "Mama" while pointing to you at 8 months; your second, at almost 10 months, says "ma" to indicate everything from his foot to the sky.

Your first child may have been walking at 10 months. She also may have been a skinny little thing, able to get up and move without much physical hindrance. If your second child is a big, chubby guy, he's probably going to be slower in the movement department, simply because he's toting more mass around. Now, you may have also been able to help your daughter learn to walk by physically supporting her and encouraging her every moment of the day — something that's much harder for you to do for your second child when you're keeping him out of trouble, chasing an older child, and trying to clean up the breakfast dishes.

The good news is that although one child may be slower in some areas than another child, most kids end up developing normally all the way around. The bad news is that parents sometimes compare children out loud — that is, at the dinner table, Dad may say to his eldest child, "You should see how your brother hit the ball at practice today. You could do that if you tried." Or, to a younger child, "Your older sister always had straight As in math. You can do better if you start concentrating." These parents are trying to stimulate healthy competition between a child who's perceived as being lazy and one who's doing well in a particular activity.

Comparing siblings to one another — especially in front of the children — is a bad, *bad* idea. The resulting competing attitudes are almost never healthy. The "lesser" child resents the "better" sibling and feels betrayed by the parent, who is, in the child's mind, showing clear favoritism toward that sibling.

Of course, when your kids are babies, you won't be comparing math grades and athletic abilities. But you may say to a screaming toddler, "Your baby brother doesn't scream. Can you be as quiet as he is?" An innocent comparison here or there isn't going to set up a lifetime of sibling rivalry — but if your toddler's personality becomes more and more disagreeable while your baby only becomes sweeter, it may be hard *not* to compare kids silently in your mind, noting that your older child has always been sort of difficult, come to think of it. She was never an easy kid — like the baby is.

Giving in to this kind of thinking may make your toddler's behavior seem worse than it actually is. Allowing yourself to compare positive and negative traits among your children can lead to an exaggeration in your perception of the kids' behavior. You may think, for example, that your baby is the best child in the world when you compare him to what your older child put you through at the same age. Try hiding that attitude from an uncooperative toddler.

Slower to talk, quicker to crawl

An interesting trend that pediatricians often notice in families is that a second-born child will often develop speech at a later age than his older sibling did — but the younger child's motor skills develop at an earlier age. These variations in development are completely normal and aren't cause for alarm. Several theories exist for why this may be true:

✔ Parents are better informed as to how to enhance an infant's motor skills the second time around.

✔ Older siblings may intervene on Baby's behalf and either talk for him or anticipate his needs so that he doesn't have to verbalize his need for his bottle, for example.

✔ Mom is busy with a toddler and the infant is left on his own in the playpen for longer periods of time. He finds ways to amuse himself early on (by learning to reach for toys, example), because he has to.

✔ The second child may simply be trying to keep up physically with an older sibling. Your firstborn didn't have anyone to chase after — or to chase *him*.

Any of these theories may be true, depending on the household.

It can be very difficult not to compare siblings — in fact, it may be impossible to never note their differences and similarities. You *can*, however, keep an open mind and an even hand when it comes to dealing with each child by assessing his or her personality traits and specific needs. Your difficult toddler is probably not trying to make you angry, for example — she may just be looking for more attention.

Also keep in mind as your kids get older that what works as discipline for one kid may seem like a treat for another, and what helps one child grasp a concept quickly may not help the other at all. Viewing each sibling in the house as a different person filled with his own unique potential that has nothing to do with his brothers and sisters can be difficult — but it's what parents strive to do in order to raise happy children who end up loving their siblings instead of competing with them.

Taking on the Grandparents: When Rules Collide

You love your parents — you really do. But why do they insist on feeding Baby ice cream and candy when they baby-sit? You've made it very clear that you're concerned about milk allergies during the first year, and you don't want your 9-month-old eating *anything* laden with fat, sugar, and caffeine. Why can't they respect your wishes and follow your rules?

Apparently, the old rules that your parents applied to your own upbringing — Mother and Father know best — have gone out the window now that you're the parent (the rule has now been revised: Grandma and Grandpa can do whatever they want). They expect that you will still yield to their whims without making much fuss about it. After all, they're the grandparents, and it's their privilege to spoil Baby. They'll point to your child and say, "Look how happy he is! *You* should give him candy more often."

It's the dance of the new parents versus the old hands. Not only will some grandparents (or friends or other relatives) call Baby's diet into question, they may also completely ignore your routines surrounding:

- **Bedtime:** You want Baby in bed at eight o'clock or else he'll be a bear in the morning? Your mother wants to visit with the tyke while she's baby-sitting, so he'll get to bed when Grandma is ready to say goodnight to him — whether that's at nine o'clock or eleven-thirty.

- **Medication:** Your sister doesn't think that Baby looks sick, so she doesn't give him the antibiotic you left behind (along with specific dosing instructions).

- ✔ **Appropriate clothing:** Your dad took Baby to the park in February without putting mittens on your child. He says it was warm enough to go without; you're checking for signs of frostbite.

- ✔ **Bathtime:** It's part of Baby's bedtime routine, but your parents thought that Baby looked clean enough and put him to bed without a thorough cleansing.

- ✔ **Allowing pets near the child:** Your aunt swears that her dog is harmless and allows the animal to sniff Baby while she holds your child.

- ✔ **Hygiene issues:** Your mother-in-law thinks the way you clean Baby's hands with a baby wipe before he eats is ridiculous. She lets you know that she never did that for her kids — and you *know* she doesn't do it for yours when he's visiting at her house without you.

How do you deal with these issues? Surely these people are wrong to disregard your rules concerning your own child — but do you really want to instigate what could be a drawn-out fight over a few pieces of chocolate? (Keep in mind that some grandparents become very offended if their judgment is called into question — never mind that by ignoring your wishes, they're putting your judgment under the microscope.)

First, rate each issue in order of importance. It wouldn't have hurt your father to put mittens on Baby — but maybe he couldn't find them, or maybe — just maybe — it really was warm enough for Baby to go barehanded. No permanent damage is done, and it's best to let this incident go. Next time your dad is planning an outing with your child, make sure you hand him the mittens and say, "You know how I worry. Please put his mittens on him when he goes outside." You're telling him that you're concerned for your child and that this isn't some arbitrary rule you've created to make Grandpa's life more difficult.

Matters of scheduling — a skipped bath or a late lunch — are usually random and won't affect Baby adversely. These really aren't worth fighting over. What's done is done, and whoever fed Baby late had to suffer the consequences (and learn the lesson) of dealing with a hungry, cranky child. (The exception to this is a late bedtime, because *you're* the one left to deal with the fallout, in the form of a crabby kid the following day. This *is* worth a fight if it happens on a regular basis.)

Hygiene issues mean a lot more to some parents than to others. Baby's hands should be cleaned before he sits down to eat finger foods. He's been crawling around on the floor, pulling himself up on everything, and generally exploring the world through his tactile senses. Wiping his hands before a meal doesn't make you obsessive-compulsive; it makes you observant of what he's been doing. Do you accept that your mother-in-law isn't going to wipe Baby's hands off, or do you insist on it? If you're not around to make sure it gets done, realize that arguing with her could make her that much more defiant on this issue. As long as he's not coming home from her house vomiting, you're probably wise to look the other way on this particular issue.

Some issues are completely non-negotiable. If Baby is on some sort of medication, giving it to him is not a debatable whim (will he get it or won't he?). Whoever is left in charge of caring for the child needs to understand this and be given explicit directions as to the timing and administration of the drug. And pets should *always* be kept at an arm's length from Baby, no matter how docile (and humanlike) their owners believe them to be.

No one wants Baby's care to cause an irreparable family rift, so before things get out of hand:

- ✔ **Assess:** Is this issue important enough to argue over, or is it possible that you can overlook it completely — again and again?

- ✔ **Plan:** If it's something that isn't negotiable, think of the *nicest* way to tell the offender that this can't happen again.

- ✔ **Lay off:** You can — and *should* — check up on matters of importance. But after you're convinced that the issue has been resolved, there's no need for you to continue to remind your aunt to keep that dog away from Baby. She gets it.

- ✔ **Find a new sitter:** If things have gotten so out of control that what's happening is effectively a power struggle between you and the errant sitter, find someone else, no matter what the financial cost. Trusting the person who is caring for your child is worth every penny you shell out.

What this comes down to in the end is a matter of respect — for your parenting skills and for your position of authority as this child's parent. No one should blatantly flout your rules. An occasional slip-up by a caregiver should be expected and tolerated (because, after all, Grandma is only human), but an out-and-out debate over what you do and don't allow your child to eat shouldn't really be of concern to anyone else — as long as your child is healthy and your pediatrician is satisfied with Baby's progress.

Part V
Keeping Up with Baby

The 5th Wave   By Rich Tennant

"You've either lost the lid to the blender, or you're introducing solid food to the baby."

In this part . . .

In the tenth, eleventh, and twelfth months, Baby makes huge strides, physically and socially. She's able to stand and move around the room, she may be walking by the time she's 1 year old, and she's communicating with you by using at least a couple of words. She's walking her way right into becoming a toddler — and you can't believe how fast the year has gone by!

Weaning becomes a concern at this point in time. Tips for easing the transition off the breast or bottle are given in this section, along with suggestions for alleviating the breastfeeding mom's discomfort during this time. And because you'll be planning for Baby's first birthday soon, this section includes a list of toys to please your almost-toddler, along with advice for planning a party that she's going to love.

Chapter 15

The Tenth Month: Chatting Up Baby

- -

In This Chapter

▶ Standing and walking

▶ Meaning behind Baby's words

▶ Caring for the active child

▶ Responding to Baby's "No!"

▶ Establishing healthy eating habits now

- -

*B*aby moves on into the tenth month — literally. He may be standing on his own two feet now, and perhaps even taking his first steps by the end of the month. He's starting to attach real meaning to his words — although he may have been saying "Mama" and "Dada" before now, during this month, he definitely begins to understand that people and objects alike have names — and he starts using them!

Along with comprehending simple directions and the meaning of "no", your child will also begin to understand the concept of doing his own thing this month — what experts refer to as Baby's *autonomy*. He's realizing that not only is he *not* physically attached to you (a realization that may have caused him some distress in the past few months), but that this lack of attachment has some definite advantages from time to time. For example, Baby doesn't always have to do what you say. Though you are well aware that you *can* force him to stop pulling on the drapes, he may not immediately comply when you tell him from across the room to let go of those curtains. He may look at you, look at the drapes, and decide that yanking on them is a pretty fun way to pass some time. He's not really being naughty; he's just doing what feels right to him at the time — while simultaneously testing your reaction.

During the tenth month, Baby inches closer and closer to the end of the first year. He's eating real foods now, and he may start to show an interest in sweets. Nipping that habit as soon as it shows signs of starting is important and is discussed in this chapter, along with tips for keeping the active child safe — indoors and out.

Checking In with Baby

Most doctors don't schedule a well-baby visit during the tenth month, so Baby can sit tight until the 1-year checkup.

During this time in Baby's development, the 1-year molars may start to erupt, which can cause intense pain in your child's jaw and ear — symptoms that may mimic an ear infection or another virus. If Baby is crabby, bats at her ear, refuses to eat, has a low-grade fever (just at or below 100 degrees), has runny stool, and is having trouble sleeping, take a peek at the very back of her lower jaw — if it's red and swollen, it's a good bet that her misery is being caused by the appearance of those molars.

Pain reliever will help to alleviate Baby's discomfort as her molars come in. Speak to the nurse in your doctor's office for advice on the correct dosage if you're unsure about how much medication Baby should be receiving at this age (and weight).

Soft foods are easiest for a teething Baby to tolerate. Though Baby isn't quite ready to handle a Popsicle on her own, you can offer her small chunks of an icy treat, along with yogurt, gelatin, soup, applesauce, or anything pureed. Cold foods may be more soothing to her sore gums.

You may be tempted to use a medicated numbing oral gel to soothe baby's gums. Many parents find that these gels really don't seem to work very well — Baby may still be crying after the gel is applied. Follow the directions on the tube; if the gel helps Baby, great — but if not, toss it. There's obviously no point in using a medication that doesn't work. Don't use more than four times daily.

Take care to wipe Baby's chin as often as you can if she's drooling a lot. Constant exposure to saliva can cause some kids to break out in a rash, which will only add to her discomfort.

If Baby's symptoms do not seem to be caused by teething, of course, call your pediatrician so that she can be evaluated in the office.

Milestones this month

During the tenth month, your child's mobility increases, as does his quest for autonomy and independence. You may notice that while he's definitely still a baby, he's showing signs of becoming his own little person — a real *kid*. Here's what he may be up to by the end of this month:

✔ Baby sits as well as you do now — and for as long as he wants.

✔ He's crawling or has created his own form of scooting from place to place. He can balance on just one hand now, which means that he can reach for objects or pull up while crawling.

- Your child will be able to crawl up the stairs, but probably won't be able to come back down.

- Baby can pull himself up to standing from a seated position or from his hands and knees.

- He *cruises* ("walks" by hanging onto objects) around the room like a pro.

- Baby may be able to stand on his own for several minutes. He may be able to seat himself nicely when he's finished.

- He's able to take steps with someone holding both of his hands.

- He may be taking his first small steps on his own.

- His pincer grasp is fully developed now and Baby is able to pick up the smallest objects with his forefinger and thumb.

- Baby understands the connection between names and people and objects. When he says "mama" now, he *means* "Mama."

- He also comprehends simple phrases and instructions. When you say, "Show me the ball," Baby will hold the ball up for you to see.

- Baby loves to mimic others. He may show an interest in combing his own hair or brushing his own teeth if he sees his parents doing these things.

- He points to objects of interest or in response to your questions. (If you ask, "Where is the dog?" Baby will point in Rover's direction.)

- Baby waves hello and goodbye.

- Baby shows affection for those he holds dear; he may be wary of strangers.

- Baby understands what "no" means, but he may test his autonomy by *not* following your simple directions.

- His singsong babbling continues, though you may be able to pick out a word or two at this age.

Baby's developing language skills

Baby's comprehension of words and their meanings continues to develop this month. You've been giving him the chance to mimic the sounds for months — now give him the opportunity to truly understand the meaning behind the words.

The following practices will help Baby understand language and begin to use it:

✔ Name everything you see, from the window to the floor and from his head to his toes.

Offer him the names of these things slowly, and wait for a response. His speech won't be perfect, but he may be able to mimic part of a word — "doe" for "window," or "ha" for "hand," for example. He may or may not be ready to move onto more challenging consonants.

✔ Ask Baby lots of questions throughout the day, and give him a chance to respond, whether by babbling, attempting a real word, or by pointing (which is a nonverbal way to show that he understands what you're saying).

✔ Repeat his words back to him to let him know that you understand what he's saying (he'll be thrilled), and to encourage him to continue trying to form new words.

✔ Use picture books to teach Baby common words that he may miss out on otherwise. You may not have a horse in your home, for example — but if there's one in his book, he's going to learn that word now, along with many others.

As a child tries unsuccessfully to express himself verbally, he may throw tantrums due to his frustration. If this happens, show sympathy, and don't push Baby to repeat what he's trying to say. Give it a rest for the time being.

Language, in particular, is a variable milestone — some kids are chatting up a storm during the second year, while other, perfectly healthy kids don't get around to speaking in sentences until much later. Baby should know and respond to his own name and be making attempts at babbling — failure to do so at this age could indicate a hearing problem. Of course, if you have concerns about Baby's speech (or lack of it), consult your pediatrician.

Keeping Baby Safe and Sound

She's here, she's there . . . wait, *where is she?*

Of course, Baby is just off playing in her room, or sitting in the closet, or trying to open the back door. And most times, she's no worse for the wear (thanks to your intense baby-proofing plan). But when you realize that she isn't where you thought she was — the fear can be paralyzing.

What can you do to prevent moments like this? You can't chain her to your leg, after all. She needs to know that she's her own person and she's allowed to explore the world around her. But she just also needs to understand the serious limits to what she can and can't do.

Updating your baby-proofing

You've already eliminated a lot of hazards with your baby-proofing — at this age, you need to double-check:

- ✔ **Doorknobs and locks:** Though most small children can't manipulate a doorknob into behaving the way they'd like it to, some can — and some end up doing so purely by luck or accident. Plastic knob covers make this an impossibility. Also make sure you don't have any doors that lock accidentally, or Baby could be on one side of the bathroom door — with the toilet, the soaps, and the tub — while you're frantically trying to get the entire knob off the door before she hurts herself. Babies can open lever doors, so be careful if your home has these.

- ✔ **Cabinets:** Opening the cabinets is an easy task for Baby at this age. Keep hazardous materials completely out of Baby's reach, but if they're in a low cabinet, make sure it has child locks — and that the locks are secure.

- ✔ **Climbing tools:** Baby may just be clever enough to learn to use one big toy to climb up to reach a shelf or the TV at this age. Keep stools and big stuffed animals away from dangerous areas.

- ✔ **Windows:** Make sure that windows are only opened from the top — for now, and for years to come. Screens pop out easily, and aren't intended to protect your child from falling from a window.

- ✔ **Gates:** For rooms that aren't baby-proofed, the gates should never come down. Gates also need to remain at both ends of the stairs even after Baby has learned to crawl up them.

Of course, nothing is a substitute for constant supervision — and every child needs it. Even children who never show signs of wanting or needing their independence should be kept within sight of their parents at this age. You just never know what a 10-month-old may do. She's physically capable of moving from one end of the house to the other. She may understand the meaning of "Don't touch" in relation to the TV, for instance — but she doesn't *truly* understand that she could be seriously injured if she doesn't comply with your order. And she's naturally curious. Up to this point, she may not have shown a real interest in getting her hands on the television — but she just may decide one day to check it out, up close and personal. If you're not nearby to put the kibosh on her plan, the results could be disastrous.

The older Baby gets, the *more* careful you need to be with her safety, until she's old enough to understand the inherent dangers of certain activities (like climbing on the windowsill or going outside by herself). And by old enough, we mean well past the toddler years. Although you don't need to keep Baby chained to your hip until she goes off to college, she'll continue to need supervision right through preschool (though less than she requires right now).

Staying safe in the great outdoors

When Baby was a tiny infant, you bundled her up, put her in her stroller, and took her out for some fresh air. There wasn't much more to her safety than making sure she was dressed appropriately and buckled into her carriage. Now that she's on the move, you need to consider many things, starting with where you take her.

If the two of you are off for an afternoon at the park, scout out the area carefully before you let her loose. Make sure the play area is well-maintained, that the baby swings aren't cracked or otherwise falling apart, and that there isn't a lot of trash on the ground for Baby to put in her mouth. Let her crawl to her heart's content — yes, she's dirty, but it's all part of her education about the world. How will she know what it feels like to crawl in the grass or what it sounds like to rustle through the leaves if she doesn't do it?

When visiting the park with Baby, make sure to pack some extra wipes. Even if you manage to keep her out of the mud, her hands are going to get dirty elsewhere — and if she's clamoring for a snack, you want to know that the only thing she's eating is the cracker you hand her.

She's old enough to explore the climbing areas of playground play sets — as long as you're right behind her. These sets are usually intended for older children and may have high, wide openings. Baby may enjoy a ride down the slide on your lap — or with you holding her hand if you prefer to send her only halfway down.

Keep a constant eye on Baby when you're outdoors. She's going to be testing her newfound sense of freedom at this point.

You may notice that she crawls away from you and then looks back to see where you are, what you have to say, and whether you're following. This is her way of testing her autonomy. She's her own person, under her own control (or so she thinks), and if she chooses to crawl back to you, she will. Otherwise, she's just waiting to see what you do. Don't be surprised if you call her back to you and she moves in the opposite direction. It's just her innate sense of freedom (and joy) calling her.

Water safety

If you live near a beach or swimming pool and you're planning on taking the plunge, call ahead to ask what type of floatation devices are allowed. (Some swimming areas only allow children to wear floatation vests.) Though Baby won't be diving into the deep water just yet, she should always have some sort of floating device whenever she's near the water — even if you're holding her. If she slips out of your arms for some reason while you're swimming at the lake, you'll know exactly where she is — as long as you've made sure she's buoyant.

Floatation devices are meant to be used in conjunction with *constant adult supervision.* Babies — and children — should never be allowed to play in or around water without a parent or another adult nearby. An adult should always be close enough to reach out and grab a child in the water on a moment's notice — or, even better, have one hand on the child at all times.

If you have a pool or frequently visit someone who does, you may wonder whether swimming lessons are a good idea for Baby. We've all seen pictures of tiny little infants learning to swim — but are they really swimming or are they just doing something that's little more than a reflexive action? And are they safer in the water than other kids?

There's nothing wrong with taking your child in the water and even enrolling her in a "baby swim" class — in fact, if she's always loved her bath and is a very active child, she may love having the chance to splash away. Very young children can learn to swim short distances (even underwater!), but most pediatricians recommend waiting until a child is 4 years old before introducing her to formal swim classes. At that age, she'll be physically ready to learn the movements — and dangers — associated with swimming.

A child who is given formal swim lessons during the toddler years may not develop a healthy fear of the water — something that every child should have.

Swimming with your child may be a soothing or stimulating experience for both of you — and something you just love to do. The problem with allowing young babies to take swim classes is that parents sometimes get a false sense of security concerning the child and water. That is, because their baby can paddle underwater a short distance, some parents assume that even if their child were to fall into a pool, she wouldn't drown. That's just not so. No child is ever completely safe from drowning. No matter how old your children are or whether they've had formal training to swim, you should always keep the gate around your pool locked up tight and use a pool alarm (one that sounds if anything or anyone falls into the water).

Feeling the effects of Baby's mobility

Chasing after a child while simultaneously being on the lookout for danger is exhausting. It's also a challenge to your sanity, because you find yourself looking for hazards everywhere you go. As Baby moves toward becoming a toddler, this is simply what life brings. You'll probably move toward a place of acceptance — looking for and removing hidden hazards from Baby's reach just becomes a normal part of your day — but you'll definitely be doing more of it in the next few years and beyond.

After you have a child, you will never again look at the world in the same way. You've always loved the beach, but now you see that the ocean is dangerous — to your child. You love a good hike in the woods, but now you worry about wild animals and the weather — and how these things will affect your child. Parents start to see — actually envision, as though they were real — the worst-case scenarios in any given setting.

It's easy to give into these fears, to throw your hands up and say, "Well, that's it. We can't go anywhere. The world is unsafe." But you'd be doing your entire family a huge disservice, and Baby will lose out on a lot of exciting new experiences if she's never allowed to leave home. Realize that yes, dangers are out there — but you can minimize them, at the very least, and even eliminate them in many cases. For more on getting out of the house with Baby, see Chapter 3.

Keeping the very active child safe without losing your mind

All of this advice is little comfort to the parent of an incredibly active almost-10-month-old — the child who has already learned to hoist himself up on the kitchen chairs in order to gain access to whatever goodies may be laid out for him on the table; the child who has already mastered the art of walking and spends his days wandering around the house and yard, making it necessary for you to follow behind (and simultaneously making it impossible for you to get anything done); the child who hates (and does his best to fight) being confined to a car seat or a crib and who certainly won't agree to being placed in his playpen anymore. The parents of this child may be beyond exhausted. They may just be on the verge of burnout. Day after day of doing nothing but following after an active almost-toddler does that to a person.

An active child needs to have a safe area of the house to play in — an area that is set up for him to jump and climb to his heart's content without the risk of injury. Consider using old couch cushions or even bringing a small jungle gym into the house to amuse your little gymnast — and to prevent him from exploring less safe options (like climbing on your bookshelves). You can also buy gymnastics mats that fold up for storage.

If your child needs to be on the go-go-go all the time, look for a playgroup or a baby exercise class for the two of you. Because your child is a natural-born explorer, Baby may benefit immensely from the interaction with other kids (whom he will probably find incredibly interesting), and you'll benefit from talking with other parents of tireless, active children (and there's bound to be at least one other child in the group whose energy level meets your kid's). You may even see a new side of your child's personality come to life, as he starts showing affection to his little playmates.

A playgroup or a Baby exercise class is also a nice change of scenery from being at home all day. Baby will have the chance to explore new territory, which may have two benefits: It may be just the thing to tire him out, and it may make him less apt to get into trouble at home, where he's become so comfortable and used to his surroundings that his curiosity drives him to explore even *more* (which is a good thing, of course, except when he's driving you crazy in the process).

Harnessing the Power of "No"

Baby may start telling you "no" at about this point, and you may not find this development entirely pleasing. It may be cute the way Baby has taken your phrase of admonishment and made it his own; you may be secretly proud that he's smart enough to turn the tables on you, but you may also be a bit worried that he's developing a bit of a stubborn streak. How should you handle a 10-month-old who loves to say "no" to you?

You may be saying "no" more often than you realize, and really, it's only natural at this point. Baby is becoming more active, and her curious bent leads her into more and more situations that aren't safe or appropriate for her. Suddenly, you're faced with teaching her right from wrong, safe from unsafe, and the easiest way to do this is to stop an inappropriate activity when you see it happening — by saying, "No, no."

Cutting back on "no"

You don't want Baby to grow up constantly hearing what she *isn't* allowed to do. Put yourself in her tiny little shoes for a minute and pretend you're a curious little imp who's constantly being commanded to stop whatever you're doing. It's far more pleasant to hear (and therefore to learn) what *is* allowed.

Here are some ways to minimize your use of the word "no:"

- ✔ **Offer Baby praise when she's doing something that you approve of.** Whether she's playing nicely, or eating her finger foods without throwing them on the floor, positive reinforcement is a powerful teaching tool.

- ✔ **Physically remove or distract her from an activity instead of just using the word "no."** Is she wearing your glasses? Take them out of her hand and give her a toy that she *can* play with.

- ✔ **Eliminate the need for "no" — at least in some instances.** If you don't want her playing with your glasses, for example, don't leave them where she can find them.

- ✔ **Reserve "no" for the most important and/or dangerous situations.** A child who hears "no" all day long becomes immune to its meaning. She learns to go about her business while ignoring your "no," even when you *really* mean it.

- ✔ **Don't say "no" in a singsong voice, like you don't really mean it.** "No" means "no" and it should be stated firmly when you need to use it.

Of course, you can't remove "no" from your vocabulary. You have limits in your household, and rightly so. Baby needs to hear "no" from time to time to know that she can't do anything and everything that she wants to. "No" means that you are looking out for her, that you are on top of things, that her safety is your number one concern.

Defusing stubbornness

Baby needs to know that she is a little person worthy of praise and accolades — and not just someone who is constantly involved in things that she shouldn't be doing. Although children this age can often get themselves involved in less-than-admirable activities (learning to remove a full diaper certainly qualifies as one of these activities, as does licking the floor), parents have to remember that these behaviors arise from simple curiosity — at least in the beginning.

But back up for just for a minute. Throughout this chapter, we've been discussing Baby's increasing sense of self — her autonomy. This is the reason she's comfortable doing more and more on her own: Because she *can*. Though it's not very common for children this age to become locked in a power struggle with their parents, it does happen from time to time. The more you say "no" to a child who is bound and determined to do her own thing, the more likely she is to continue doing it. (You don't like removal of the dirty diaper? Well, that just makes it all the more appealing — or funny — to her.)

Using diversionary tactics is a great way to distract a child who uses her own "no" as a way of testing her power with you. By responding to her with anger, you either scare her half to death or ensure that the behavior will continue — and both of you lose in the end. Next time she's pulling at the tabs of her diaper, consider that perhaps she finds a dirty diaper very uncomfortable. Change her — and don't put it off. If it turns out that she's removing the diaper just because it's amusing, make it impossible for her to do so by dressing her in one-piece outfits.

Find the source of the power struggle and eliminate it right away — and you may find that you're eliminating a lot of your "no's" throughout the day, as well.

Making "no" really count

When it is necessary for you to use a firm "no" with Baby — for example, when he's managed to climb on the couch and is about to dump the cup of coffee you left on the table there — follow through with a teaching lesson so that he understands that you aren't angry, but that you are concerned about his well-being.

In the case of the child who is about to reach for a cup of coffee:

1. **Stop him in his tracks with a loud, stern warning.**

2. **Remove the cup from his reach.**

3. **Take the time to teach him two important concepts:** "hot" and "burn." (Or "ouch" or whatever word you feel fits best here.) Take his index finger and lightly touch it to the side of your coffee cup to teach him "hot."

   Don't do this if the coffee is scalding hot — lukewarm is safest. You don't want to teach him about burns by accidentally giving him one.

Consider the difference between simply telling him "no" and teaching him the reasoning behind the "no." In one case, he's been saved from a burn — this time. In the other, he's learning not to touch Mom's coffee cups because he could get hurt. (Of course, you should keep those cups completely out of his reach anyway.) He's also learning the meaning behind the word "hot." You can transfer this concept to teaching him to keep away from the stove and teaching him not to touch the faucet in the bathtub.

Feeding Your 10-Month-Old

By now, Baby has sampled a veritable buffet of solids. Because he likely has a couple of teeth at this age, you may be tempted to give him harder-to-chew foods, like pieces of apple or chunks of meat. Remember that he is still relying on his gums to do the work, so keep his foods semi-soft and small enough to prevent choking.

Foods that you should avoid feeding to Baby at this age include:

- Honey (which may contain *botulinum* — spores which can cause botulism)
- Cow's milk (which can cause a milk allergy or inflammation of the gastrointestinal tract if introduced during the first year)
- Egg whites (some children show a severe reaction to the whites at this age)
- Strawberries
- Shellfish, which can cause severe allergic reactions
- Peanuts — peanuts and any peanut-containing products should actually be avoided for two years according to current allergist recommendations

Chapters 11 and 18 discuss food allergies in more detail.

Otherwise, Baby's meals are probably starting to be similar to your own — although his foods are minced, mashed, or pureed versions of what you and the rest of the family are eating. Baby is still consuming about four 6-ounce servings of formula or breast milk at this age (including whatever his cereal is being mixed with). His schedule may look something like this:

- **Breakfast:** Baby will be starting the day off with a serving of iron-fortified cereal, and topping that off with a nursing session or a bottle of formula.
- **Midmorning snack:** Half a jar of fruit or a handful of cereal, perhaps.
- **Lunch:** May consist of half a jar of prepared baby food along with some finger foods and ½ cup of fruit juice.
- **Snack when he wakes up from his nap:** A bit of cheese, yogurt, or a bagel along with a bottle.

✔ **Dinner:** He's probably having whatever you've made for everyone else in smaller, mashed or minced portions. Offer him a balanced meal of meat, starch (bread or pasta), and vegetables and allow him to eat as much or as little as he wants.

✔ **Bedtime feeding:** He's ready to nurse or suck down a bottle. He tops off the day with another serving of cereal.

Basically, you want to strive for a healthy balance of foods at this age as well as a good variety. A 10-month-old needs about 2 to 4 tablespoons of protein foods a day (most meats provide a good amount of protein, as do legumes, fish, cheese, and egg yolk). His iron-fortified cereal prevents anemia.

By and large, babies know when to say when, and when to continue chowing down. However, if you're worried that Baby isn't eating enough, or that he's eating far *too* much, make sure to ask your pediatrician for his take on the matter. He can assess Baby's weight and growth patterns and let you know whether you're right to be concerned.

Baby should continue on his normal growth pattern, falling roughly in the same percentiles for height and weight at each checkup. If he's falling behind and he never wants to eat, your pediatrician may want you to cut back on Baby's formula or nursing sessions. If Baby is still hovering around the same percentile for his height but his weight percentile takes a huge leap, your pediatrician may want to know what, exactly, your child has been eating.

Continue to offer Baby new foods one at a time — and allow four to five days between introducing foods. This way you can watch for any adverse reactions (a rash, cramps, diarrhea, itchy or watery eyes) and know exactly which food has caused it. Providing Baby with a variety of new tastes at this age will hopefully translate into healthy eating habits when he's a toddler — and less likely to comply with your mealtime wishes. (If he's been eating carrots all along, he's less likely to balk at them a year from now.)

Avoiding food fights

Some kids aren't big eaters — or eager eaters. Ideally, introducing Baby to new foods during the second half of the first year creates enough of a novelty that he's just excited to sit in his highchair and taste the culinary delights you've prepared for him. Sometimes, a 9- or 10-month-old is just too busy to be bothered with much of a meal. Rarely, a child this age may show a definite preference for certain foods — and an abhorrence for others.

There are two things that you can do to prevent "food fights" between you and your baby. First, keep the sweets and junk foods to a minimum. Think about it: Why do older kids and adults love chips, doughnuts, and candy? Because they taste good — and, as far as most of us are concerned — they taste much better than, say, carrots. Don't encourage Baby to develop a taste for candy and grease. If your child is already hooked on a diet loaded with sugar and fat, you're going to have a heck of a time convincing him that a sweet potato is delicious. (If you're wondering if you need to deprive Baby of sweets altogether, the answer is no. Fruits are a wonderful, healthy choice for dessert, not only during the first year, but throughout childhood and beyond.)

Secondly, don't ever force your child to eat. He should be his own regulator where food is concerned. You may want to teach him that "dinner" is a special block of time when you all sit down together as a family. That's fine — just keep in mind that Baby may be far more interested in getting back to his blocks than in eating the chicken you've minced for him. Have realistic expectations of the child. If he's not interested in eating, don't make him sit for 30 minutes while you and your spouse catch up on your respective days. And realize that he's a fickle little thing. He may just *love* carrots this week only to refuse them next week. Offer him something that he finds palatable at this point in time and work those carrots back into his food repertoire in a couple of weeks.

Don't make Baby stay in his highchair until he's eaten the food you've laid out before him. This is a fight you shouldn't even start. Forcing your child to eat even when he clearly isn't hungry ebbs away part of his autonomy. Because every person has an internal feeling that tells us when we've had enough, it's risky to try and judge when someone *else* is full. Allowing Baby to decide how much he's going to eat in one sitting allows him to get used to that "I'm full" signal that tells him when he doesn't need any more. Forcing him to eat more than he can comfortably stomach may lead to him ignoring that signal, putting him at risk for becoming overweight or developing life-long issues with food. Sit him in his highchair for 10 to 15 minutes for the meal, and then let him down if he's done. Don't have books and toys at the table. Concentrate on the meal, and then let him go play. Try not to have him in his highchair while preparing the meal — he'll already be tired of being in the chair when it's time to eat.

Combating childhood obesity

Several decades ago, a child in elementary school could name the overweight kids in the school — because there weren't that many. Today, parents walk into their kids' schools and notice that the children seem, well, larger than the kids from the 1970s and 1980s.

One of the biggest problems facing kids today is childhood obesity. And although it's perfectly normal — and healthy — for Baby to be a little butterball during his first year, the eating habits he establishes now could very well determine whether he ends up being plump throughout his school days and beyond. It's not up to Baby to decide *which* foods he's given at meals and during snack times. It's your responsibility to make those choices for him — and to make the healthiest selections possible.

All foods aren't created equally, healthwise. A banana is a much healthier snack than a cookie, for example, even though they may have the same amount of calories. The cookie provides Baby with little more than a sugar rush; the banana is providing him with potassium and fiber, two essential nutrients for a growing child.

In theory, kids should be able to burn off that excess weight as they grow taller and become more active. The problem in today's world is that kids just aren't very active. Twenty years ago, children came home and played outside after school. Today's kids play video games for hours on end. They chat online with each other. They watch a lot of TV. There's not a lot of opportunity for these children to burn off any excess weight they're dragging around. The earlier they put on weight, the harder it may be for them to lose it, because eating habits can be incredibly difficult for a child to change — plus, the more weight kids gain, the harder it is for them to do anything about it.

Childhood obesity can lead to a myriad of problems, among them:

- ✔ Low self-esteem
- ✔ Diabetes
- ✔ Sleep apnea
- ✔ Knee and hip problems

And we're not talking about these problems surfacing in adulthood. These are issues that overweight kids deal with *as children*.

On the other hand, Baby needs to eat as much as he wants at this age, so cutting back on the amount of food he's given isn't a good idea. Remember, he has a built-in shut-off switch to tell him when he's full. Don't mess with that. Allow Baby to eat to his heart's content so that he can recognize the feeling of being full. Kids who aren't allowed to make this determination on their own (whose parents either stuff them or dole out scanty portions of food to their hungry children) are *more* likely to develop weight problems later in childhood, when Mom and Dad aren't there to watch every morsel that passes the kid's lips. These kids simply aren't able to recognize when they need to eat, or how much food is enough, and they're prone to overeating for these reasons.

Help your child develop healthy eating patterns that will benefit him for a lifetime by doing the following:

✔ **Be a good example.** Don't expect your child to sit down to a healthy
meal of minced grilled chicken breast and pureed veggies if you've
served yourself a heaping plate of fried chicken and French fries.
Prepare your own meals at home as much as possible. Fast food and
many frozen prepared meals are loaded with fat and sodium.

✔ **Look for ways to cut the fat.** Preparing low-fat meals for the entire family
has never been easier. There are so many organic and low-fat products in
the supermarket these days that all it takes to make the switch is to reach
for the fat-free mayo instead of the heavy-duty stuff. Getting used to the
low-fat taste may take some time, but after you do, you never *want* to go
back to regular.

✔ **Eliminate sugary drinks.** Although it's all right to give Baby diluted fruit
juice once in a while, he shouldn't be drinking an entire jug of it daily.
Soda should be outlawed in your home. It's one of the leading causes of
obesity and tooth decay in children.

✔ **Turn off the tube.** Get baby outside as much as possible — or, if you
happen to be snowbound for months on end, get him to an indoor playgroup as often as you can. At the very least, set up a safe area in your
home where Baby can be as active as he needs to be. Allowing him to
become hooked on TV at this age may set a dangerous precedent for
his entire lifetime (he's less likely to get any exercise and more likely
to mindlessly consume snacks in front of the tube in years to come).

✔ **Don't use food for comfort or as a reward or diversion.** If Baby bumps
his elbow, he doesn't need a brownie to make it all better. You don't
need to distract him from pounding on the piano by offering him a
cookie. He should be learning to associate food with hunger, not with
other behaviors.

✔ **Don't deny food.** On the other hand, don't withhold food as punishment.
If Baby is throwing food from his tray, you have every right to take him
out of his highchair until he's ready to eat nicely. But when he's a toddler
and he smacks your mother, don't send him to his room without dinner.
He needs his nourishment. Meals are not a negotiable part of childhood.

Eating healthfully is a commitment that the entire family needs to make
together — and it doesn't have to include a promise to never ingest another
piece of candy in your collective lifetime. Just grilling your meat instead of
frying it is a healthy change. Allowing Baby to have one treat instead of three
is another. Live by the motto "Everything in moderation" where food is concerned, and you'll find that making the changes to healthier eating habits
isn't as difficult — or as overwhelming — as it may seem.

Chapter 16

The Eleventh Month: Walking the Walk

- -

In This Chapter

▶ Taking a look at Baby's growth

▶ Nipping unsafe behavior in the bud

▶ Adjusting to weaning

▶ Establishing good bedtime habits

- -

*W*here has the time gone? The first year flies by in what seems like a nanosecond, and before you know it, your little one is running out of your reach, exploring new things by himself, saying a few words, and becoming his own person.

Changes are in store for you at this point, too. As your child becomes more and more independent, you may miss those days not so long ago where he would stay in your arms until you put him down. Baby's becoming quite the active little person these days, and he may seem to be changing and growing as you watch. Read on to find out what's in store for both of you during this time of transformation.

Checking In with Baby

Most pediatricians don't schedule a well-baby checkup this month, so Baby's off the hook for another month. As he becomes more and more active (and possibly injury-prone), though, and is exposed to germs through daycare or playgroups, you may find yourself in the doctor's office anyway.

If you do have to make an unscheduled trip to the doctor's office, make sure you ask your pediatrician any questions you may have about Baby's injury or illness. When the doctor is giving you advice or instructions, have a pen and pad handy to write them down. Caring for a sick child can be confusing at times, especially if you're losing sleep and not quite as sharp as you normally are. Writing down the information and repeating it back to the doctor or nurse ensures that you've gotten it right.

Of course, if you feel as though you missed something, or new issues with an illness or injury pop up, call your doctor's office. Always choose to be safe instead of sorry.

Milestones this month

What kind of milestones does Baby hit by the end of this month?

- ✔ She's able to stand on her own, either for a short time or for several minutes.

- ✔ Baby *cruises* ("walks" by hanging onto furniture or other sturdy objects) like a champ.

- ✔ She may be taking her first tentative steps or may even be able to walk well (by the end of the month).

- ✔ Roll a ball to her, and she's able to roll it back to you.

- ✔ She can feed herself finger foods and drink from a cup independently.

- ✔ Baby can now pick up very small objects.

- ✔ Baby is able to follow simple instructions ("Come here," "Don't touch," and so on).

- ✔ She can say "Mama" or "Dada" with meaning.

- ✔ May be able to say at least one or two other words.

- ✔ Can indicate her wants either by pointing or by grunting or using her own made-up words. (She may even talk to herself in her own language at this age, which she understands completely, although you probably won't.)

- ✔ Mimics expressions and movements of others.

- ✔ May love to drop things so you'll pick them up (which is indicative of a growing sense of object permanence — and a little sense of humor).

- ✔ Engages in *parallel play* with others. (Baby plays next to other kids, but not with them yet.)

- ✔ Understands the word "no."

Planning ahead

An interesting thing happens to babies in the last few months of the first year: Their brains kick into overdrive, and they're able to figure out how to get what they want by planning ahead, which means you may see the gears turning in your child's little head sometimes as she thinks, "Hmm . . . If I want to see Mom during my naptime, all I have to do is climb out of this crib." Or she may pick up a long, skinny toy to reach something that's up on a shelf. She may lead you to something she wants, like to the refrigerator for a drink, or to the front door to go outside to play. (Yes, you have a little smarty on your hands!)

With this ability to think logically comes the potential for Baby to get herself into some trouble (climbers at this age aren't thinking first and foremost about their own safety, for example). Keeping one step ahead of the clever almost-toddler takes some planning of your own, something we discuss in the next section.

Keeping Baby Safe and Sound

Although a baby this age is capable of some rudimentary reasoning, he's not old enough to fully appreciate the consequences of his actions. As your seemingly fearless child becomes more and more active, you may find that the best investment you can make is in a good pair of running shoes, because chasing after Baby seems to take up the bulk of each day. Even the most mild-mannered babies (those who are content to sit right on the blanket they were placed on, playing nicely with their toys) can sometimes surprise their care-givers by engaging in a dangerous activity (exploring the back of the TV, for example).

The differences among children become more pronounced at this age. Some just can't sit still; others never need to venture any further than where they're placed by Mom. The most important thing to remember about an active child is that he's simply programmed to be this way. He isn't naughty, and he isn't trying to drive you crazy. He's simply exploring his world the only way he knows how: by *doing*. (Hey, you're getting some exercise by chasing him, and he's learning new things every day, so there are definite benefits to having a busy kid.)

Double-check your past baby-proofing efforts and make sure they're toddler-proof. Look for things Baby can reach while standing and for tools he can use to reach even higher.

Curbing crib climbers

Naptime can become a real battle when Baby decides she'd rather scale the side of the crib than sleep in it. She's less than 1 year old, so she isn't ready to give up her daytime rest yet, but active children sometimes have a tough time settling down for a nap.

If you have a child who finds it difficult to switch gears and go from playtime to rest time just because it's one o'clock, stop playtime 15 minutes before her nap and institute some transition time:

- ✔ Read a story with her.
- ✔ Turn on soothing music in her play area, where she can listen to it and relax a bit before turning in.
- ✔ Put away the noisiest toys.
- ✔ Steer clear of activity that may rile her up — no chasing the cat or tickle sessions with Dad.

By the time you put her in her crib, she may just decide that climbing out isn't worth it, now that she's had a head start on her rest time.

If Baby still doesn't settle down, she may be feeling frightened in her crib all by herself. You can try a small stuffed animal or another comfort measure. Rub her back for a minute before leaving her, or turn on some soft music, if that helps. If she's climbing out of her crib because she simply doesn't want to be there, though, or because she thinks it's fun (notice the big grin on her face when she appears in the doorway of the kitchen?), a stuffed animal isn't going to help matters.

If she's still determined to get out of that crib, take a look at her sleeping set-up to determine whether escape is just too easy. Just because she's capable of climbing out of the crib right now doesn't mean that you can't make it a bit more difficult: Make sure the mattress is moved to its lowest level. Check to see that the rails are at their highest level. Is she using a crib toy or bumper pad to climb on? Get rid of them.

Don't move her to a toddler bed just yet. She's not quite ready for that kind of independence (and neither are you). Invest in a tentlike attachment for the top of her crib. (See Figure 16-1.) They're made specifically for this purpose. Baby will be hopping mad when you put her in there, especially if she's really been enjoying her liberty at naptime, but remember: She's probably not ready to give up her nap, and this is the safest way to corral her.

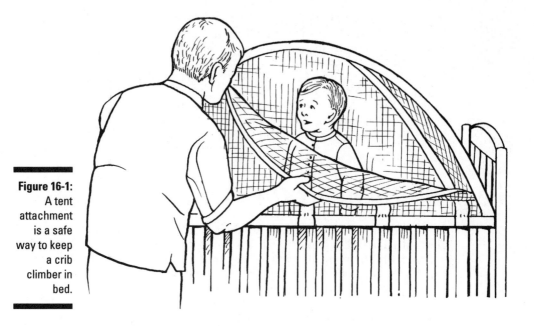

Figure 16-1:
A tent attachment is a safe way to keep a crib climber in bed.

Reining in roaming babies

A baby closing in on 11 months is a very curious creature: He wants to know more, see more, do more. By extension, he's highly distractible, especially in new or interesting situations. He may not see the steps going down to the yard as he chases a butterfly. He may not realize how far toward your property line he's wandered in pursuit of a squirrel.

Fortunately, wandering off doesn't become a real issue for most children until the toddler years (which, by the way, are right around the corner) — because parents are so vigilant with little ones. Also, most children under 1 year tend to stick pretty close to their caregivers; they're still leery of strangers, and they like the security of having Mom or Dad nearby. Still, a few nearly-1-year-olds pull the disappearing act in the house or in the yard, making their parents prematurely gray.

Children this age, whether they're very active and constantly on the move or content to be by your side, need constant adult supervision. Don't ever assume your job is done when it comes to baby-proofing. Check and recheck your baby-proofing measures (see Chapter 20) to make sure nothing has changed or come undone. (Did someone uncover an outlet and forget about it? Are the drapery cords up high, out of Baby's reach? Has someone dropped loose change where Baby can pop it into his mouth?) Because Baby has the capacity to climb (or will very soon), make sure that all furniture and overhead items are secure.

Got a real climber or jumper on your hands? Create a safe space for your little acrobat. Use old couch cushions or a foam interlocking floor. Your main goal is to let this child expend his energy without hurting himself.

Paranoia? Perhaps. But a teeny dose of paranoia and overprotectiveness can go a long way toward preventing injury to your child. Going to the extreme — managing every move he makes, hovering over him as he explores the great outdoors — isn't healthy, for him or for you. Vigilance and common sense are the keys to keeping Baby safe while giving him a bit of freedom.

Weaning Baby off the Bottle or Breast

Before you know what's happened, Baby's first birthday is coming down the tracks like a speeding train. This is about the time when your pediatrician will probably recommend weaning Baby from the breast or bottle. Not only does Baby need nutrition from other sources at this age, but weaning him at close to 1 year will be much easier than attempting to remove his bottle (or your breasts) from his grasp during the toddler years. Tips for making this process easier on both of you are included in this section, along with a look at how a nursing mom's body may change during and after weaning. For a more complete look at breastfeeding and weaning, check out *Breastfeeding For Dummies* by Sharon Perkins and Carol Vannais (Wiley).

Don't try to wean Baby from his bottle (or cut him off the breast cold turkey) the same week you're moving into a new house, or right after you've switched his day care or nanny. It may seem logical to throw him two curveballs at once and get it all over with (thinking that maybe he'll even forget about his bottle when he's in this new situation). That's probably not going to be the case. A change in his normal routine is a big deal to the 11-month-old, even if he seems complacent about it. More likely than not, he's going to need some extra comforting measures during a major change in his life, and if he gets it from his bottle, then so be it. Wait until he's made the adjustment before attempting to make the bottle disappear for good.

Doctors recommend weaning Baby from breast and/or bottle when he's about 1 year old to prevent the possibility of baby bottle mouth: Breast milk and formula contain enough sugar to create cavities in Baby's developing teeth, which could cause him a lifetime of dental problems. (For more on baby bottle mouth, see Chapter 11.)

Stopping breastfeeding

When Baby can scarcely spare time out of his busy daytime activity schedule to nurse, and/or when you start to view nursing him as more of a chore and less of a special bonding time between the two of you (perhaps *because* he's so fidgety and reluctant to nurse), you should think about weaning the child.

Many doctors recommend weaning at about the 1-year mark, citing Baby's need for increased independence and the decreasing benefits of mother's milk. Some moms find that their children self-wean, little by little, as they become more interested in the world around them (leaving little time for cuddling with Mom); some mothers find that after a year of nursing and the nine months of pregnancy preceding Baby's arrival they just want their bodies back.

Weaning can be a time of intense emotional upheaval, even if you know that Baby isn't all that interested in nursing anymore. Letting go of nursing entails breaking a bond between yourself and your child, and even if you're mostly ready for it, the break can still be a little sad. Weaning ushers in a whole new era, one where Baby isn't physically dependent on you. Even though you're excited by every one of his newest accomplishments, each one takes him further out of babyhood.

Don't wean an older baby from the breast to the bottle. You're just creating another habit to break him of. If he's old enough to hold a cup, wean him directly to it.

Taking a gradual approach

Most moms and their babies are able to gradually cut back on nursing — over a period of weeks or even months — and do it naturally, as the child's demand (or lack of demand) for nursing dictates. Daytime feedings are usually the first to go, one by one, little by little. You may notice that Baby is most eager to nurse before his nap and before bedtime. Because sucking soothes him and settles him down for a long rest, these feedings are usually the last vestments of what used to be a round-the-clock nursing schedule. These feedings may gradually decrease in length, until Baby's only sucking for a few minutes before he's ready to turn in. This is a good indication that he may be ready to give it up all together and only cuddle with you before settling into his crib.

Putting Baby into her crib without nursing her for the first time may seem strange. Rest assured, she'll suffer no long-term effects being weaned from the breast. It's a natural step in her life — and in yours, too — no matter how sad it seems to you right now.

Don't stop nursing cold turkey. Not only can this upset your child, it can also cause you considerable discomfort and increase your risk of developing a breast infection or clogged milk ducts. Abruptly weaning your child from the breast could cause a significant hormonal crash for you. A sudden decrease in *prolactin* (a hormone that stimulates milk production and lifts your mood) can seriously affect your mood, especially when coupled with the mild anxiety and sadness that often accompany the weaning process. If you're prone to depression, wean your breastfed child as gradually as possible. This will give your body plenty of time to adjust to the decreasing levels of prolactin and will help to prevent a major mood plunge.

If you're ready to give up nursing at night and you're not opposed to pacifiers, offer one to Baby at these times. Combined with a good snuggling session, this may be all she needs to prepare herself for sleep at this point.

Remember that the sugar from breast milk will stay on baby's teeth all night and can cause tooth decay. If you nurse to sleep, wipe baby's teeth with a wet washcloth before putting her to bed for the night.

Don't panic if Baby shows no signs of giving up these final nursing sessions. Although many doctors suggest weaning Baby around the age of 1 year, most won't bat an eye at your comforting your child in this way before she drifts off. If she's not ready at 12 months, she may be ready at 13 or 14 months; pay attention to her signals. If she doesn't cut the nursing back on her own, do it for her. Keep track of how long she nurses before her naps and subtract a minute every few days. Then do the same thing with her nighttime nursing.

Decreasing your discomfort

The discomfort you experience during weaning won't even come close to what you went through when your milk came in. Your breasts may be a bit sore and engorged at times, but this varies from woman to woman, and also depends on how gradual your weaning schedule is. The discomfort may be more significant for the mom who is actively cutting out one feeding every few days than for the mom who has been slowly tapering off Baby's feedings for several weeks.

Here are some tips to help you alleviate the discomfort of weaning:

- ✔ **Take a pain reliever, like acetaminophen.**

- ✔ **Express some milk if you need to.** Engorged, sore breasts are more likely to become infected or develop clogged ducts. Try not to express any more milk than you absolutely must: If you pump regularly (and continue the demand), the supply will continue.

- ✔ **Cut back on the sodium.** Salty foods encourage fluid retention, and you'll notice it most in your breasts right now. Remember, too, that if you haven't had your period the entire time you've been nursing, it'll be returning soon. If you're prone to bloating during your menses, you have all the more motivation to cut back on the salt.

Although you should decrease your sodium while weaning your child to prevent water retention, don't cut back on your fluid intake. Dehydrating yourself isn't going to do you or Baby much good, and it's not a very effective way to slow milk production, anyway.

✔ **Step into a warm shower.** The heat will soothe sore breasts and you can also express a bit of milk as you bathe.

✔ **Wear a supportive bra, but make sure it's not too tight.** Have your nursing pads on hand, because you may leak.

✔ **Try drinking sage tea, which contains an ingredient that some weaning moms swear helps to dry up breast milk.** Two to three cups a day, one about every six hours, is the recommended dosage.

✔ **Wrap your breasts in raw, cold cabbage leaves.** This home remedy has been passed along for generations, though no scientific explanation exists to explain why it helps to alleviate the engorgement associated with weaning. You need a fresh head of green cabbage. Wash the leaves, dry them, and put them in your fridge. After they're cool, wrap one leaf around each breast, positioning them so that they're comfortable and soothing. Leave them on all day if they help, but change them when they start drooping (the leaves, not your breasts).

Don't bind your breasts when you're weaning. This just isn't done anymore. Binding lactating breasts can lead to serious side effects, like infections and clogged milk ducts. Plus, it hurts.

Getting acquainted with your new breasts

So, after you wean your baby off the breast, you're going to have a pair of perky, pre-pregnancy breasts again, right? Hate to tell you this but . . . probably not. Your breasts may be very different, so don't break out those old bras just yet. When you're finished weaning your child, you may notice that your breasts look saggy and possibly much smaller than you recall. This is completely normal. Remember, you've not only been through a year of nursing but also almost a year of pregnancy. Those physical and hormonal changes have resulted in some changes in your breasts, and your genetics are coming into play here, too: Some women have remarkably elastic skin, which allows those breasts to pop right back into shape after months of nursing, and others . . . don't.

Most women find that their breasts fill out and perk up again, at least somewhat, in about six months, though some never do return to their previous cup size or shape. There's just no way to determine what each individual woman's experience will be, so prepare yourself for any eventuality — and tell yourself that it was all for the greatest cause.

Packing the bottle away

Whether you weaned Baby months ago from the breast to a bottle or Baby has always been bottlefed, now's the time to kiss that bottle goodbye. We know of several reasons for breaking the bottle habit at this age, most notably the risk of baby bottle mouth (tooth decay), and the fact that a child who's toting a beloved bottle around may not be very interested in solid foods (for more on baby bottle mouth, see Chapter 11). At this age, Baby needs nutrients from all of the major food groups.

Putting the bottle away for good seems like an easy enough task, but if your little one is really attached to his bottle, having it disappear in the span of one day isn't the best plan of action. The cold-turkey method of bottle weaning should be used only when it's clear Baby has absolutely no intention of giving up the bottle after you've tried to ease him off it gradually.

Some tips for bottle weaning:

- ✔ Offer a sippy cup to him instead of his bottle at mealtimes, removing the bottle from one feeding at a time. To do this, add the cup to (and remove the bottle from) one mealtime a week, until he's eventually taking the cup at all meals.

  If Baby is just starting on the cup, find one that he can comfortably handle (and one that doesn't leak).

- ✔ When trying to break the bedtime bottle habit, shake up the nighttime routine. If you normally snuggle up with him and his bottle in your family room, try reading to him in his bedroom. Doing things differently will encourage him to give up that last bottle of the day.

- ✔ Make sure you offer Baby lots of extra cuddling and attention during this time, especially if he was extremely attached to his bottle.

- ✔ Don't leave bottles (or bottle parts) around. Out of sight, out of mind. In fact, pack away all of the bottles and only use one, if possible, to show Baby that the endless supply of bottles has come to an end.

- ✔ Stick to your plan. Don't insist that he use the cup one day and then allow him to have the bottle the next. After you've weaned him from the bottle at a particular feeding, the bottle is gone from that feeding forever.

- ✔ After the bottle is gone from all feedings for good, don't bring it out to comfort a sick or crying child. This will only confuse him and force you to start the process all over — only this time, it may be harder, because Baby knows that bottle is *somewhere*.

✔ Many babies balk at the taste of cow's milk, but it's an essential part of building healthy bones. Introduce it into Baby's diet *only after* he's 12 months old, and do so gradually, using a 1:1 ratio of milk and formula. This will not only make the milk more palatable, but will allow you to watch for any signs of a milk allergy. (For more on food allergies, see Chapters 11 and 18.) If Baby liked his formula warm, he may reject cold milk. Warm the milk at first and gradually warm it less and less until Baby takes it straight out of the fridge.

✔ Expect those nighttime and naptime bottles to be the last ones to go. These are the bottles that are most likely to contribute to tooth decay, so it's important to wean Baby from them by the time he's around 1 year old. Read to him, rock him for an extra minute or two before he goes in for the night, and make sure he has any security objects he hangs onto during the day.

It can be as sad to wean Baby from the bottle as it is for a nursing mom to wean her child from the breast. Another sign that he's not an infant anymore. Tell yourself that weaning is the right thing to do, that it's best for his development (after he's off the bottle, he may become more interested in new foods and activities), and that it's easier to do this now than it will be in a year.

If Baby cries for that bottle while he's in bed, give him a bottle filled with plain water (make it warm if he's used to having a warm bottle of formula at night). It's hard to do, but stand firm on this rule. The longer he takes a bottle of formula, breast milk, or cow's milk to bed, the better his chances of developing tooth decay from the sugars contained in these drinks.

Bye-bye, binkie

With all this talk of weaning, you may be wondering how pacifiers fit into the picture.

One thing at a time. Remember, Baby derives a lot of comfort from sucking — that's just the nature of small children. So although you may be anxious to move on to the next phase of your child's life — the phase where you're no longer hunting for bottles and pacifiers at naptime — just keep in mind that taking all of her comfort measures away at once may unsettle her.

If you have a child who wants that pacifier in her mouth around the clock, you must start easing her off it, for many of the same reasons babies are weaned from the bottle: Constant use of a pacifier can affect her attempts at speech, her interest in food, and, if the dependence is long-term enough, the development of her permanent teeth.

Easing Baby's need for the pacifier during the day is easier if you have something that will (at least temporarily) take the place of this habit — if she's sitting there on her blanket, just like she does every morning, looking for that binkie, you can be sure she's going to cry for it. But if you break her out of her routine for a week or two — by taking her out of the house, or by engaging in playtime in another room of the house — she may just forget what she's missing.

Shoot for cutting the pacifier use down to only naptime and bedtime, and then decide where to go from there. Some kids carry that sucking impulse with them right into the preschool years, and taking the pacifier away may only encourage her to suck her finger or thumb, which can be a very hard habit to break (and if this habit stays with her into her school-aged years, the orthodontist is going to *love* you).

She's almost 1 year old: Too old for you to take her pacifier away cold turkey, and too young to express her distress at not having it anymore. If you're cutting the pacifier use back to bedtime and she seems to really need it, leave the weaning until she's old enough to understand a reward system for giving it up. Will this be harder to do in a year? Maybe; but she may still really need it. This is something you have to determine on your own, keeping in mind that some children do need to suck to relieve tension. In any event, most dentists recommend that the pacifier go in the garbage can by 18 months.

Tucking Baby In Now

At this age, Baby should have a good bedtime routine going. If your child is still rather unpredictable in this area, you can — and should — take control and encourage a nightly schedule as soon as possible. Baby needs adequate sleep for many reasons — most importantly for his growth and development (kids really do grow while they sleep, for one thing, and for another, a tired and crabby child isn't likely to be interested in exploring his world).

Good bedtime habits

Helping Baby settle down at roughly the same time every evening is beneficial to everyone in the household, even if you personally abhor schedules. You need to know when this child is going to drop off so that you can have some time to yourself, or time to catch up on the things you're just not able to do during the day. And Baby needs to know what's going to happen each night.

Children thrive on repetition. It makes them feel safe and secure.

Even if it was darn near impossible to get your child on a schedule during the first half of his first year, you should be able to do so now. He's eating more during the day, he's much more active (and should be good and tired when nighttime rolls around), and he's able to comfort himself with a security object or two.

What kind of activities promote a sedate settling down every evening? We're glad you asked. Here are some good ideas:

- ✔ **A bath:** Schedule a nice, warm bath for early in the evening as a way of heralding that bedtime is approaching.

- ✔ **A snack:** Make it something small — applesauce, a cracker, some yogurt, or cheese. Just enough to tide Baby over till the morning.

- ✔ **Brush those teeth:** Before Baby gets very sleepy, clean those pearly whites. Making it a habit now will alert Baby to the fact that bedtime is drawing near and, as a bonus, ensure that Baby always thinks of his teeth right before bed.

- ✔ **Snuggle time:** Obviously, you have to be involved in bedtime — but you *really* need to get into the routine with Baby to achieve maximum sleepy results. Sit and read with him, sing some lullabies, or just rock together for a while.

- ✔ **Routine:** Make sure Baby has his favorite blanket when you put him into his crib. You may want prayer to be a part of his routine; if so, start now. He probably won't be able to memorize anything just yet, but he'll come to accept this as part of his nighttime ritual.

If Baby's having trouble winding down for bedtime (or staying asleep during the night), take a look at how much and how long he's sleeping during the day, and cut his naps back — little by little — accordingly. At this age, most children sleep between 12 and 14 hours per day. So if he's taking a 2-hour nap in the afternoon, he should sleep at least 10 to 12 hours at night.

Baby should be awake when he goes to bed so that he falls asleep on his own. If you always rock or comfort him until he's asleep, he'll come to depend on you to perform this service. He needs to find his own ways to usher himself off to Dreamland; otherwise, it's more likely that he'll need your help to fall back to sleep in the middle of the night and at naptime, too.

Most kids wake up once or twice in the middle of the night. Baby should be able to comfort himself and put himself back to sleep at this age. If he's still crying for you at two and three in the morning, give yourself a few minutes before responding to him — and then a few minutes more, and then a few minutes *more*. Rushing to his side is only depriving both of you of sleep, and this will continue right into his toddler years if you don't stop it now.

Baby trusts that you'll come to him when he needs you. It's up to you to separate his *needs* from his *wants*. Although you should avoid the urge to rush to Baby every time he whimpers in his crib (because he merely *wants* to see you), your motherly instincts will tell you when something's really wrong. If he's screaming in pain or out of fear (babies can have bad dreams), he *needs* you, and of course you should comfort him.

Not-so-good bedtime habits

So now we know what kinds of activities help kids settle in for the night. What kinds of activities are counterproductive?

- **Roughhousing:** Can you have a tickling session, roll around on the floor, chase your spouse around the house . . . and then settle down to sleep? Neither can Baby.

- **General noisiness:** Your child may be sensitive to loud sounds. Turn down your rock and roll music when bedtime rolls around.

- **TV as a pacifier:** Allowing Baby to zone out while watching a video is a bad idea. He's not learning to accept sleep as it comes to him; he's not actually engaging in the process of falling asleep at all. Instead, he's probably fighting sleep to stay awake and watch TV — and he'll become dependent on the TV to put him to sleep.

- **Rocking him to sleep:** Again, he's not learning to comfort himself and accept sleep as a normal part of the day, and he's more likely to want more rocking in the middle of the night.

- **Varied bedtimes:** It can be very difficult for working parents to leave a rigid office routine and come home to a rigid bedtime routine, but it's best for Baby to establish these nighttime rituals. Even though you may be hankering to keep him awake so that you can all watch the late show together, he needs to have a pattern of going to bed at roughly the same times every day and night.

A child who hasn't followed any sort of a nighttime schedule up to this point will need some time to adjust. That's perfectly fine, but establish the routine and stick to it. He needs it, and so do you. He shouldn't need you to come in and calm him (or feed him) in the middle of the night, every night. He's physically capable of having a normal sleep pattern now — and you're long overdue in returning to yours.

Chapter 17

The Twelfth Month: Who's This Toddler?

So you and Baby made it — she's turning 1 year old at the end of the month. The past year has been pretty amazing. Why, 12 months ago, you didn't even know each other, and now you probably know exactly what makes this child tick (and run, and scream, and giggle). After the first birthday, children are officially in the toddler years, so you'll see that word pop up in this chapter from time to time.

The last month of the first year is very exciting. You've reached a huge milestone in parenting (and although it would be nice to say that the hardest times are behind you, they're really out there looming in the teen years). Let's just say you came, you saw, you lost sleep, and you prevailed as an amazing parent to an incredible child. Celebrate this accomplishment along with Baby's first birthday!

It can be a bit melancholy to watch her first year come to an end (so quickly!), but realize that it doesn't mean that she's not your baby any more. You know how your mother tells you that you're still *her* baby? Now it all makes perfect sense.

Checking In with Baby

Gone are the days when Baby was in the doctor's office almost every month for a well-baby visit. After the 1-year visit, things slow down considerably.

During the second year, you can expect to pop into the pediatrician's office for just two or three well-baby visits; otherwise, you'll only be seeing the doctor when Baby is sick or hurt. (You've spent so much time with him and his office staff this past year, you're really going to miss them!) The goal now becomes to stay *out* of the pediatrician's office, because going in usually means Baby's not feeling well.

The 1-year checkup

This month, your doctor continues to monitor Baby's growth and development, keeping in mind that this child is actually close to becoming a toddler. In Chapter 6, we discuss the significance of height and weight charts (and you can take a look at the charts at www.cdc.gov/growthcharts). Your doctor is largely concerned with whether Baby regularly falls into the same percentiles. In other words, don't worry if your child is either large or small, worry if he's much larger than other babies at one checkup and much smaller at another. You want his growth to on the same general scale.

Keeping in touch with Doc

Just because you won't be having regular visits with the doctor doesn't mean that he doesn't ever want to hear from you. Questions about raising a child don't just stop when Baby blows out her first birthday candle. Many offices have a *phone hour* — a set time each day when the doctor takes calls from parents. (Baby's been throwing major temper tantrums and you want to know whether this is normal? Call during the phone hour and the doctor will answer your questions.) In their off hours, doctors have answering services that relay urgent messages to your pediatrician. (Baby has a fever of 103 degrees and you're not sure what to do? Leave a message with the service, and the doctor will call you at home.)

Parents sometimes hem and haw about whether they should call their pediatrician about an issue. If it's a medical thing and Baby is sick, call. You can't be expected to know everything about every illness and how serious it is or could be. Put your own mind at ease and get the answers you need. But do remember that your doctor is at home with her family and try to save after-hours calls for emergencies, not routine questions or medication refills.

If it's a behavioral thing, use your best judgment — and call during office hours (unless it's a radical and disturbing change in behavior, like nonstop crying, which could signal an acute illness). You don't need to call the doctor to ask him if it's normal for Baby to rub his face on his blanket before he goes to sleep. It's adorable, yes, and quite normal. If Baby is banging his head into the wall in order to fall asleep, however, you should really run that past the doctor and get his opinion on why your child is doing this.

Questions your pediatrician will probably ask during the 1-year checkup include:

✔ What is Baby's sleeping pattern like? How much is he sleeping now? Does he sleep through the night? How many naps during the day?

✔ Is Baby talking? How many words does he say?

✔ Can Baby indicate what he wants by pointing?

✔ What is he eating? How much?

✔ Is he standing, cruising, or walking?

✔ How many teeth has he cut so far?

✔ Is he a sociable baby? Does he make eye contact, appear to listen when you speak directly to him, engage in playtime with you?

✔ Does Baby appear to hear and see normally?

✔ Is he able to stack blocks or manipulate his toys? (This is an evaluation of his fine motor skills.)

The doctor will also want to know whether you have any areas of concern. You won't be back for another well-baby visit until your child is 15 months old, so don't be shy — lay your questions on the doctor.

Immunizations

Baby's due for several shots this month. These shots come complete with a series of confusing initials. Don't worry, we break all this down in Chapter 18 for you, where we tell you exactly what the initials mean and how the shots themselves protect your child. The following vaccines can be given between 12 and 15 months:

✔ MMR

✔ Hib #4

✔ PCV #4

✔ Varicella

Your child may also receive DTaP #3 and/or HBV #3, which can be given between the ages of 12 and 18 months. It just depends on Baby's immunization schedule.

As always, remember to ask the doctor or nurse about the common and possible side effects of each vaccine, including comfort measures and which side effects warrant a call to the office.

Milestones this month

During the twelfth month, Baby seems to be learning new tricks every day — there's just no end to what she can do! Here's what you can expect by the end of the month:

- ✔ She can sit well and pull herself up on things.

- ✔ Baby is probably able to stand on her own at this point.

- ✔ She can probably also walk, either holding onto your hand or by herself. Many babies don't walk well until the thirteenth or fourteenth month, so don't panic if she's not quite up and running just yet.

- ✔ Baby is at least trying to use a spoon and cup.

- ✔ She may try to assist you with dressing her — by holding out her foot for a sock, for example.

- ✔ She may be an expert climber at this point, which means that you need a baby-proofed house (see Chapter 20). You also need to keep a constant eye on her.

- ✔ She can probably stack blocks or stack cups with success.

- ✔ Baby can probably roll a ball back to you.

- ✔ Baby is talking, probably using at least two words with meaning. She may be creating her own little language, in which she mimics voice inflections of the adults around her, but doesn't say anything that you can understand.

- ✔ She probably points to things she wants or lets you know what she wants without crying.

- ✔ Baby can follow simple directions, like "Come here," or "Put that down."

- ✔ She enjoys showing affection to others.

- ✔ She's still too young to play with other kids, but will play near them *(parallel play)*.

- ✔ Baby recognizes herself in the mirror now and may love to watch herself.

Marking the milestones

Go ahead: Look back on the last year and revel in how far Baby has come! In the past year, she has doubled her height, tripled her birth weight, gained mobility and independence, and learned to communicate with others. Her achievements are nothing short of incredible.

Not all children reach milestones at the same rate. Some milestones, such as speech, are particularly variable. Some kids start chatting away soon after they turn 1 year old, while others may not start to communicate effectively until they're 2 or 3. Your doctor will be more concerned with Baby's progression toward the milestone (is Baby at least attempting to talk?) than with reaching the milestone by a given date.

If your doctor shares your concerns about Baby's development, keep in mind that early intervention is often key to nipping certain developmental delays in the bud.

Keeping Baby Safe and Sound

With the advent of the toddler years comes new parenting territory. Your child is learning more and more about the world every day, and that knowledge can sometimes create fear. Think about Baby's position: He's surrounded by all of these things that he's beginning to take note of and that he's very curious about . . . but he doesn't truly understand them.

On the flip side of this coin, some parents have children who seem to have a major fear deficiency. Things that should scare these kids (a barking dog, a honking horn) don't, and their parents worry themselves sick with the thought of what kind of trouble their offspring may end up in.

Facing new fears

Where *does* the water go when you pull the plug in the tub — and why *wouldn't* it also pull Baby down the drain? That's a terrifying thought for a child. Come to think of it, it's a terrifying thought, period — but as adults, parents understand how the world works and that certain things are just not going to happen, or are very unlikely to happen, or are completely out of our control and not really worth worrying about. Baby doesn't have that kind of life experience or the ability to reason with himself to allay his own fears.

New fears are considered a very normal part of a child's development and are quite common in the toddler years. You may be able to pinpoint an event that made Baby fearful of something — perhaps a dog snapped at him or he slipped under the water in the bathtub — or he may develop a fear out of (seemingly) nowhere. And although you may have a child who has only one fear, some kids have a generally fearful disposition, either because this is simply the way they are or because they have a parent who is also very fearful and the child picks up on Mom or Dad's heightened anxiety level.

Sometimes, you simply can't predict what's going to scare the wits right out of your child, but there are some fears that are more common among the toddler set, among them:

- ✔ Loud noises
- ✔ Animals
- ✔ Water
- ✔ Darkness
- ✔ Separation from parents

These last two fears often go hand-in-hand: Baby is put to bed in a dark room without his parents. The resulting drama can be pretty hard to take.

Periods of major change or stress in Baby's life (a move, a new baby in the house, a new caregiver or day-care situation) can result in his developing new fears — or the worsening of an already-existing fear.

So what can you do to help your child deal with his fears? Several things, actually:

- ✔ **Acknowledge the fear and don't belittle it**. Don't try to make your child pet your neighbor's dog when the kid is screaming in a blind panic. Whether the fear is justified or not, your child's feelings are very real. If you force him into a scary situation, you're going to confuse him. (He *thinks* you love him, so why are you doing this?)

- ✔ **On the other hand, don't play up the fear too much.** All right, so he doesn't have to pet the neighbor's dog. Don't talk about the "bad dog" all day long. React when the situation presents itself and then drop it. Giving it your undivided attention to the fear for hours on end only reinforces it.

- ✔ **Resist the urge to protect him from everything.** In order to overcome his fears, your child has to be exposed to them little by little and see that these objects or situations really are safe. This can be hard, especially if you have a child who's afraid of (seemingly) everything. Stay nearby and support him when you see fear on the horizon, but don't shelter him altogether.

- ✔ **Look for obvious solutions.** If your child is afraid of the dark, buy him a nightlight. If your neighbor's dog really *is* nasty, keep Baby far away from the animal. If Baby's afraid of the tub, hold his hand while he's in there, and make sure the water doesn't run down his face when you wash his hair. A little adjustment could make all the difference and help him overcome his fear altogether.

Paging Dr. Scary

You're sitting in your pediatrician's waiting room and all you can hear is a child screaming in one of the examination rooms. Is the doctor torturing this poor kid? It's possible that the crying is due to a shot, or an illness — or another common fear that children around this age develop: Fear of the doctor and/or nurse. If co-author Dr. Gaylord sees a child wide-eyed with fear when he enters the examination room, he examines the child on the parent's lap. Don't be afraid to ask your pediatrician to do the same. No one wants a child to fear the doctor's office any more than he has to (because of shots or memories of unpleasant illnesses) — and especially not because of the doctor himself.

Children often develop fears of things that never bothered them before. Your little one may suddenly scream in terror when your husband turns on the lawn mower, when he wasn't scared of the noise at all a month ago. Again, this is normal behavior for kids this age.

Most kids outgrow these fears, though some may hang on to remnants of them for years to come. Fear isn't really a major concern unless the fears turn into real *phobias* — where your child is completely paralyzed by his fears, and they prevent him from developing physically or socially. This is more common in older children and unlikely to happen to your 1-year-old, but if you have some concerns about his fearful temperament, talk to your pediatrician.

Your fearless little crusader

Parents of burgeoning toddlers who seem to lack the fear chromosome are often left shaking in their own boots. Good heavens, how can a child get herself into so many perilous situations day after day?

Again, this is just part of her disposition. She's curious. She's active. She sees no reason *not* to explore her options, even if that includes climbing on the front of the TV or standing on the back of the toilet. It's just good fun, as far as she's concerned, and you're *way* overreacting, Mom and Dad.

Of course, you're not really overreacting. Every parent's main mission is to keep his children safe. Parents of fearless 1-year-old children simply have a harder job than the parents of more sedate kids.

Here are some tips to help you keep Baby safe:

- **Make things as easy on yourself as possible.** You've seen what she's capable of. She's not going to stop her explorations simply because you want her to. Keep the bathroom door closed. Limit her to areas where she can't get into trouble.

- **Get creative.** Become the child. Think of the most dangerous thing she could get into in each room she has access to, and beat her to it. Remove or rearrange whatever she can get herself into trouble with in the house. This is a step beyond basic baby-proofing, as you may be forced to remove ottomans, move chairs and stools out of her reach, and block off areas like your entertainment center (where she tries to pull herself up on the shelves). Your mantra: Whatever it takes to make home safe.

- **Say "no."** When she's jumping on the couch and teetering on the edge, make her stop. Don't allow her to stand up in her highchair.

- **Don't trust her.** She's still so young, and yet so active, and so *not* going to listen to your explicit instructions to stay out of the dryer. You still need to keep her in your sights at all times.

Create a safe haven for Baby to be active in. Get creative using padded materials for jumping on and providing her with appropriate climbing materials (a baby jungle gym, for example).

When you leave a fearless child with a sitter, whether it's a relative or a teenager from the neighborhood, make sure the person understands that your child is *very* active (it's actually best to have a sitter come several days before you're going to leave her with Baby so that she can see your child in action). Some folks have really never had any experience with children like this, and you want to educate them so that Baby is being left in capable hands.

Last words here: Get used to this. Her activity level will probably only increase throughout the second year, though in time she may calm down. And if she doesn't, she'll probably make a great gymnast or an amazing trapeze artist.

Happy, Happy Birthday, Baby: Planning the Party

Keeping Baby's first birthday in perspective can be difficult — especially if you love to throw a good party. Kids' parties these days are nothing like the parties children had a generation ago — caterers and wildly expensive entertainment are *de riguer* these days, so why should you keep your child's first birthday on the down-low?

Well, because it's a party for your child, and his enjoyment should be your top priority. Ask yourself what would make the day extra-special for your child and move in that direction. Chances are, he's not going to give a hoot about booking the hottest band in town, but he'd probably love a cake and spending some time with his friends, cousins, and grandparents.

It can be hard to rein yourself in on the first birthday party, but Baby is going to have lots of other birthdays — and in the future, he'll actually understand what all the fuss is about. You're better off scaling things down for now and saving the extravagant stuff for subsequent birthdays.

Consider the following elements to make sure your party is kid-friendly:

✔ **Other kids:** Invite the littlest relatives, and if Baby has a little friend or two, invite them also.

✔ **Size:** Some people would advise having only an intimate gathering for Baby's first birthday, but if you have a large family, he's already used to crowds (and they wouldn't miss this for the world, anyway). Don't overwhelm him with strangers or a huge number of guests if he isn't accustomed to being around a lot of people, though.

✔ **Finger foods:** You don't want to be feeding sliced bananas to your in-laws, but make sure you have some treats on hand for Baby and the other kids.

✔ **Activities for the kids:** Have some games planned for your smaller guests (and prizes on hand). If weather permits, consider having the party outdoors, where the kids will be free to run.

✔ **Timing:** Don't plan an all-day affair, and do plan the party around Baby's naptime. He's not going to care who came to wish him a happy birthday if greeting these people means he's going to miss his afternoon snooze.

✔ **The cake:** Give him his own small cake, or a piece of the larger cake, and let him dive in.

Allow Baby to open his presents in front of his guests if he's interested in doing so. If he's just too busy running around with his pals, don't force it. You can open them later and make a list of who gave him what. (You and Baby will be busy with those thank you notes later in the week!)

Choosing Toys for Your Child

Now that you're starting to pack away some of the baby toys, make sure that Baby is prepared to move into and through her second year with interesting, entertaining, and educational play things.

You want to make sure that Baby has toys that are safe and that actually encourage her development, like:

- **Musical toys:** The more noise it makes, the better. Drums, baby pianos, rattles — whatever you can find.

- **Shape sorters:** Children this age also love to put things inside of other things. Not only will Baby be putting all the shapes inside of the container, but after she gets the hang of sorting those shapes, her fine motor skills will also be employed. And she'll clean up after herself! Picking up toys and putting them in the toy box can also be a fun activity.

- **Stacking blocks or nesting cups:** Toddlers love to stack them up and knock them down. Kids this age also enjoy putting things in and taking things out, which is why they also love nesting cups.

- **Push toys:** These large, sturdy toys help Baby become steadier on her feet.

- **Pull toys:** As Baby becomes an expert walker, she'll enjoy pulling a toy duck or dog along behind her.

- **Puzzles:** She'll become better and better with her motor and cognitive skills over the course of the next year. Puzzles with just several large pieces are a thrill for toddlers to complete.

- **Activity tables:** They deliver on their promise — they're chock-full of activities. Many have flashing lights and music, too.

- **Bath toys:** Baby needs a friend or two in the bath. Nowadays, you can find waterproof versions of stuffed animals. You may also be interested in supplying her with foam rubber letters and numbers that stick to the side of the tub when they're wet. Boats and toys that shoot water are big hits.

- **Crayons and a workspace:** For the child who loves to draw at the tender age of 1, drawing materials and a kid-sized table to work at can be a dream come true.

- **Books:** Continue to look for books with colorful, interesting pictures and sturdy pages. Avoid books that are too long or that have too many words at this point. Books with pop-up pages or flaps to turn are an incredible source of amusement for toddlers.

- **Pop-up toys:** Baby pulls a lever or presses a button, and a little head pops up.

- **Activity tables:** Baby hits a button and something happens — the button lights up, music plays, something spins, and so on.

- **Music:** You know what kind of music she likes. Buy her a CD, just for her room.

> ✔ **Playhouses:** Little kids love little houses. If you have the room, set one up for her. Tents are fun too.
>
> ✔ **Play sets:** Toy kitchens are a big favorite among the toddler set, as they offer countless activities for a child to get involved in.
>
> ✔ **Car seat toys:** Do you sense boredom in the back seat? She may enjoy a toy steering wheel, complete with a squeaky horn.

Although Baby may be interested in a TV show or two already, try not to load her down with videos for her first birthday. Toddlers should be spending the bulk of their day exploring and learning from doing — things they aren't going to engage in if they're sitting in front of the TV.

Of course, these are only suggestions. You know your child best, and you know what kinds of activities she best enjoys. Just remember to buy her toys that are appropriate for her age and activity level. You may be dying to buy her first real guitar, but she's not going to be able to do much with it at this point.

Don't be surprised if Baby is more interested in pots and pans than in actual toys: They're shiny, they're loud, and Baby can fit *lots* of stuff inside of them.

Safety concerns

Baby should continue to have age-appropriate toys to play with. When purchasing toys, read the labels. Most will have an age range on the package. Don't buy toys that are intended for older children. For instance, don't give your almost-1-year-old child a toy that's meant for a 6-year-old, even if it catches his eye and he just loves it.

Choking is the number one toy-related risk to small children. Toys that are intended for older kids often contain small pieces that can break off and pose a threat to Baby's airways: wheels, googly eyes, buttons, chunks of foam rubber. All of these materials (and many, many more) may be contained in older kids' toys and may present a choking hazard to Baby.

Toys and gender

Most toys for children of this age are made for boys *and* girls. It's when children get a bit older that gender comes into play (and into marketing) where toys are concerned. If you've tried hard to keep your child's playthings gender neutral, you may be surprised to find your 2-year-old daughter wants nothing except the items in the pink aisle of the toy store or your son bites his toast into the shape of a gun.

Going with the flow

Should you accept that your child may strongly exhibit the stereotypical mannerisms of his or her gender (if your little boy is incredibly active, for example, or your little girl is fairly subdued)? Of course. But within reason. You shouldn't try to force a child into a different personality altogether, but you can and should step in to teach him or her what's appropriate and what isn't.

Yes, boys will be boys, but a little guy who's constantly beating on other little guys should be reined in. (Natural instincts are one thing; unacceptable behavior is quite another.) If your little girl, on the other hand, is constantly the victim of other toddlers taking things from her, you're well within your rights (and responsibilities) as a parent to teach her to stand up for herself.

Although little people of both sexes seem very similar at this age, each sex has very different hormones running through their veins. These potent chemicals are at least partially responsible for your little girl's nurturing her stuffed toys or your little boy's throwing them.

Now, there's nothing wrong with offering your almost-1-year-old son a play kitchen or your daughter a set of trucks. They'll probably like them, in fact — at least until friends come into the picture, and TV commercials start affecting their vision of life. Some kids are able to shut out these messages; others just truly enjoy playing with the stereotypical toys for their own gender and aren't interested in those meant for the opposite sex.

So when choosing playthings, keep a few things in mind:

- ✔ **Respect your child's choices in playthings.** Don't force toys on your child that he or she doesn't want to play with. If your little boy has no interest in playing with a dollhouse, you can't make him become interested.

- ✔ **You can raise a caring, kind, politically correct child even if he or she isn't accepting of toys that are commonly purchased for the opposite sex.**

- ✔ **Your overall outlook and points of view on issues will carry much more weight in developing Baby's attitudes toward life than any toy will.** If you constantly tell your little girl that she's strong and smart, expect her to view herself that way.

Bringing Up Brainiac

There's a push in our society to have our children stand out from the masses — and to make sure that if a child doesn't demonstrate exceptional abilities on his own, we find her gifts and cultivate them for and with her. Not that there's anything wrong with expecting a child to live up to her potential — indeed, talents should be nurtured and encouraged. The truth is, *every* child has her own unique talents and abilities, and whether a child is labeled as being gifted or not, she should be allowed to explore her own possibilities.

Even if your child doesn't show an aptitude for books and vocabulary, she may be an amazing budding athlete (those climbing kids) or a blossoming musician (the kids who can seriously pick out a little tune on the piano when they're very small). Every child should be supported and encouraged in whatever strengths she has — and as long as you recognize your own child's interests and abilities, she'll develop into a capable person down the line.

Is Baby gifted?

"Gifted" is one of those loaded terms — some children are held up as shining examples while others are labeled as merely "normal." When we hear the word "gifted," we tend to think of a brilliant Baby, one whose mind works levels above our own, a child whom we may never really understand, but who may just grow up to change the world. There are some signs that may indicate — even at this early age — that you've got an extremely bright youngster on your hands. They include:

✔ **A tendency to hit milestones early and with bravado.** This child not only pulled up at 6 months, he walked at 9 months. Now he's running. His motor skills (fine and gross), in general, may be advanced.

✔ **The ability to notice similarities or discrepancies in his world.** He sees a man with brown curly hair in the park and says, "Dada," because his father's hair looks like this. Or if you suddenly stop wearing your glasses, favoring contacts, he'll bring you whatever he can find (maybe your sunglasses) to put on your eyeballs.

✔ **He may have a great sense of humor because he recognizes discrepancies as being funny.** But he could also swing to the opposite end of the spectrum and be a very serious little person because he's just so busy observing everyone and everything.

✔ **He really pays attention to things.** He loves to look at books or have stories read to him, he "sings" along to his favorite music.

✔ **His comprehension is advanced for his age.** At this age, he may understand the concept of "up" and "down," for example, or of "in" and "out," "off" and "on." He also demonstrates a comprehension for language. Sure, he understands what you're saying to him, but he also understands people who don't necessarily talk to him like he's a baby.

✔ **He has mastered all of the toys meant for his age group and needs advanced stimulation.** At the age of almost 1 year, he may be able to solve a puzzle meant for a child six months older without any hesitation.

As Baby moves through the second year, he may continue on this course — he may be a kid who can memorize an entire book upon hearing it once, know his alphabet by the age of 2, or count to 100 by the time he's 2½ Children who exhibit these skills often tend to read and write much earlier than their peers — and often teach themselves these skills.

You can encourage Baby's intellect, but remember that he's a small child. He needs nurturing more than anything else. In other words, follow his lead and resist the urge to push him to accelerate too much. He'll let you know what he's ready for. Here's how you can encourage his burgeoning intellect without going overboard:

- **Provide him with level-appropriate toys.** If he's able to put a simple puzzle together, find one that's a little more difficult. But be careful not to go overboard to the point where you've made playtime so difficult or serious that his own toys overwhelm him. And always check carefully, of course, for choking hazards.

- **Allow him lots of opportunities for seeing the world.** You don't have to hop a flight to far-flung locales; just take him on lots of outings (to the park; to the zoo; to the children's museum; to outdoor concerts or shows — anywhere he can see or do something new) and let him take his time exploring.

- **Talk to him.** This also gives him the opportunity to expand his vocabulary — and you can bet that he will.

- **Continue encouraging whatever it is that he's interested in.** Reading. Music. Puzzles. You can try to diversify your child's interests, too, but stick with his main areas of attention. If you can clearly see that this child has an aptitude for spatial relationships (he's able to actually *build* with his blocks instead of simply piling them on top of each other), let him go with it. But don't label him as the next Frank Lloyd Wright just yet. He may have *other* amazing talents, too. Do your best to uncover them while *keeping* him interested in the blocks.

Raising a Nice Kid

The toddler years are coming and along with them come increasing independence and assertiveness on your child's part. This is a good thing, really — it shows that she's developing her own opinions and ideas, even though she may be driving you a tad bit nutty in the process of expressing herself.

At this point, you become not just a caregiver but also a disciplinarian, and the change in roles may be difficult for both you and your child. Figuring out how to stop the behaviors you don't want and encourage the ones you do takes some trial and error but pays big rewards in the long run. For a more complete look at parenting beyond the first year, read *Parenting For Dummies* by Sandra Hardin Gookin and Dan Gookin (Wiley).

Your goal in disciplining your child is to not only let her know that there are limits and boundaries in your house, but also to help her make the right decisions in the future.

Using age-appropriate discipline

The average 1-year-old has very little understanding of "good" and "bad" behaviors. There's only what feels right, what's fun, and what isn't so fun. So if your daughter has, for the third time today, thrown her meal on the floor, she's most likely doing it because it's fun, at least as far as she's concerned. She's not considering that you have to clean this mess, nor is she thinking about the time and effort you put into preparing her dinner, which the dog is now thoroughly enjoying.

Keep Baby's point of view in mind, and monitor your own expectations of her behavior. Babies are babies — and toddlers are really just older babies. It's unfair and unrealistic to hold them to rigid behavioral standards meant for older kids. This *doesn't* mean that your child should be allowed to run roughshod through your home and the homes of your friends.

Keep in mind that it's far easier to introduce her to your minimum expectations now rather than a year from now, when she'll be going through the *terrible twos* (a normal phase of childhood where Baby discovers that she has very strong opinions that are often contrary to her parents').

Every parent has her own style, but you should steer away from being either way too lax or far too strict. Boundaries are actually comforting to small children, who are faced with a great big world filled with possibilities. Not having anyone to rein them in once in a while means that anything can happen — and that's a scary thought for a little person. It's an old adage, but it's so true: Kids need to know that they have limits, especially as they move into the toddler years.

By having almost no discipline in your own home, you could also set your child up for future social failures, in school or at a playmate's home, where she'll suddenly be faced with a set of rules for acceptable behavior that she's never encountered before.

Conversely, adapting a very strict, regimented style of discipline for your small child could have the effect of making her a very scared, timid person who's afraid to explore her world the way she should.

The following guidelines are tried and true for disciplining toddlers:

✔ **Choose your battles wisely.** Decide which behaviors are important and let the others go. She isn't allowed to draw on the wall. That's a huge issue, and rightly so. Breaking this rule warrants a stronger response than a rule that isn't as important to you (say, making a mess with her blocks).

✔ **Stop certain behaviors before they even start.** If you see her headed for the wall with a crayon, stop her before she realizes that she's a great muralist. Distract her from this activity, and it may never become an issue.

✔ **Stick to your guns and follow through.** Don't stop her from drawing on the wall one day and allow her to do so the next day. Your response to a particular activity should be the same each time it happens, as in the case of Baby tossing her dinner across the room. Switching responses — from very stern one day to not-so-stern the next — only serves to confuse her.

✔ **Use an appropriate level of response.** If she's committed a first offense by drawing on the wall, your reaction should reflect that. Take the crayons away, give her a stern "no," and hand her a cloth so she can "help" wash it off. If she's done this many times over the course of several weeks, your reaction is more stern: The crayons go away, for one thing, and she may have a short *time out,* which at this age consists of you sitting her down for one minute — don't expect her to stay put by herself. She'll probably react strongly to this confinement, and that's the point. You're teaching her that negative behavior has negative consequences — in this case, she's not free to move about as she pleases (which is *everything* to a child this age). After the one-minute mark, she can "help" to clean the crayon off the wall.

Baby's brain is very different from yours — and it takes time for her to get the message that a particular behavior is unacceptable. She may very well continue to do something you've told her not to do ten times, but as long as you're consistent in your message and you follow through in your response, she will eventually understand right from wrong.

Offer your child alternatives to the forbidden behavior. All right, so she can't draw on the wall, but she *can* draw on paper. Don't just tell her what isn't acceptable — show her the right way to do things.

Here are some things to avoid when disciplining a child this age:

✔ **Telling her she's a bad kid.** She's far too young to appreciate the difference between a little angel and a bad seed.

✔ **Yelling.** Again, she's too young for this. When a parent *really* yells at a child this age, the child gets scared. She cries. You'll probably end up comforting her, realizing that you lost it for a second there. The lesson she was supposed to be learning about her behavior is gone. A seriously raised voice should be reserved for only the most dangerous behaviors.

✔ **Making everything into an issue.** You're trying to instill important lessons here about what's acceptable in your house and in society in general — don't dilute your message by correcting everything she does. Let some things slide — at least for now.

✔ **Spanking.** Spanking should be used in only the most extreme — and dangerous —situations. Check out the upcoming "To spank or not to spank?" section for more.

In the end, *you* have to decide which behaviors are acceptable in your home and which aren't. Just remember that children are naturally curious and that they need *guidance* first and foremost. (Baby wasn't born with an internal gauge for determining right from wrong.) Punishment (in the form of time outs at this age) should be reserved for the most important issues so that it doesn't lose its impact.

Tackling tantrums

A 12-month-old who throws himself on the ground and screams because he's displeased with something in his little life is about a year ahead of schedule. You thought you had another year before you had to deal with the horrors of the terrible twos — and now you're scared to death of what your tantrum-throwing child will be like 12 months from now.

The main culprits for throwing little people into big tailspins include:

✔ **Fatigue or hunger:** If Baby seems to be unhappy at certain times of the day, he may just need a snack or a nap. Try keeping track of his grumpy times while observing him. Is he angry and looking beat? Put him in his crib for a while. Or, if it's been hours since he had lunch, offer him some fruit or cereal. His mood may change drastically (and for the better).

✔ **Frustration:** Not being able to accomplish a task or communicate your needs is incredibly frustrating. Try helping Baby out or temporarily removing a toy that's upsetting him.

✔ **Not feeling well:** If he's had a cold or virus lately and is really feeling out of sorts, he may just need some extra comfort from Mom or Dad. He may also need extra rest.

✔ **Not understanding why he can't have what he wants *now:*** Baby's still-developing brain can't quite handle the concept of delayed gratification. Not much you can do about this except ride out the storm.

Temperament, temperament: Hypersensitivity and tantrums

Kids who suffered through colic may be more prone to throwing tantrums as toddlers. Research suggests that these kids may simply be hypersensitive to the world around them. Things that wouldn't bother other kids their age — bunched-up socks or a funny smelling dinner — can set off kids whose senses are set to a "high" level. For more on this subject, see Chapter 8.

Before you label this child as "difficult" or "unhappy," realize that sensitivity is just part of his make-up; this is simply who he is. He can no more change his level of sensitivity than you

can — and right now, he's too young to tone down his reaction to certain things.

A little prevention can go a long way with a child like this: Make sure his clothes are comfortable, that his beloved blanket is in his crib at naptime, and that his schedule doesn't go through any major upheavals if at all possible. These are things that any 1-year-old would be miffed over; the highly sensitive kid may just be pushed over the edge into a tantrum, and if you can stop it before it happens, both of you will be happier.

The best tactic for dealing with a 1-year-old's tantrum is to simply ignore it. Easier said than done, sure, but chances are if you don't pay too much attention to his fit, he'll stop in a relatively short time. You can then act as though it never happened, instead of chastising him for this behavior, which isn't going to help at this age. He won't understand why you're angry with him, and he'll either be frightened by your tone of voice or he'll ignore it altogether. (Either way, he's not learning anything from your lecture.) Just avoid the urge to give into this behavior, if Baby is having a tantrum over something you've taken away from him, for example. If he learns that all he has to do in order to get his way is to throw himself on the floor and scream, you'll be dealing with these tactics for years to come. (Charming, it ain't.)

Before you ignore a tantrum, however, assess the situation. If Baby is already a hitter or a thrower, make sure he doesn't have anything around him that he could harm or that could harm him (a window, for example) if he decides to pull out all the stops. He's probably not strong enough to do too much damage at this point, but it's better not to take the chance.

To spank or not to spank?

You were raised in a house where a little spanking went a long way, and so you see nothing wrong with a well-timed smack to Baby's bottom when she needs it.

Most child-rearing experts disagree with this point of view — but there are plenty of parents who feel that spanking, when used correctly, is an effective form of discipline. This is a debate that has been going on for years and another one of those parenting issues that divides its advocates and critics into clearly delineated camps.

Experts shun spanking for several reasons:

✔ Spanking may stop the child from doing whatever he's doing, but it doesn't teach the child an appropriate action in its place.

✔ Spanking a child may damage his self-esteem, as he's often left feeling confused, embarrassed, and angry.

✔ Kids who are spanked seem to get better at not getting caught, but don't necessarily stop the offensive behavior.

Proponents of spanking, on the other hand, point out that toddler-aged children can't be reasoned with, and they feel that spanking is an appropriate measure for teaching children what's acceptable and what isn't. Many parents (and even some of the experts) feel that spanking should be used sparingly and *only* in situations where Baby has placed herself in danger so that she'll get the immediate message not to repeat the behavior. When she's older and capable of understanding why she can't play in the road, you can explain the danger to her.

Try one of these alternatives to spanking:

✔ **Physically remove your child from a situation.** If it's time to leave a play date, for example, and your child refuses to comply with your order to come along with you, pick him up and put him in the car. That's the beauty of being the bigger person in this relationship.

✔ **Use a series of distractions or diversions.** Helping him switch gears (and move from jumping on the couch to playing nicely on the floor with toys) may stop the behavior and give him an acceptable alternative.

✔ **Put yourself on his level.** For serious or dangerous infractions, like reaching up toward a hot stove, get down to his eye level, hold his hands, and sternly tell him no. He'll realize by the tone of your voice that you're serious.

✔ **Make sure you don't set him up for failure.** He's a kid. He needs supervision. Your house needs to be kid-proofed. Leaving your priceless antique teacups on the coffee table and spanking him when he shatters them just isn't fair. Do your part to prevent putting him in situations where he can't win.

Your job is to teach your child right from wrong. Using spanking as your only form of discipline is a far cry from getting involved and showing him what kinds of behaviors are acceptable, and could have serious, long-lasting effects on his self-esteem. You also run the risk of damaging the relationship between yourself and your child and of having a kid who learns to hit others as the main way of resolving conflict.

Part VI
Protecting Baby's Health and Safety

The 5th Wave   By Rich Tennant

"Your baby's fussiness, whining, and general discontent isn't anything to worry about. It should clear up on it's own in about 18 years."

In this part . . .

The signs of illness can sometimes be difficult to recognize. In this part, we discuss some of the more common first-year illnesses, let you know when to call the doctor, and tell you how to help Baby at home. We also fill you in on the benefits of immunizing Baby. This section also includes a discussion of the special-needs baby. We give you a good idea of what to expect if your child must visit the neonatal intensive care unit.

We also include a chapter giving you advice on what to do when Baby hurts himself. We give you advice on how to handle these situations to best help your child. Hint: Stay calm! We tell you what to keep in your first-aid kit and let you know how to treat bumps, bruises, and burns. We also tell you when you need to call the doctor.

Keeping Baby healthy extends to keeping him safe, and baby-proofing your home is a major project you never quite finish. Find out how to make your home as safe as possible.

Chapter 18

Keeping Baby Healthy

*W*hen Baby first arrives, her immune system is still maturing. Breastfeeding boosts her immunities to some things (she's protected from certain allergies, for example, and she's less likely to suffer from ear infections and certain skin disorders), but unfortunately, there's no magic supplement to keep her germ-free for life. She'll eventually catch her first cold, and you'll suffer right along with her, feeling her misery. This chapter will explain some of the most common first-year ailments and how to treat them.

Preventing Illness with Immunizations

During the first year, most of Baby's checkups will often include at *least* one shot. If you've never been a big fan of needles, you can't stand to see Baby cry, or you've been reading some information that suggests that immunizations can do more harm than good, you may be thinking about opting Baby out of his shots.

Don't.

Though serious adverse reactions to immunizations do occur, they're very rare. The chances of Baby becoming ill because he missed out on his shots are far greater. If you're feeling as though immunizing Baby is akin to gambling with his life, the opposite is actually true.

Times have changed since you were a kid, and the newest vaccines provide protection from illnesses that were fairly common not too long ago (measles, chickenpox, ear infections). You may wonder, then, whether modern medicine has gone too far — are doctors immunizing children *too* much? Not when you consider the potential hazards of these illnesses. Measles and chronic ear infections, for example, can lead to hearing loss, and chickenpox can lead to pneumonia and *encephalitis* (swelling of the brain). Mumps can cause male sterility. Pneumococcal meningitis can cause permanent hearing loss or death.

Side effects of immunizations are rarely severe, and most often include pain, redness, and swelling at the injection site; fever; sleepiness; and crankiness. Your doctor or nurse will advise you on pain relief measures and more serious side effects to watch for.

Baby has a whole slew of shots in her near future. Table 18-1 contains a list of the common immunizations and what they protect against.

Table 18-1	First Year Immunization Schedule	
Vaccine	*Purpose*	*Age*
Hepatitis B (HBV)	Provides lifelong defense against hepatitis B, which can cause liver damage and cancer in adulthood.	#1: Birth to 2 months #2: 1 to 4 months #3: 6 to 18 months
DTaP	A three-in-one shot that protects Baby from diphtheria, tetanus, and pertussis (whooping cough).	#1: 2 months #2: 4 months #3: 6 to 18 months
Hib	Protects against Hemophilus influenza B, which can cause meningitis and other serious (and potentially fatal) bacterial infections.	#1: 2 months #2: 4 months #3: 6 months #4: 12-15 months
IPV	Polio vaccine.	#1: 2 months #2: 4 months #3: 6 months or 15 months

Vaccine	Purpose	Age
PCV	Pneumococcal conjugate vaccine. Pneumococcol bacteria can cause pneumonia, meningitis, and ear infections.	#1: 2 months #2: 4 months #3: 6 months #4: 12-15 months
MMR	Protection against measles, mumps, and rubella (German measles). Each of these illnesses can have quite serious complications.	12-15 months
Varicella	Provides immunity to chickenpox, which also carries the risk of serious side effects and/or complications. (Now required for admittance to school in some states.)	12-15 months

One more vaccine for you: Because complications from the flu can be very serious, especially in young children, pediatricians strongly recommend the flu vaccine for children between the ages of 6 months and 2 years. If Baby is younger than 6 months when flu season hits, doctors recommend that the rest of the family be immunized to prevent any flu in the house.

Outlining the First-Year Ailments

Baby wakes up one morning with a stuffy nose and cough. Before the week is out, she's crabby and has a fever. What's going on with her, and what can you do to help her feel better? Despite your very best efforts, you can count on the fact that your child is going to get sick from time to time. Infants are also prone to skin conditions that will have *you* scratching your head trying to figure out what's going on. This section gives you information on the most common first-year sicknesses and rashes, how to treat symptoms, and when to call the doctor.

You can't keep Baby isolated from every ailment, but you can prevent some of them by practicing good hygiene. Keep in mind that germs lurk on your hands and in your nose! Handwashing is the key to stopping the spread of germs.

Recognizing common illnesses

During her first year, Baby will be exposed to a host of brand new (to her, anyway) germs. She'll be able to fight some of them off, but others will take hold and leave her feeling down and out. The following sections list some common first-year illnesses, their symptoms, how to treat them, and when to call the doctor.

Common cold

- ✔ **Symptoms:** Runny or stuffy nose, cough, low-grade fever during the first 48 hours (100 or below), loss of appetite, sleepiness. Contagious.

- ✔ **Treatment:** Symptomatic. Treat runny or stuffy nose, cough, and fever with over-the-counter cold medicine (call your doctor for recommendations and dosage information). A cool-mist humidifier may be helpful in Baby's bedroom to keep his nasal passages moist (and free from further irritation).

- ✔ **Call the doctor:** If fever is above 100.5 degrees and baby is younger than three months, if fever in an older baby is 101 degrees for 3 days, if cough becomes constant, if loss of appetite continues or increases (may be signs of infection). Most common secondary infection is otitis media (see the "Otitis media" section).

Conjunctivitis (Pinkeye)

- ✔ **Symptoms:** Crusty, oozing, itchy, bloodshot eye(s). Very contagious from person-to-person and from eye-to-eye.

- ✔ **Treatment:** Warm eye soaks (a clean wash cloth soaked in lukewarm water) will clean the eye and alleviate irritation.

- ✔ **Call the doctor:** Pinkeye is usually short-lived and resolves itself. However, it often needs treatment with antibiotic eye drops or ointment (available only by prescription, which means a doctor visit) so that a child can return to day care.

Croup

- ✔ **Symptoms:** Barking cough, hoarseness, wheezing, difficulty breathing, fever. Croup is a virus that narrows baby's airway. It tends to strike at night, panicking parents and children alike. Croup is contagious.

- ✔ **Treatment:** Turn on the hot water and let your bathroom steam up. Steam or cold night air work wonders for opening up Baby's airway. (If one isn't working, try the other without delay.) Keep baby calm. Anxiety tends to worsen the situation. Use a humidifier in Baby's room until croup clears up.

✔ **Call the doctor:** *Immediately* if Baby is clearly struggling for breath, if his lips are blue, or if steam/cold air treatments aren't working within several minutes. You may be advised to take Baby to the emergency room.

Gastroenteritis

✔ **Symptoms:** Fever, nausea, vomiting, watery diarrhea.

✔ **Treatment:** Continue feeding Baby normally (is he's breastfed, keep nursing; if he's on solids, he may not have much interest in food, but offer it to him anyway). Increase his fluids to prevent dehydration. Frequent, small amounts of fluid are best. If Baby doesn't urinate often, call the doctor immediately.

✔ **Call the doctor:** If Baby appears to be dehydrated (shows signs of excessive thirst, dry mouth and tongue, irritability, dry diapers for hours on end, sunken soft spot or eyes, restlessness or lethargy), call your pediatrician immediately.

Hand-foot-mouth disease (Coxsackie virus)

✔ **Symptoms:** Fever, possibly sore throat, loss of appetite. Tiny blisters appear on Baby's palms, soles, and/or the inside of his mouth (also may appear on his bottom or on other parts of his body). The mouth lesions are very painful. Contagious.

✔ **Treatment:** Symptomatic for babies with mouth lesions. Pain reliever may help. For the older baby on solid foods, keep his diet cold and soft.

✔ **Call the doctor:** You can call to describe Baby's symptoms and rule out other illnesses.

Influenza (Flu)

✔ **Symptoms:** Sudden onset of fever, chills, lethargy, cough. Baby *looks* ill. (His eyes are glazed and have circles underneath them; he's pale; he has little energy.) May be clingy and/or miserable. Contagious.

✔ **Treatment:** Symptomatic. Increase fluids, as babies tend to dehydrate quickly.

✔ **Call the doctor:** Baby should be seen if he looks and/or acts terribly ill (he's either inconsolable or completely lacking energy). Your pediatrician will want to evaluate Baby and test him for influenza. (This is done to rule out sepsis, meningitis, or pneumonia, all of which can produce symptoms similar to those of influenza.)

Otitis media (Ear infection)

✔ **Symptoms:** Usually follows or coincides with a cold or allergy congestion. Baby has a fever, is having difficulty sleeping. May refuse to nurse or take his bottle due to pain. Bacterial infection; not contagious.

✔ **Treatment:** Pain reliever and antibiotic. A warm compress may help alleviate the pain and pressure until Baby is feeling better. Wrap a moist, warm washcloth in a plastic baggie, wrap *that* in a thin towel, and lay Baby on affected side.

✔ **Call the doctor:** Call if Baby has symptoms and has recently had a cold.

Pneumonia

✔ **Symptoms:** Baby starts out with a cold, which gets worse. He has a fever. Cough is persistent and productive. He may be wheezing. There are two types of pneumonia: viral, which is contagious, and bacterial, which is not.

✔ **Treatment:** Symptomatic for fever and aches. Over-the-counter pain reliever is recommended for both. Call your doctor for dosing information.

✔ **Call the doctor:** Call for breathing difficulty, rapid breathing, or wheezing. Check with doctor before giving a cough suppressant (you may be advised to use it only at night). Increase fluids. Doctor may prescribe an antibiotic.

Respiratory syncytial virus (RSV) infection

✔ **Symptoms:** Cold symptoms, cough (lasting more than two weeks in some cases), labored or rapid breathing. Infants may be irritable or lethargic. Decrease in appetite. Symptoms can last from a few days to a few weeks. Very common and very contagious. Premature babies and babies who have chronic lung disease are at risk for developing serious (even life-threatening) complications from RSV.

✔ **Treatment:** Symptomatic. Your focus is on making sure Baby can breathe easily. To that end, eliminate any irritants (smoke, cold air, and so on) and consider using a vaporizer in his bedroom.

✔ **Call the doctor:** Call your pediatrician if you suspect RSV, because the virus can occasionally cause significant respiratory distress, which may require specific therapy (such as bronchodilator meds) or monitoring in the hospital. Your pediatrician can also test for RSV to confirm the diagnosis.

Roseola infantum

✔ **Symptoms:** Baby just doesn't feel well. Fever, runny nose, loss of appetite. He seems to be feeling better, and suddenly, he's got spots! They're pink, and they're everywhere. Contagious when the fever is present; once spots appear, no longer contagious.

✔ **Treatment:** Symptomatic, until the spots appear. After he's got the rash, he's probably feeling better, anyway.

✔ **Call the doctor:** Call to describe symptoms and rash, to confirm the diagnosis. Also call if fever persists, or if Baby doesn't seem to be feeling better.

There are, of course, other illnesses lurking out there (on the handle of the grocery cart, in the air at the doctor's office, on the table of your very own home). Don't feel silly about calling your pediatrician when Baby is sick, even if it turns out to be a mild illness in the end. Your doctor will realize that you're a mom, and he won't think any less of you for having your child's best interest at heart.

Your baby's doctor won't prescribe an antibiotic unless Baby has a bacterial infection. This is sometimes a complication of a virus (as in the case of an ear infection — Baby initially gets sick from a virus, and the congestion leads to a bacterial infection in his ear), but they're two separate entities. An antibiotic won't cure a viral infection; it has to run its course. Overuse (or misuse) of antibiotics leads to new antibiotic-resistant strains of bacteria. The bottom line here: If Baby doesn't have some sort of bacterial infection, your doctor won't (and shouldn't) give him an antibiotic.

Chafing, itching, and scratching

As though the runny noses and the fevers aren't enough, every now and then, Baby may turn up with strange skin issues. Moms often learn through trial and error that treating a rash incorrectly can make matters worse — and sometimes the only treatment is no treatment (as in the case of infant acne). In this section, we go over common infant skin problems and the best ways to care for them.

Cradle cap

✔ **Appearance:** Flaky or crusty patches of dry skin on Baby's head. Can be quite thick. Not contagious, just unpleasant to look at. May also be itchy.

✔ **Treatment:** For mild cases, try mineral oil or petroleum jelly (and a comb) to loosen the scales while bathing baby. Tougher cases may require the use of special shampoos and/or ointments, especially if cradle cap has spread to Baby's face and neck. For more on treating cradle cap, see Chapter 6.

Diaper rash

✔ **Appearance:** Raised or flat red patches on Baby's bottom. If it occurs on the buttocks or labia, it's called *contact dermatitis;* diaper rash that appears as small pink or red dots around the edges of the rash in the creases of the skin is *candida* (yeast infection).

✔ **Treatment:** For contact dermatitis, protect Baby's skin with diaper ointment. Use antifungal cream (available over the counter) on candida.

Eczema

- **Appearance:** Itchy, red, bumpy, oozing or weeping, crusty, painful, tiny red bumps. Usually appears on Baby's chin or cheeks and in a family with a history of eczema.

- **Treatment:** Consult doctor for persistent cases of eczema. Treatment may consist of applying unscented skin cream, changing your laundry detergent, limiting baths, changing Baby's diet, and/or using a topical steroid ointment.

Heat rash

- **Appearance:** Bright red rash around neck, armpits, or diaper.

- **Treatment:** Cool Baby off by removing a layer of clothing or giving a cool bath.

Hives

- **Appearance:** Itchy, raised welts on the skin. May be red and widespread.

- **Treatment:** Hives are sometimes due to an allergy; sometimes they have no apparent cause. Call your pediatrician to rule out allergic reaction. Calamine lotion helps to soothe itchiness.

Impetigo

- **Appearance:** Yellowish crusty blisters that break; weeping skin underneath. Very contagious if not treated properly.

- **Treatment:** Call your doctor if you suspect impetigo. Antibiotic skin ointment will be prescribed. Change and wash any bedding or clothing that may have been exposed to the blisters.

Milia

- **Appearance:** Teeny white or yellow dots on Baby's face. Usually pops up in the first two weeks of life (if at all).

- **Treatment:** None. Goes away on its own.

Neonatal acne

- **Appearance:** Tiny pimples on Baby's face. Usually appears between 2 weeks and 6 months.

- **Treatment:** None. Even if you can't stand to look at it, leave it alone. It will clear up on its own. Scrubbing the pimples with soap won't get rid of them, and may make them worse.

Taking Baby's Temperature

Sooner or later, you have to pull out the thermometer you got at your baby shower and use it on your baby. You have two options when taking an infant's temperature: You can take it rectally or under the armpit (which your doctor will call an *axillary temperature*).

A rectal temp is the most accurate because it actually measures Baby's temperature from inside her body. Axillary temps can be off by half a degree or more, depending on the temperature taker's skills. For a baby 3 months old or younger, rectal temps are usually recommended. You can take Baby's temp in the armpit after this age, but *always make sure you tell your pediatrician how you took the temperature*. He'll decide how to evaluate it.

Generally speaking, a doctor will subtract a degree from a rectal temp and add a degree to an axillary temp. Doing this will usually get you in the ballpark range of Baby's true temperature.

So how do you take a rectal temperature? First, be calm. Baby's not feeling well, and she needs a cool, collected parent to reassure her that everything's just fine. For obvious reasons, mark this thermometer for rectal use only. To take the temp:

1. **Wash off the tip of the thermometer and lubricate the end.**

2. **Lay Baby on her side on a safe surface.**

3. **Insert the thermometer in about ½ inch.** Never force the thermometer in, and don't insert it any further than ½ inch.

4. **When the thermometer beeps, remove it.** Read the temperature.

To take an axillary temp, again make sure Baby is quiet and calm. Here's what to do:

1. **Lay her down and remove her shirt.**

2. **Put the thermometer in the center of her armpit and then hold her arm to her side.** It's important to get a good "seal" in her armpit in order to get the most accurate reading.

3. **Hold her in this position for several minutes (usually four to five minutes, depending on the brand you use).** The thermometer will beep before that; ignore it and do anything you can think of to amuse this child so that you won't have to start all over again.

4. **When the time is up, remove the thermometer and read the temperature.**

Babies aren't old enough to have their temperatures taken orally (in the mouth). Remember, taking a temperature requires cooperation. Your infant just isn't capable of sitting still and keeping the thermometer under her tongue right now.

If you need to actually go out and buy a thermometer, you'll be faced with several choices. Obviously, if you need to take Baby's temperature, you don't want to fool around with thermometers that won't do the job correctly. Here's the lowdown on what you'll find:

- ✔ **Digital thermometers:** Best during Baby's first year. Very, very easy to use, and generally pretty reliable. Find a reputable brand (B-D is a good one), and have two or three on hand. Label one for rectal use only.

- ✔ **Ear thermometers:** Very popular these days, and very easy to use. However, a child has to be able to sit still in order to get an accurate reading, and a baby's ear canal may be too short and too flexible for an accurate reading. For these reasons, ear thermometers shouldn't be used during baby's first year.

- ✔ **Mercury (glass) thermometers:** Generally discouraged by doctors nowadays, because there are so many other safer choices. There's a risk of mercury poisoning if the glass breaks (not to mention the risks involved with broken glass).

- ✔ **Forehead strips:** Not all that reliable, and so not all that recommendable.

- ✔ **Pacifier thermometers:** The problem here is that taking an infant's temperature requires cooperation. If you have a baby who is screaming in pain from an ear infection, she's probably not going to take that pacifier (because the sucking will only hurt her ear more).

Sneezing and Wheezing: When Allergies or Asthma Enter the Picture

If you're a sneezer or wheezer (or your baby's other parent happens to be one), be on the lookout for allergies and asthma in your child, particularly if your allergies developed in childhood. Some of these conditions are thought to have a hereditary link. The good news is that children often outgrow allergies and asthma; the not-so-good news is that they can cause misery while they're around. This section will tell you what to look for and what you can expect from Baby's allergies or asthma.

Environmental allergies

Baby's been sniffling for weeks on end. Does he have a cold, or is it a seasonal or indoor allergy? Even when you're the one experiencing the symptoms, it can be hard to differentiate between the two. Generally speaking, though, some telltale signs of allergies are:

- ✔ **Duration:** A cold will usually clear up in 10 to 14 days; allergies linger, sometimes throughout a season (if it's a seasonal allergy) and sometimes even longer (if the culprit is a pet or household dust).

- ✔ **Sneezing:** Nasal irritation is really common with allergies.

- ✔ **Thin, clear drainage from his nose:** Nasal discharge from a cold tends to be yellow or green, and thick.

- ✔ **Dark circles under the eyes:** Also, redness and itchiness in and around the eyes.

- ✔ **Itchy nose:** May be indicated by Baby rubbing his nose with his hand or rubbing it on something.

- ✔ **Dry cough:** Due to postnasal drip.

- ✔ **Rash:** Indicates a sensitivity to an allergen.

- ✔ **A tendency to breathe through the mouth:** Because Baby's poor little nose is stuffy.

The predisposition for allergies is inherited in many cases. Because allergies develop over a period of many months (and repeated exposure), environmental allergies are not as common in babies as food allergies are.

If you suspect Baby has an allergy and can't find any obvious cause, call your pediatrician. He may recommend taking Baby to an allergist for testing.

Finding food allergies

Introducing food to Baby is an exciting step during the first year, but remain aware of food allergies and the types of symptoms they can cause. The most common allergy-causing foods are cow's milk, strawberries, egg whites, wheat, and soy. Shellfish and peanuts can also cause allergies, triggering severe (even life-threatening) reactions in some cases, and most doctors recommend that you avoid feeding these to Baby during his first year of life. For more information on food allergies, see Chapter 11.

Common reactions that indicate a food allergy include:

- A rash
- Itchy mouth
- Gastrointestinal distress (cramps, diarrhea, vomiting)
- Wheezing
- Hives
- Runny nose
- Abnormal crying

A more severe reaction called *anaphylactic shock* involves some of the above symptoms (cramping, hives, a tingly feeling in the mouth, especially if the allergen is a nut) as well as difficulty breathing, a loss of consciousness, and possibly death. If you notice that your child is reacting severely to a food, get him to the hospital without delay.

Studies suggest that introducing solids to infants before their digestive systems can handle it (before 4 to 6 months) may actually cause certain food allergies. In any event, try to introduce one food at a time, waiting several days before introducing another new food so that if a reaction does occur, you can easily pinpoint the cause.

Identifying asthma

Baby may wheeze for all sorts of reasons, and not all of them indicate that she is asthmatic. Many viruses can further narrow an infant's already-small airway and cause her to wheeze. However, *asthma* (a lung condition in which overly-sensitive airways constrict in reaction to an irritant) is definitely on the rise in this country, and whether it's because of an increase in environmental causes (such as pollution) or because it's being diagnosed earlier and better than in past generations, the fact is it's the most-diagnosed chronic condition in children.

Because infants' lung capacity can't be measured effectively, it's difficult to diagnose asthma until a child is a bit older and able to cooperate in lung function testing. Wheezing is a common symptom. Rapid breathing, and overuse of the chest and neck muscles while inhaling are other asthma indicators. Many doctors take a family history into consideration when determining an infant's symptoms: Do the child's parents have asthma? Does this child have other allergies? These conditions make asthma more likely.

The mayhem milk may cause

There's sometimes a bit of confusion between milk allergy and lactose intolerance. A *milk allergy* is actually caused by the body's immune system reacting adversely to the proteins in milk; lactose *intolerance,* on the other hand, occurs when the body is missing an enzyme needed to digest the sugar in cow's milk or in formula. If Baby is allergic to milk, he may develop hives, eczema, bloating, diarrhea, blood in the stool, nausea, and vomiting. Lactose intolerance tends to cause the gastrointestinal upset without the skin reactions. The good news is that most children will outgrow a milk allergy by about 18 months. Lactose intolerance, however, may persist.

Treatment for infants with asthma usually entails using a *nebulizer,* a machine that vaporizes asthma medicine so that the child can easily inhale it.

Be aware that infants may wheeze for reasons other than asthma. Babies have smaller airways than older children, and a bout with an upper respiratory virus may be enough to make Baby sound like he's whistling while he breathes. Nevertheless, call your pediatrician if Baby is wheezing; the doctor can make the determination as to the cause.

Correcting Crossed or Lazy Eyes

During Baby's regular checkups, she'll be screened for the most common infant vision problems, *strabismus* (crossed eyes) and *amblyopia* (sometimes called "lazy eye"). (For an example of what strabismus looks like, see Figure 18-1.)

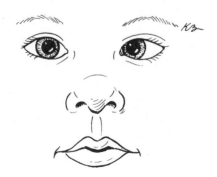

Figure 18-1:
Strabismus
in an infant.

Parents sometimes notice that something seems amiss with Baby's eyes. Maybe one is crossing, or one is slower to track an object than the other eye is. If you're concerned about Baby's vision, make sure to mention it to your pediatrician during your next visit. Depending on Baby's age and how severe your doctor judges the problem to be, he may recommend sending Baby to an ophthalmologist right away, where a more in-depth exam of the eyes can be done.

The good news is that when these conditions are diagnosed early, they're very treatable with glasses, surgery, or a combination of both. (Allowing them to go untreated, on the other hand, may result in the loss of vision in one eye). Family history tends to play a part in the diagnosis of these particular vision problems.

Loving Your Special Needs Child

Some parents go into the delivery room knowing that there's a problem with the pregnancy and that their child will be born with an abnormality; for others, a birth defect or premature labor comes as a complete shock. Either way, accepting the reality of having a sick child can be extremely difficult. In fact, it's every parent's worst fear come true.

Regardless of whether you had forewarning about Baby's condition, you can't truly prepare yourself for this experience. You may feel devastated, terrified, angry, or guilty, thinking that you could have done something to prevent this from happening. Accept your feelings. Allow yourself to be angry or sad — but don't try to handle overpowering emotions on your own. Look for support — from your partner, from family members, from a support group, or from a therapist or counselor.

Keep in mind during this difficult time that becoming a parent can be an overwhelming experience, even when a child is completely healthy. Knowing that your child — for whom you feel completely responsible — may have to endure even a short period of illness and/or discomfort can make you feel like the entire world is crashing down around you. This isn't what you expected. It isn't fair. You'd change places with Baby in a nanosecond if you could.

Get information on your child's condition. Knowing what to expect can help ease your mind — often, what you fear may happen to your child is worse than coming to terms with the reality of his condition. The March of Dimes provides parents with pertinent information on birth defects; there are also national groups presenting information on specific conditions — the Spina

Bifida Association of America, for example. You can ask your doctor or NICU staff for the names of groups they recommend. Also check out your local library and the Internet, if you have a connection.

After the initial shock and fear subside, you'll feel that bond between parent and child begin to grow — don't let fear stop you from holding, talking to, and most importantly, loving Baby. No matter what his prognosis is, he's your child, and this is your parenting experience. There's no point in comparing it to what you expected (even parents of healthy newborns have to let go of predelivery fantasies). Cherish him for who he is — your precious child.

Birth defects

Many birth defects can be prevented. Folic acid is an incredibly effective preventive measure — some estimates state that as many as 75 percent of neural tube defects (including spina bifida) can be prevented by adequate intake of folic acid during pregnancy. Other recommendations include:

- ✔ Wait to get pregnant until any underlying medical conditions (such as diabetes or seizures) are under control.

- ✔ Avoid alcohol and tobacco in the months prior to and during pregnancy.

- ✔ Avoid illicit drugs (you hate to think it, but many people think marijuana is no big deal).

- ✔ Lead a healthy lifestyle during pregnancy. Eat well, get plenty of rest, and follow an exercise plan.

- ✔ Talk to your obstetrician before taking any prescription or over-the-counter drugs during pregnancy.

But, of course, not every birth defect is preventable. If your child is born with an abnormality, your may want to curl up and disappear — but you *must* deal with what's happening. Although your child is in good hands with the hospital staff, you're his number one advocate. You need to find out what can be done to minimize the effects of his condition.

Depending on your child's specific condition, he may need the intervention of several specialists, including medical specialists and physical, speech, or occupational therapists. Providing him with early care can have a profound effect on the quality of his life. A child who is born with clubfoot, for example, may benefit most by being treated as early as possible, even in his earliest weeks and months. Left untreated, the foot may not grow properly; the child will be limited in his activities; and his emotional state may suffer because he's different from his peers.

Other birth defects are obviously more severe and their long-term effects can be far more devastating, as in severe cases of spina bifida. But many children can be taught to care for themselves to a large degree — and the earlier they're taught, the more successful they're bound to be. The level of self-care a child is able to undertake also affects his level of self-esteem by giving him a measure of control.

Premature births

A child born three or more weeks before her due date is considered premature (often called a *preemie*). There are differing degrees of prematurity, of course, and a child who is born at 35 weeks gestation is going to suffer far fewer short- and long-term effects than a child who is born at 30 weeks. Simply put, the longer Baby stays in the womb, the more time she has to finish the business of developing her internal organs and nervous system — the areas that are most often seriously affected by premature birth.

A premature child's weight is measured in grams instead of pounds; preemies can fall anywhere between 500 grams (about 1 pound) and 2,500 grams (about 5½ pounds). The more a preemie weighs at birth, the better. One problem that's common to premature infants is their lack of body fat — something we all need for insulation. Premature babies just can't regulate their body heat, even if they're wrapped up in a nice, warm blanket. This is why you see preemies in incubators or radiant warmers.

Feeding difficulties are another common issue with preemies. A child who is born prior to 32 to 34 weeks hasn't developed the sucking reflex necessary for breast- or bottlefeeding. Because preemies also have immature digestive systems and are at risk for an infection of the intestine, they often need to be fed through a tube inserted through the nose into the stomach.

A baby born prior to her due date will be catching up on those weeks for some time to come. Take a look at a child who has been born two months early: The parents of this child would subtract two months from their child's age to determine where she is developmentally. For example, at 4 months, she'll be doing what a typical 2-month-old can do. Children catch up at different times, depending on the severity of their conditions. Some catch up within the first couple of years; some will always lag behind a bit.

Getting to know the NICU

Most new parents don't expect to spend Baby's first few days or weeks in the Neonatal Intensive Care Unit (NICU) — but it happens in cases of serious birth defects and premature births. With all the life-saving equipment, high-tech gadgets, and medical jargon whirring all around you, you may feel over-whelmed. Babies in the NICU are often hooked up to monitors and feeding tubes, and are sometimes placed in incubators. In some cases, holding your newborn may be impossible because of health concerns. Your doctors will explain exactly how much contact is allowed between you and your baby.

Although all new parents have many questions for their doctors and nurses, the parents of a child who is in the NICU may feel too stunned to speak — or too scared to ask anything of anyone. The staff in the NICU will help your entire family through this experience; they know how difficult and frightening it is to have a sick newborn. They will welcome your questions and do their best to answer them, so don't be afraid to ask. If you do run across someone who doesn't seem inclined to answer your questions, ask someone else. Keep asking until you get a satisfactory answer. Remember: You are your child's number one advocate, and you have every right to know what's going on with her condition.

The good news is that medical science continues to forge new paths in the treatment of birth defects and premature births. In the past decade, the age of a viable premature fetus has dropped from 27 weeks to 23, and new advances in the study and management of birth defects are being made all the time. Your baby is in a safe place with a very competent and caring staff.

Your *neonatologist* is a pediatrician who has spent four years in med school, three years in a pediatric residency, and another three years studying neona-tology, the care of sick newborns and infants. Most large NICUs have a team of neonatologists working around the clock, along with dozens of well-trained nurses, several respiratory and physical therapists, and a nutritionist. Your child will be well-assessed and receive all the care that she needs.

Most NICUs allow parents to visit 24 hours a day, but may have restrictions on other family members, particularly small children. Check the visitation policy before bringing a younger sibling by to see the baby.

Forging the connection

Parents of children who are born with birth defects often feel left out of the "new baby scene," because their children tend to have developmental delays. Your parenting experience will differ from the average mom and dad on the street; in addition, you may be faced with difficult personal situations. You're not alone. This section addresses some of the things you may be experiencing at this time and suggests ways to move through them.

By this time, you've probably accepted and have figured out how to cope with your child's specific health problems and special needs. If you haven't, though, or if each day is bringing you only sadness or depression, you must seek professional help in the form of a therapist, counselor, or support group. No one is going to chide you for feeling the way you do, but you need to move toward acceptance — for your sake as well as your child's.

It's easy for parents of special needs kids to get overwhelmed (and stay that way); it's normal to feel angry or sad from time to time; you may even question whether you love this child as much as you *would* have if he had been born without any problems.

It can be extremely difficult to let go of the images you formed while you were pregnant: You had the perfect baby in the perfect home, and everyone was happy, happy, happy. Realize that this *was* just a fantasy (because even parents of comparatively healthy children sometimes have a very difficult time settling into life as parents) and discover how to live in the here and now. You've been dealt *this* hand of cards: What are you going to do with it?

Depression is a common reaction, especially if your child needs constant medical care (or intermittent testing or surgery). Recognize what you can handle on your own, and when it may be time to seek out professional advice. And then do it. You have nothing to lose, and everything to gain in the process.

Don't know where to find a good therapist or counselor? You can start by asking your primary physician or your child's pediatrician. You may also begin by calling your health insurance company for a list of providers and then ask your doctor for his recommendations based on the names on that list. Your pediatrician may be able to lead you in the general direction of a support group.

Keeping your relationship with your mate together also becomes a major issue when dealing with a child who has special needs, especially if one or both of you are the primary caregiver to a child who needs constant care. Look for ways to help one another, accept outside offers of assistance, talk to each other about how you're feeling, and look for a couples' therapist if you need to. You can work this and get past these feelings of doubt and sadness, and you can do so together.

Dealing with the public

"What's wrong with your baby?" Kind of makes your stomach churn and your hair stand up on end, doesn't it? Although this may be nothing new to you at this point, especially if your child's birth defect or special needs are physically apparent, as time goes on, the developmental differences between your child and other kids may become more pronounced. You'll no doubt be faced with answering this question at some point — and the questioner may not be a complete clod, which will probably only upset you more — you wonder how anyone who seems like a decent enough person could be so insensitive. (Because, in fact, you know there's nothing *wrong* with your child — he has health issues that most kids don't have. That simply makes him different.)

So how do you answer this question? It depends on a few things:

- ✔ **Who's asking:** Obviously, you're obliged to be a bit more open with family members and close friends than with total strangers. First, you know that your loved ones are asking because they are truly interested in your child; you also know that they're going to accept what you're telling them.

- ✔ **How much you feel like disclosing:** A stranger doesn't need to know all the details of your child's condition — unless you feel like getting into the whole story, and this person happens to be truly interested. Be aware that this person could be asking about your child to be polite — don't overload her with a two-hour tale.

- ✔ **Your level of tolerance for this discussion**: You're never obligated to disclose any details to anyone, but be aware that the less you're willing to say, the more people are going to assume. It's perfectly all right to give the person just the basic facts and to say no more.

This is all fine and well when you're dealing with someone who is sensitive — what do you say to someone who asks what *you* (or your spouse) did to cause your child's condition? Or, in the case of adoption, how should you answer someone who asks why you would have ever brought a child with such problems into your home?

In these cases, you're well within your rights to tell the other person the truth — that despite your child's problems, and perhaps *because* of them (after all, this is a part of who he is), you love him. Depending on the situation, you may strive to give this person a brief tutorial — separating the facts from fictitious fears — regarding your child's condition (if this happens to be a family member who'll be in your child's life on a regular basis), or you may choose to walk away (if you hardly know this person anyway and/or you know there's nothing you can do to impress upon him that your child is the love of your life).

Walking away is just fine, by the way. Though informing people goes a long way toward quelling fear and misunderstanding of birth defects in many instances, some misguided people spend their days judging not only your child, but everyone else. See that attitude for what it is and let it go. It's their loss, not yours.

Chapter 19

Making It All Better: When Baby Has a Boo-Boo

*P*arents seldom want to read about *potential* injuries (the thought of Baby bleeding is just too much to bear), so if you're leafing through this section, chances are you need help either determining the severity of an injury or dealing with the reality of one. We give you an overview of common mishaps and what to do about them.

This chapter is not a replacement for your intuition as a parent. If Baby has suffered a fall or other injury and is crying uncontrollably, is unusually groggy, or is otherwise showing signs of distress, call your pediatrician without delay. Some injuries can have internal effects that may not be obvious.

Playing the Part of the Calm Parent

Remaining calm when your child is hurting can be very difficult. You can almost feel Baby's pain, and her fearful reaction is hard to watch. That's exactly why it's so important to put your own fears on hold and to soothe her.

She learns almost everything by watching you. Her immediate reaction to a cut finger may be to cry — it hurts, after all. *Your* reaction may determine how long she cries, and how she reacts to future injuries, as well. Imagine two scenarios: In the first, you calmly pick her up, sing to her as you wash out the cut, dry it, and bandage it. Depending on Baby's temperament, she may continue to cry, or she may be satisfied by your no-big-deal attitude that this injury is, in fact, not the end of the world. Either way, you have demonstrated through your actions that you believe she is going to be just fine.

In the second scenario, you see your child's blood and freak out. You're calling for your partner, neighbor, mother, mailman — anyone available to help you wash out a cut and apply a bandage to it. Baby sees the look of pure panic on your face and decides that this is a bad situation — it's very, *very* bad. She wails in terror, and becomes inconsolable.

No one is going to blame a parent for reacting strongly to her child's injury — but concealing those emotions (at least temporarily) is often best. As time goes on, you figure out which injuries are serious (dangling limbs, profuse and uncontrollable bleeding) and which aren't (scrapes and minor bruises). You also discover how to save your emotional energy for when it's most needed (say, for soothing a child who has taken a serious tumble versus icing and elevating every tiny bump). Otherwise, especially if you have a very active child, you wear yourself out.

Calm reaction to injury is also important because Baby is learning — and she needs the space and confidence to trust her new abilities, or else she may be so fearful of every little fall that she won't try anything new. This isn't to say that you shouldn't protect your precious child from dangerous situations: If Baby is pulling herself up using a rickety table, you're right to make a dramatic save. But if you insist on holding her every time she tries to take a step on her own, she's not going to learn much about the physics of walking.

Stocking Your First-Aid Kit

Every home should have a first-aid kit stocked and ready for action. A kit differs from what you most likely already have on hand in your medicine cabinet (thermometer, medicine spoons, and the like), and should be in its own mobile container (something like a tackle box — with dividers and drawers). Your first-aid kit needs to be accessible and portable. Take it along on day trips or vacations.

Make sure you include:

- Bandages in all sizes
- Antibiotic ointment or cream

- Sterile gauze (roll and pads)
- First-aid adhesive tape (to secure gauze)
- Sharp scissors (to cut the tape)
- Liquid soap (to wash out wounds)
- Alcohol wipes (you may be without water for cleansing a wound)
- Tweezers (for removing splinters, gravel, thorns, and such)
- Pain reliever (acetaminophen or ibuprofen — *not* aspirin)
- Sunscreen
- One percent hydrocortisone cream (comes in handy for soothing bug bites, sunburn, and even inflamed diaper rash)
- Benzocaine (for sudden teething attacks)
- Insect repellent
- Benadryl (diphenhydramine) for allergic reactions
- Your doctor's phone number

You can buy prepared kits in most drug stores. Before you purchase one, make sure it includes everything on this list — and add your pediatrician's number immediately.

Playing Dr. Mom

Bumps, cuts, and scrapes are common injuries babies encounter in the first year, especially when they start moving. Rolling, crawling, pulling up, and walking are major milestones — but each one comes with an inherent risk of injury. Most such injuries are fairly mild and nothing for you to lose any sleep over. Some, though, will leave you wondering whether Baby should be whisked off to the emergency room. This section covers the ins and outs of treating mild injuries and helps you to determine what kinds of injuries qualify as emergencies.

Caring for scrapes, cuts, and bruises

As Baby becomes more independent, he may also become more injury-prone. Knowing how to judge the severity of an injury becomes incredibly important. Not every injury, of course, is life-threatening — but not all serious injuries present themselves as such immediately. In other words, what seems to be a not-so-serious hurt may be worse than you think. Fortunately, most children make it through the physical trials and tribulations of early childhood no worse for the wear.

Scrapes

Scrapes are usually fairly mild injuries, even though they're sometimes awful to look at. Wash out a scrape as soon as you can. This will probably sting, so the best way to do this is by using warm, soapy water and distracting Baby by singing or talking to him. And of course, be very gentle. Take as much time as Baby will allow, wash out as much debris as you can, apply an antibiotic ointment, and bandage the scrape.

If Baby has fallen on gravel or dirt, you may have to remove tiny rocks or other foreign objects from the wound. If you're at home (or when you return home), let him soak in the bath to remove any rocks or dirt you weren't able to get at. (You can use tweezers if Baby will allow you to.) If you're not at home, find a clean water source (a sink is good; a puddle is not) and wash out the scrape as much as possible, as soon as possible.

Cuts

You can't always tell how deep cuts are. Wash a cut out with warm, soapy water. If it's a minor bleeding laceration, bandage it and send Baby on his way. Make sure to change a bandage at least daily, and more often if it gets dirty. If a bandage is sticking to Baby's skin like glue, rub it with some mineral oil. This should loosen its grip on Baby within a few minutes. As soon as a cut forms a scab, it doesn't need a bandage anymore. If a cut becomes red, swollen, or otherwise infected-looking, call your pediatrician. Most cuts will heal on their own with no need for medical intervention (other than a kiss from Dr. Mom).

Minor cuts don't always need a bandage; in fact, some cuts heal more quickly if they're exposed to the air.

If a cut is bleeding profusely, *elevate* it (hold it up so it's above Baby's heart), if possible, and apply pressure with a clean paper towel or sterile gauze, if you have some handy (See Figure 19-1). For example, if Baby has cut his hand, raise it up over his head while you gently press down on the injury. If his foot is bleeding, lie him down and raise his foot above his chest level. Applying pressure should stop bleeding within ten minutes. If Baby's cut is still going strong after this time, call your doctor right away. Baby may need stitches.

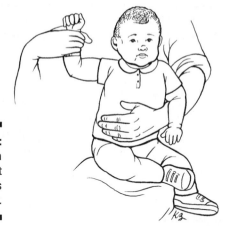

Figure 19-1:
Elevate a
cut that
bleeds
profusely.

Never use a tourniquet on a baby! Tourniquets can do more harm than good, and should be used only in the most extreme cases where nothing else will stop the hemorrhaging. Firm pressure will stop the bleeding in almost any wound.

The following signs let you know that a wound needs to be stitched up:

- **Leaves a gaping wound.** Those edges won't close themselves, leaving the wound open to infections and scarring.

- **Is more than ¼-inch deep.** That's too deep for the edges to close on their own.

- **Has jagged edges.** Clean cuts are more likely to close and heal without scarring.

- **Is significant and located on the face.** You can't rush Baby in every time he scratches himself on the cheek, but deep facial cuts are likely to leave scars.

- **Is significant and located in an area unlikely to promote healing.** Chins. Knees. Fingers. Places where the skin is not going to stay closed without a little help.

Puncture wounds

Because puncture wounds are difficult to clean, infection is a concern. Wash the wound with warm, soapy water for several minutes and evaluate any bleeding. Profuse bleeding that doesn't stop with elevation and direct pressure (applied for ten minutes) is cause for concern. Call your doctor's office right away to determine whether Baby needs to be seen (and stitched up) in the office.

If the offender was a neighbor's pet, you need to make sure — and see in writing — that this animal is up to date on his shots, and in any event, *call your pediatrician.* If Baby cut herself on a rusty nail or something equally unsanitary, call your pediatrician right away. Watch for foreign bodies in the puncture wound (cat/dog teeth, pieces of a thorn). If left in the wound, these will cause infection. Baby may need antibiotics.

Bruises

Bruises usually don't need any special treatment. Basically, as kids learn to stand and walk, they take their tumbles. And after they perfect their walking, the bruises will probably be even more plentiful, because they can do even *more.* Black-and-blue marks are most often just a sign that Baby is a busy guy.

Bruises that come on suddenly with the onset of a fever, however, should be evaluated by Baby's doctor.

Handling head injuries

Cuts to the head bleed *a lot.* The head is chock-full of blood vessels, which is what often makes these cuts seem worse than they really are. You may think Baby is losing every ounce of blood he has, and then you realize that the cut is actually pretty minor. Same rule of thumb applies here as to cuts elsewhere on the body: Apply firm pressure. Evaluate the bleeding after ten minutes. Anything jagged or deep or both or located on Baby's face needs further evaluation by your doctor.

Bumps to the head are common injuries sustained by babies everywhere — and the resulting anxiety over these bumps is shared by their parents. Watching your child fall and hit his head is traumatic. If he pops right back up and seems fine — and continues to behave normally — he's probably all right, even if he has a "goose egg" where he hit his head. These huge bumps are evidence of the injury sustained to the blood vessels in your child's head — a goose egg (horrible looking as it is) doesn't indicate any injury to Baby's brain. Put an ice pack on it for 20 minutes to help alleviate the swelling.

An *accelerated head injury* (falling off the counter, into the wall, or down the stairs, especially in a walker, which holds an infant in an upright position) is more likely to cause a concussion or serious brain injury than falling from a standing position onto the floor. (These latter types of falls rarely cause significant brain injury.)

A *concussion* is an injury to Baby's brain and is a serious matter. If Baby has sustained a knock to his head, keep an eye out for the warning signs of concussion for the next 24 hours and contact your pediatrician immediately if your child exhibits any of the following symptoms:

- Loss of consciousness
- Unusual pallor
- Dilated or large pupils (one pupil may look larger or not react when a flashlight is shined into the eye)
- Irritability (included prolonged crying) or lethargy
- Vomiting
- Loss of physical coordination (unable to crawl, walk, or move as he did before he bumped his head)
- Discharge from ears (bloody or watery), which could be a sign of a skull fracture

If Baby bumps his head in the evening, he can go to bed, but do check on him frequently throughout the night — at least once every two hours. Make sure his breathing is normal, he isn't in any sort of distress, that you can wake him, and he appears to recognize you.

Dealing with mouth injuries

Mouth injuries, like head injuries, tend to bleed a lot. Fortunately, when an injury in the mouth is a cut or an abrasion, stemming the flow of blood is pretty easy. An ice cube is usually sufficient to stop any bleeding.

Occasionally, though, teeth get involved in the act. Baby may fall and chip a tooth on the coffee table — or she may knock it out completely. And after baby teeth are out, they're out for good. Your main concern is an infection in the gums (which appear red and swollen or are oozing pus) or, in the case of a badly chipped tooth, Baby's appearance.

If Baby has sustained a major injury to her teeth and gums, call your pediatrician during normal office hours. You want to make sure that Baby's teeth haven't been knocked completely out of line and you also want to make sure she hasn't injured any of the surrounding teeth. Your doctor can tell you whether Baby needs to see a dentist. A tooth that has turned brown or gray may have sustained a sufficient injury to kill the root. If you notice this, go ahead and call your dentist yourself.

Surviving sprains and fractures

Although a baby's bones are more flexible than an adult's (making actual *breaks* rare), those little bones contain growth plates that are easily damaged by trauma. Baby's long bones can sustain what's called a *greenstick fracture.* (Picture trying to break a fresh branch. It doesn't snap cleanly; it just kind of separates.)

If Baby sustains a major fall or injury, he can suffer a *sprain* (a torn or stretched ligament) or a *fracture* (a break or crack in a bone). The two injuries have some of the same symptoms, including:

- ✔ Bruising
- ✔ Swelling
- ✔ Extreme pain
- ✔ Inability to use an arm or leg or to bear weight on it

A fracture also has the following symptoms:

- ✔ Crookedness or deformity of the limb or extremity (including a protrusion of the bone)
- ✔ Increase in pain with movement of affected area

Ice and elevate a suspected sprain or fracture and call your pediatrician right away. Any injury that causes pain and swelling of a bone needs to be evaluated as soon as possible. Your pediatrician may ask you to feel around the injured area to locate any obvious areas of pain. Tell your doctor if there is a cut or open wound over the area of concern — this could be an open fracture and needs antibiotics to prevent infection.

Nursemaid's elbow

Dads, especially, love to swing their children 'round and 'round, holding them by the hands or wrists. This can lead to a common problem called nursemaid's elbow (official name: radial head sublaxation). When a child's extended arm is pulled in this way, it may lead to discomfort or flat-out refusal to use the arm. (Your child may, for example, reach for a toy and hold her arm bent at the elbow and across her chest.) The injury can also be caused by pulling up on the arm of a child who is just learning to walk. Fortunately, this is usually easily remedied with a painless procedure in the pediatrician's office in which the elbow is popped back into place.

Caring for Stings and Bites

You and Baby are lying on a blanket in the grass, loving the lazy summer afternoon, when suddenly — without warning or provocation — Baby howls in pain. Her first sting. Ouch. If your child is very upset, distract her with a treat or a TV show (this is one of the only times when it's okay to use the boob tube to calm your child).

Then use the blunt edge of something — your nail, a butter knife, a stiff piece of paper to remove the stinger. *Don't use tweezers*, and don't try to pinch the stinger between your nails, because this could release more venom into Baby's skin. Scrape the stinger out of the wound, wash the area with soapy water, and apply an ice pack. However, the stinger will usually leave with the offending insect right away.

Applying a paste of baking soda and water to a bee sting is an age-old remedy — and one that really seems to help reduce swelling and itching. Another popular home remedy involves rubbing meat tenderizer on the sting. You may want to try these, or you may try calamine lotion.

Stings carry the risk of severe allergic reaction in some children. These kids will usually show signs of being hypersensitive before they develop the *actual* allergy to an insect bite, which indicates that they are developing an allergy to the venom — and any future bites could be deadly. Because the signs of hypersensitivity are not always severe (and because your child may be stung when you're not with her), there's always the possibility of missing the signs of hypersensitivity — in which case, you won't even know that your child is at risk for a major allergic reaction to her next sting. What this means, in a nutshell, is this: Your child can be stung several times and appear to be okay. If she has a hypersensitivity to the venom, her next sting could send her into a severe allergic reaction — even though she's never had one before. If you didn't notice the signs of hypersensitivity, you won't see the allergic reaction coming.

If your child is short of breath or has extreme pain or swelling following an insect bite, call your doctor immediately. These are signs of hypersensitivity. Baby may enter *anaphylactic shock* (a severe, life-threatening allergic reaction), which could result in death. If your child exhibits any of the following symptoms after being stung by any insect, seek medical attention without delay:

- ✔ Hives
- ✔ Nausea and/or vomiting
- ✔ Hoarseness and/or coughing

✔ Difficulty breathing (including wheezing)

✔ Swelling of the face, tongue, lips, ears, eyelids, palms, soles, or mucous membranes

✔ Headache, dizziness, or fainting

A child who is diagnosed with a hypersensitivity to stings may be prescribed an emergency syringe of epinephrine, which you'll need to keep on hand whenever you go outdoors. This medicine temporarily counteracts the effects of the venom and prevents your child from going into anaphylactic shock.

Ticks

Deer ticks can carry and transmit *Lyme disease,* which is caused by a toxin that can be transmitted from a deer tick to a human. Long-term effects may include stiff joints, rashes, and flulike symptoms.

If Baby has a tick, smother it with petroleum jelly to kill it and then try to remove it with tweezers (the petroleum jelly should ease its removal, as well). Get as close to the tick's head as possible, and pull it up and straight out. Don't try to pick at it, or to remove it by twisting it. Also, don't try to remove the tick by using the head of an extinguished match or applying kerosene to kill it. You're putting your child at risk by using these potentially harmful agents.

You need to get as much of the tick as possible out from under the skin. Leaving bits and pieces behind defeats the purpose and puts Baby at risk for developing Lyme disease

After you remove the tick, kill it, save it in a plastic sandwich bag, and call your pediatrician. He'll determine whether this is a deer tick, for starters, and then decide if treatment is necessary. Some doctors are very proactive and will prescribe antibiotics for any child who has had a tick removed, but many are more laid-back, opting instead to wait and see if the child develops the tell-tale bull's-eye rash (a rash that forms around the bite site and looks exactly like it sounds) before prescribing treatment.

Prevention is key with Lyme disease. Though it's most prevalent in the Northeastern United States, there have been cases reported across the country. If you're headed into the woods or Baby is playing in the grass, cover her as much as possible. Tuck those pant legs into her socks, and give her long sleeves to wear. Do a thorough tick check when you return home, especially focusing on Baby's head.

Remove a tick as soon as you spot it. It takes a tick at least 24 hours to "share" enough of his bacteria to cause Lyme disease in a human host.

Treating Burns

Burns can blister and lead to infection, so it's important to evaluate and care for a burn properly. Ideally, it's best to prevent burns altogether, of course. Chapter 20 provides tips for keeping Baby burn-free. This section will give you an overview of what burns may look like, how to soothe them, and when to call the doctor.

Thermal burns

When most people think of burns, they think of *thermal burns* — burns from fire, scalding, or contact with a hot object. These burns are classified by how many layers of skin have been affected. The signs of each are listed in Table 19-1 (first- and second-degree symptoms are also used to classify sunburns).

Table 19-1	Classification of Burns and Their Symptoms
Burn	*Symptoms*
First degree or superficial burn	The top layer of the skin is involved. Expect the area to be dry, pink or red, and somewhat painful. No blistering is involved.
Second degree or partial thickness burn	Burn goes into the deeper layers of skin. Dark red, swollen, quite painful, blistered. Skin may "weep" or appear moist due to exposed underlying tissue.
Third degree or full thickness burn	All layers of skin affected. Skin may appear pearly white or charred; painless (nerve endings destroyed).

If Baby suffers a relatively mild thermal burn at home, remove clothing from the area and cool the skin. If he has burned his hand, fill a large bowl with cold water and stick his hand in it (or put him in a cool bath — whatever will work better) for 20 minutes. If he has burned his face, apply a wet, cool compress. Burns to the hands or face should always be evaluated by Baby's doctor.

Don't use any home remedies that advise applying butter or oil to burns. These materials hold heat inside the skin, making the burn even worse.

Increase Baby's fluids, and give him acetaminophen or ibuprofen to alleviate any pain. Cover any blisters with an antibiotic ointment and a loose bandage. Don't break the blisters! Not only does this put the wound at risk for infection, it also disrupts the healing process. Call the doctor for further evaluation for all but the most minor burns. There is a risk of shock (the body shutting down its major systems) involved with some burns.

If Baby shows signs of third degree burns (charred or pearly skin) get him to the hospital immediately.

Sunburns

Nowadays, everyone knows that exposing bare skin to the sun is a bad idea. Ideally, children younger than 1 year old should be kept out of the sun; their skin is just too sensitive. We know, though, that sometimes babies *are* out in sun, so we offer some tips for keeping her burn free. And if you're only reading this after allowing Baby to play outside on a hot, sunny day, or if Baby's sunscreen didn't do its job, this section will tell you how to care for Baby's burn.

Here are some tips for keeping Baby sunburn-free:

- ✔ Protect children older than 6 months with sunscreen of at least 30 SPF.

- ✔ Use sunscreen liberally, and apply it at least 20 minutes before your child goes outside to give it time to absorb into her skin. Reapply according to label instructions (every couple of hours and after swimming).

- ✔ No matter what the label says, though, if your child is *looking* red and burned — even though she's wearing 45 SPF — she's *getting* red and burned. Get her inside and keep her there.

- ✔ Get Baby a sun hat — and do everything you can to keep it on her head. For best results, look for something with a wide brim so that it will shade her face and the back of her neck. (Boys' hats also come with wide brims and/or "tails" that hang down from the back of a baseball hat.)

Don't use sunscreen on babies younger than 6 months. Kids this age tend to have their hands in their mouths all the time, and because they're not really mobile, it's easy enough to keep them out of the sun and/or in long clothing, which is your safest option.

If Baby does get sunburned, she'll be very unhappy. You can expect her skin to be red and hot. Help her feel better by:

- ✔ Increasing her fluid intake to prevent dehydration
- ✔ Dipping her into a cool bath
- ✔ Giving her pain reliever (acetaminophen or ibuprofen)

✔ Using a lotion or cream that contains aloe, which soothes the skin and feels cool as it evaporates

Avoiding regular skin cream, as this only "traps" the heat and makes things worse

✔ Keeping her completely out of the sun

Don't pop any sunburn blisters — this can lead to infection. Leave them alone, and call your pediatrician. They may be signs of a second-degree burn. Also call your pediatrician if your child develops any signs of heat stroke (vomiting or loss of consciousness).

Chemical and electrical burns

Household cleansers can also cause serious burns to the skin and mucous membranes. If Baby has somehow managed to get under the kitchen sink, remove her, brush off any powdery substances, and give her a thorough washing. If you know which cleanser she's been into, read the label; often, it will include instructions about what to do if the cleanser has gotten on the skin or in the eyes. (Poison Control will also have this information; the number is listed on the Cheat Sheet in the front of this book.) Follow these instructions and call your pediatrician right away. It's safest to keep all poisons and cleansers where Baby has absolutely no chance of getting into them — up high or out in the garage, for example.

If Baby suffers an electrical burn (from exposure to an outlet or a wire), seek medical attention immediately. Although these burns can appear mild, they carry the risk of electrical shock.

Chapter 20

Preventing Injuries at Home

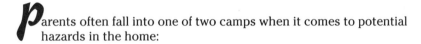

Parents often fall into one of two camps when it comes to potential hazards in the home:

✔ Everything is a deathtrap.

✔ It'll never happen to us.

Each of these mindsets comes with its own unique set of issues. For example, viewing the entire world as a place that can only harm your child may lead you to become *way* overprotective of your tyke, not just in these early years, but for the rest of time. Your child will have no choice but to take one of two roads: She'll either become a person who's almost paralyzed by fear, or she'll rebel against you with everything she's got. Either way . . . not such a healthy relationship to have with your child.

Thinking that nothing bad will ever happen to your child (reasoning that there are millions of little kids in this country, and *most* of don't ever sustain serious injuries) is just living your life in the dark. There are real hazards out there. It's your job to scout them out and prevent Baby from innocently wandering into them. Failing to do so may either ensure that Baby will, indeed, get hurt, or may possibly leave her feeling as though she's pretty much on her own and can do whatever the heck she wants — which, to a child, is a frightening thing.

The key is to find some kind of middle ground here, one that's dictated by the very real possibilities of what could happen if Baby's environment is not properly safeguarded — but one that is also tempered by common sense.

Babies are curious, they're quick, and no parent can prevent every single mishap — but you can prevent the most serious, life-threatening injuries. Take a proactive stance and evaluate the dangers within your home before Baby has a chance to snoop them out for herself. Get down on your hands and knees and look at life from an infant's perspective. You may be surprised by what you see.

Making Home Sweet Home a Safe Haven

Making your home baby-safe is no small task; within the first year, your infant will change from a helpless little angel to a holy living terror — at least as far as your most precious possessions are concerned. Baby won't discriminate between your grandmother's teacups and your pots and pans; after all, both make lots of fun noise when dropped on the floor.

Protecting your collectibles is one concern; a much larger concern, of course, is protecting Baby from the inherent dangers of, say, smashing a tea cup, or discovering that certain things actually fit inside an electrical outlet, or finding that a tablecloth is something to pull herself up on (and pull things down on top of her head simultaneously).

When you bring a child home, you have to make certain accommodations for his safety. That's part of the deal. No one wants to decorate with cabinet locks and fireplace gates, but these devices are only temporary additions to your household. Before you know what happened, your baby will be replaced by a big kid, and not only will he not want to play in the garbage can under the sink anymore, he won't want to touch it at all (especially when you ask him to take out the trash).

Baby-proofing your home is like redecorating — certain things must go, and certain things need to be added. Nowadays, you can buy just about everything you need to make your home a secure place for your child. Each baby-proofing product is out there for a reason: some kid, somewhere, got into something, and a particular product was born to prevent other children from doing the same thing. If you can remember to keep that bathroom door closed, for example, you may not need the toilet seat lock — but would it really hurt to install it just in case Baby finds his way into the bathroom? (Your baby-proofing motto: Better safe than sorry.)

Making the house completely safe may feel like an overwhelming task at first, but chances are, after you get into the job, obvious hazards will start popping out at you.

Getting a jump on safety

Don't wait until Baby is crawling around your house to start baby-proofing. Get going as early as possible — even while you're in your last trimester of pregnancy, or as soon as you bring your infant home. Make safety a priority. Even though you may feel like you have lots of time before Baby will be any-where *near* independent, she'll be rolling around before you know it, and you'll be in a cold sweat, blocking those outlets, padding the fireplace, gating the stairs — and trying to keep an eye on Baby at the same time. Make the necessary changes before you're chasing Little Miss Mobile 'round and 'round the house.

Never assume your house is safe enough. Keeping your home a safe haven for your child is a neverending process. After you make your preliminary sweep through the house, blocking access to some hazards and removing others, sit back and observe Baby's movements. You may have overlooked a potential hazard or two (and with so many potential dangers out there, it's really quite easy to miss something). Remember, as Baby progresses into each new devel-opmental stage, your safety plan needs re-evaluation.

Baby-proofing, step by step

Everything needs to be baby-proofed. More specifically, anything that poses any sort of potential harm to Baby, and anything that Baby can get into with-out your instantaneous knowledge needs to be made as safe as it can possi-bly be. This means anything on the floor, anything that Baby can reach or pull herself up on, and anything Baby can climb onto needs to be safeguarded.

The floor

Get down on the floor and take a look at what an inexperienced roller or crawler may get into. Be sure to:

- ✔ Remove all small objects that Baby can choke on.
- ✔ Place plants, which can be toxic, up high where Baby can't get to them.
- ✔ Move litter boxes to the basement or any other area where Baby has absolutely no access, to prevent Baby from playing in them.

✔ Block access to low-slung furniture that Baby can get stuck under.

✔ Install a fireplace gate or a bumper cushion around a raised hearth. Gate off a fireplace so that Baby can't get into ashes.

✔ Gate or block off wood stoves completely, or don't use them at all. Wood stoves can cause serious burns on contact.

✔ Remove or pad any furniture that has sharp edges.

✔ Gate stairways but never use a pressure gate at the top of stairs — it can pop out if Baby pushes on it and cause a serious tumble. Only use a gate that can be screwed into the wall.

✔ If you have a landing at the top of your stairway surrounded by railings, purchase a clear guard to prevent falls through the railings.

✔ Tack down any loose carpeting to prevent a novice walker from tripping or slipping.

Around the house

Consider what Baby will be able reach. She'll have easy access to electrical outlets and cords. Cabinet doors and drawers open to reveal hidden hazards. The list goes on and on.

Keep Baby safe by doing the following:

✔ **Purchase and install electrical outlet faceplates.** Choose those with covers that automatically close over open outlets or purchase plastic outlet covers. Pop them in outlets everywhere.

✔ **Tuck electrical cords behind furniture when able**.

✔ **Install cabinet, drawer, and toilet locks.**

✔ **Check tables and chairs to see which tip easily or are top-heavy.** Baby may pull these over on herself if she tries to pull herself up on them.

✔ **Remove tablecloths or anything else dangling from a table.** Baby won't be able to pull herself up with a tablecloth, but she may well be able to bring your centerpiece crashing down.

✔ **Bolt large, top-heavy furniture, like bookcases, entertainment centers, baker's racks, and dressers into the wall.** Baby will use anything that's the right height to try to pull herself up. Save her from herself (and a barrage of books) by making sure these items are secure.

✔ **Remove doorstops with small rubber stoppers and replace with a larger rubber doorstop.** Small coiled doorstops with rubber tips are choking hazards.

✔ **Install finger-pinch protectors on doors.**

✔ **Cut Venetian blind cords so that they no longer form a single loop (a choking hazard) and so that they're completely out of Baby's reach.** Or wrap the tails on a holder on the wall so they won't dangle down.

✔ **Turn your water heater down to 120 degrees to prevent scalding.**

✔ **Purchase a rubber faucet guard for the bathtub so that Baby won't hurt his head.**

✔ **TVs are extremely top-heavy and should be kept well out of Baby's reach, and not on a shelf or table.**

✔ **Don't hold Baby in one hand and a hot cup of coffee in the other.** In fact, keep all hot beverages far from your child. She can swat and grab at a mug, causing serious burns to herself (and you).

✔ **Don't hold your baby while cooking — let her cry!**

Special concerns

Some babies are strong enough (and clever enough) to open up a refrigerator, oven, dishwasher, washer, dryer, and so on. A child trapped in a refrigerator can suffocate; ovens may be hot; dishwashers may have sharp objects inside; children can become trapped in front-loading washers and dryers.

Babies learn to climb and grab during the first year — be ready to protect Baby from herself by taking the following precautions:

✔ **Purchase and install appliance locks, which are used to keep Baby out of the oven and refrigerator.**

✔ **Safeguard your stove by purchasing covers for the burners, and kid-proof knob covers to prevent curious would-be cooks from turning on the heat.**

✔ **Remove all furniture from underneath windows.** Children may peer out too far, jump on furniture, and fall out the window, or use the furniture as a ladder to open a window.

✔ **Open windows from the top.** Screens can pop out with very little force and are intended to keep flies out of your house (they're not intended to save your child from a fall).

✔ **Make sure your automatic garage door has a self-acting "bounce up" feature (the door opens if it hits anything on its way down).** Older doors don't, and a child can be crushed if he's under the door when it closes. Test your door to make sure it's working properly by setting a garbage can in its path and closing it. It should bounce up without making a dent in the can.

✔ **If you've been thinking about installing a home security system (or you have one already), make sure you choose one with an option to sound an alarm whenever windows and doors are opened.** Leave this feature on even when you're home. You'll know for certain that Baby isn't slipping out into the back yard while you're preparing his lunch.

Environmental hazards

You're not quite finished yet. Don't forget that chemicals you have closed up in your cabinets may be dangerous and that you need to be very proactive in making sure your smoke detectors have batteries.

Make a list of what needs to be done, and make sure it includes the following:

✔ **Move any poisonous or hazardous chemicals completely out of the house.** Keep them in the garage in a locked cabinet.

✔ **Install smoke detectors.** Have at least one on every floor of your home. Change the batteries every year even if they still work.

✔ **Install carbon monoxide detectors.** Place one near your furnace and one near your bedrooms.

✔ **Make sure the paint in your older home is lead-free.** Chips of paint containing lead can cause brain damage if Baby eats them. (Check out the section "Get the lead out: Addressing harmful paint" for more information.)

✔ **Consider keeping all your toiletries completely out of reach.** Toothpaste is hazardous in large quantities, as are the medicines commonly kept in bathroom medicine cabinets. These things will be more difficult for Baby to reach if they're in a linen closet on the highest shelf.

Get the lead out: Addressing harmful paint

Now that Baby is rolling all over the house, sticking his hands in his mouth, and preparing to become even more of an explorer, you need to think about his exposure to lead. It's not paint itself that poses a threat — it's the dust. Children who inhale lead dust are at risk for developing severe neurological defects that may affect them for the rest of their lives. These defects may include an inability to concentrate, hyperactivity, developmental delays (including slow weight gain), and brain damage. Adults aren't immune to the effects of inhaling lead dust, but children are particularly susceptible to irreversible damage because their brains are in the process of developing.

Most experts agree that it's far more dangerous to try to sand the paint off the wall than to leave it alone: You're going to create far more dust by removing the paint than by maintaining it. Your best bet is to make sure that the paint isn't chipping and to immediately clean up any paint dust in high-friction areas like windowsills and underneath doors. You should also keep your child from playing in those areas. Keeping your home clean and in good repair goes a long way toward preventing lead poisoning in your child.

You can find many kits on the market that test for lead in the home. The health department may be able to do more extensive testing.

Remember that your home isn't the only source of lead-based paint exposure. A few years back, certain window blinds were found to contain lead. Toys manufactured in some foreign countries may contain high levels of leaded paint.

If your home was built after 1978, the year that lead-based paint was banned, there's almost no chance of the paint in your home containing lead. This is not to say that a home built in 1970 is lead-laden; some paint manufacturers started to lose the lead from their products as early as the 1950s.

I recommend a *lead test* (a simple finger prick that's screened for high levels of lead) at one year for every child, regardless of your home's potential for containing lead.

Checking for Choking Hazards

Because babies love to stick everything in their mouths, choking is a major concern of parents everywhere. When kids reach the oral stage, they're really exploring the world through their mouths, discovering textures, shapes, and tastes by using their oral cavity. (Remember, a small baby isn't all that good with his hands; it's much easier for him to grasp something and shove it in the general direction of his face than it is for him to actually grasp and feel it with his fingers.) This goes on into the second year and sometimes even into the third. Removing small items from Baby's reach is a good start; doing a thorough exam of the floor each and every time you put Baby down on her blanket is also a good idea. But this is another area where constant vigilance is needed, because children most often choke on toys and food — the very things that are given to them by their parents. In this section, we give you tips on how to avoid a choking child. We also go over the basics of the Heimlich maneuver for babies and infant CPR. We also recommend that you take a class to find out more about these techniques.

Safe snacking

You can cut down the risk of choking just by knowing which foods are safe for babies and toddlers and which aren't. The following foods are known choking hazards:

- Hot dogs
- Grapes
- Raisins
- Nuts
- Chunks of firm food (vegetables, cheese, meat, or fruit, for example)
- Thick, sticky foods like peanut butter or marshmallows, which can actually clog Baby's throat
- Hard candies (including lollipops)
- Popcorn

Beyond sticking to safe foods, you can take further steps to help prevent your child from choking on her food:

- Make sure Baby is sitting up and not giggling or talking while she eats.
- Cut any firm foods into tiny pieces that can't get stuck in Baby's airway.
- Cut any round foods (grapes, hot dogs, carrots) into small pieces or strips before feeding them to Baby.
- Don't allow her to stuff her mouth full of food.
- Avoid sticky or hard foods (like nuts or sticky or hard candies) altogether. Baby doesn't need them anyway.

It's also important to know the Heimlich maneuver and infant CPR — just in case. See the sections on these techniques for more information.

The Heimlich maneuver

If Baby is choking, have someone call 911. But knowing the Heimlich maneuver may save your baby's life.

Here's how to do it:

1. **Place her face-down on your forearm, supporting her neck with your hand.** For a visual, take a look at Figure 20-1A.

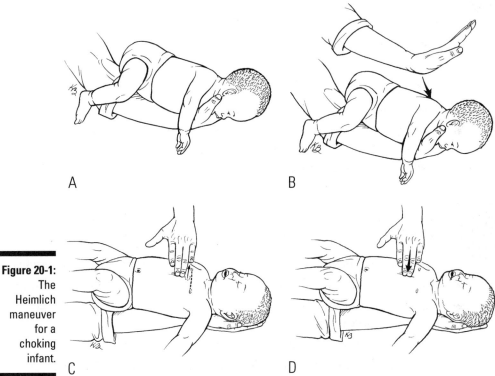

Figure 20-1:
The
Heimlich
maneuver
for a
choking
infant.

A

B

C

D

2. **Give five solid blows with the heel of your hand to her upper back, between the shoulder blades.** For a visual, take a look at Figure 20-1B.

3. **If this doesn't work, turn her over and center your index and middle fingers right between the nipples.** For a visual, take a look at Figure 20-1C.

4. **Give five chest thrusts with your index and middle finger.** For a visual, take a look at Figure 20-1D.

5. **Repeat above steps.**

Infant CPR

If Baby is unconscious and not breathing, have someone call 911. Lay her on a flat surface. Tilt her head back and look into her mouth. If you can see the object, crook your index finger and try to "sweep" the object out of her mouth. If she still isn't breathing or you don't see the object, begin infant CPR.

1. **Lay Baby on a flat surface.**

2. **Tilt her chin and head back to open her airway.**

3. **Cover her mouth and nose with your mouth. Give her two gentle breaths (about two seconds each).** Her chest should rise each time.

4. **Place your index and middle finger in the middle of her chest about an inch below the nipple line.** Give five quick, gentle compressions, pressing down half an inch to an inch.

5. **Repeat steps, using one breath and five compressions until Baby rouses or help arrives.**

Eradicating other hazards

Because an active, crawling Baby will try to slip just about anything into his mouth, keeping your home free and clear of choking hazards is a full-time operation. Before you let Baby play in any room, do a thorough sweep of the floor, the tables, the couch cushions, and anyplace else Baby has access to (check underneath the recliner, for example, to make sure no one has dropped any loose change).

Choking hazards to be on the lookout for include:

✔ Coins

✔ Buttons

✔ Small, round batteries (used for watches, remote car locks, hearing aids, and similar items)

✔ Bottle caps

✔ Marker or pen caps

✔ Thumbtacks

✔ Paper clips

✔ Small toys that compress and expand (like foam balls or balloons)

✔ Raisins, peanuts, snack foods

✔ Toys with small pieces (wheels from toy cars are especially hazardous, as are plastic eyeballs)

The previous list is only a starting point, because so many small items in any given household could pose a choking hazard to your child. Always be on the lookout for pieces of larger toys or common items that could come loose in Baby's mouth. It may seem safe enough, for example, to let Baby chew the top of a soda bottle — but that cap can twist off in his mouth and create a life-threatening situation.

Two rules of thumb about choking:

- ✔ **If a toy fits into the center of a cardboard paper towel tube, it's too small for Baby to play with.** The opening of the tube is roughly the size of Baby's airway.

- ✔ **Don't think that because something will taste bad (like a penny) or feel sharp (like a tack) that Baby won't pop it in his mouth anyway.** His main concern is exploring the world through his oral cavity, so make sure you're providing him with safe options to this end — and doing everything you can to keep the unsafe options out of his reach.

Playing It Safe with Your Pets

Bringing Baby into a home already occupied by a beloved family pet can spark intense jealousy from your dog or cat. Your pet may act strange — depressed, hyper, nasty — and you may wonder whether it's safe to have him in the same room as your child.

You're right to worry. Pets are often as special to their owners as children are (or at least it seems that way until you actually have a child), and although you love and trust your animal completely, all bets are off when an infant comes into the house. Your previously docile animal may exhibit behavior you didn't know he was capable of.

The bottom line on pets is this: Never trust an animal around your baby. Always physically put yourself between the two. To an animal, your infant is just a smaller animal who makes strange noises. Even if you would trust your pet to save your life (and even though he very well may pull you from a burning building), Baby is a stranger to him, and he may not particularly like strangers — particularly small ones who cry, smell strange, and take all of your attention.

Even when your child is older, don't leave him alone with an animal. Children are often known to pull fur, bite, and pet too hard. Your pet may not respond by running and hiding — instead, he may decide to teach Baby a lesson by biting back.

Keeping Your Little Sleepyhead Safe

Putting Baby to bed sometimes feels as though you're removing him from the perils of the world, tucking him in where he can't get hurt. But in order for *you* to get a good night's sleep, you have to know beyond the shadow of a doubt that Baby's bed and bedroom are a safe haven. Make sure everyone is going to have a secure rest by giving the nursery a good once-over.

Crib notes

The crib can be a safe, secure spot for sleeping or an accident waiting to happen. Make sure yours is in tip-top shape and perfectly safe by following these guidelines:

- **Use only newer cribs.** Those built before 1992 don't meet current safety standards and shouldn't be used.

- **Make sure the crib is sturdy.** If a crib's been taken apart 12 times and passed around the family, make sure the screws are still holding everything together as they should. Never use tie-wraps (plastic strips that are sometimes used used in lieu of screws) to secure various pieces of the crib.

- **Measure the distance between the slats.** If slats are more than 2⅜ inches apart, Baby could get her head caught in between them.

- **Buy a firm mattress that fits snugly in the crib.** If you can fit more than one finger between the mattress and the sides of the crib, it's too small; buy a larger one. Baby could get stuck in the side.

- **Put the crib in a safe spot.** Venetian blind cords pose a strangulation risk to your child; keep them as far from the crib as possible, and cut them so they don't form a loop.

- **Hang mobiles out of Baby's reach, and remove them as soon as Baby starts pulling up on the sides of the crib.**

- **Remove the bumper pad as soon as Baby pulls up so that it isn't used as a stepping stool to the outside world.**

- **If you paint or stain a crib, make sure you use a product that's safe for Baby.** Your child will be up and mouthing the side of that crib soon enough; you don't want him ingesting any hazardous substances. Check the rails often after Baby is pulling up and teething; look for any rough surfaces that could cut Baby's mouth or pose a choking hazard.

- **Don't use a crib with corner posts.** They pose a strangulation hazard if Baby's clothing gets caught on them. The same goes for pretty cutouts in a crib's headboard: Clothing can get caught in them, and so can Baby's head. Choose a plain crib instead.

Babies should be put to sleep on their backs to reduce the risk of SIDS (sudden infant death syndrome, for more on this see the following section). Also, keep the crib clear except for Baby. He doesn't need pillows, stuffed animals, or heavy blankets in his bed, and they pose a suffocation hazard.

Bumper pads are cute, but not necessary. Be sure to remove them by 6 months so baby doesn't use them to climb. Keep the mattress at the lowest level possible to prevent falls from leaning over the edge when baby begins to pull up.

Preventing Sudden Infant Death Syndrome (SIDS)

Sudden Infant Death Syndrome (SIDS) is the term used to describe the death of a baby who seemed to be completely healthy. At one time called *crib death*, SIDS typically occurs in children under the age of 6 months during naptimes or in the overnight hours. There are some measures you can take to minimize your child's risk of SIDS, including:

- ✔ **Use a firm mattress and the lightest blankets.** Soft, plush bedding and coverings increase the chance of your baby's face becoming covered by or snuggled into material that will cut off her oxygen. Doctors think that soft mattresses simply don't give a Baby enough support. Imagine you were a weak little thing lying on your back on a waterbed, for example. It would be much easier for you to breathe if you were lying on something firmer.

- ✔ **Lay Baby on her back.** This doesn't eliminate the need for a firm mattress.

- ✔ **Keep Baby's room and clothing cool enough.** Overheating the room and/or bundling Baby up too much for naps or bedtime may be contributing factors in SIDS. Keep your thermostat set at a reasonable temperature (not a balmy 80 degrees). One layer of clothing and a light blanket are sufficient coverings in the crib.

- ✔ **No smoking!** Second-hand smoke may be a contributing factor in SIDS.

- ✔ **Breastfeed, if at all possible.** Breastfeeding provides Baby some protection against respiratory and gastrointestinal illnesses, sicknesses that seem to coincide with some SIDS cases.

Some babies are at an increased risk for SIDS, including those with a sibling that has died of SIDS, babies who have been exposed to drugs in the womb, low birth-weight babies, and babies who have already had an episode of respiratory distress in the crib. Your pediatrician will assess your child's risk factors; if it's determined that your baby is at a higher risk of SIDS than her peers, you may be advised to use a monitor that evaluates Baby's breathing and heart rate.

Pajama-rama

Not so very long ago, all children's sleepwear had to conform to governmental safety regulations. Every pair of infant and kid jammies had to be made from flame-retardant material. This rule has eased up in the last few years, and the recommendation now is for children over the age of 9 months to wear close-fitting pajamas made from either flame retardant fabric or natural fiber.

The theory is that close-fitting clothing doesn't provide the oxygen fire needs to spread. Children under the age of 9 months don't move around enough to whip up mass amounts of oxygen, and are considered less at risk for inadvertently fanning any flames on their pajamas.

Baby's pjs should be snug, but not tight. Loose-fitting pajamas carry a risk in case of fire and are also a strangulation hazard for an older child (if a loose neckline gets caught on something in the crib, Baby could be at serious risk).

Sleeping tight

When Baby starts making regular escapes from his crib, you may think you need to move him to a bed. Resist the urge to buy a toddler bed for your baby. Most kids stay in their cribs for at least the first year, and well into the second, so don't rush things. Cribs are safe, confined spaces — you know where Baby is, and you know what he can and can't get into. When you put him into a bed, all bets are off. He's too young at this point to be left unattended and completely free to explore every corner of his bedroom (which may well happen during the middle of the night or during naptime). Keep him safe and keep him in the crib for now.

Instead of buying a new bed, try placing the mattress down at its lowest point and hitch those rails up to their highest point — you may just make the climb difficult enough so that Baby gives up on it, at least for a while.

If he insists on scaling the walls of his bed, the safest option is to purchase a tentlike attachment for the top of his crib. These tents are designed to keep little escape artists safe in their beds. Refer to Chapter 16 to see what they look like.

Don't let Baby sleep in a regular-sized bed, even if it has side rails. Beds are fraught with peril for babies: Infants can roll off, get their heads caught under side rails, or become stuck between a wall and the bed. If you're visiting Grandma and there's no crib available, it's much safer to let Baby nap in his stroller or on a clean blanket on the floor while you sit close by. Baby should also be kept out of the parents' bed to prevent suffocation (by someone rolling over on him or by pulling the blankets over his head). Waterbeds are too soft and are unsafe for infant use.

Water Safety and Your Baby

Your baby can drown in less than a minute and in only 1 inch of water. Keeping Baby safe when water is nearby requires constant vigilance. Bathtubs and pools are danger areas for small children, as are ponds, hot tubs, wading pools, ice chests, and drainage ditches. In addition, some very real drowning hazards — like toilets and buckets — don't *seem* hazardous at all.

Your safest bet when you're aware of a water hazard is to maintain close and constant physical contact between you and your child. This is easy enough with an infant — but it becomes even more important as your child becomes more independent.

Tips to prevent drowning:

- **Empty all buckets, ice chests, or other containers filled with water as soon as possible and *put them away*.** (Containers filled with rainwater are a hazard to Baby, too.)

- **Never allow an older child to supervise Baby in the tub or pool.** Not only is a child easily distracted, but she may not be able to save Baby in case of an emergency.

- **Keep your small child away from the ocean.** Large waves can surprise even the most seasoned beachcombers; Baby is too small to fight a strong tide.

- **Never leave Baby alone in the tub — not for a minute, not for any reason.** If you have to answer the door or phone, wrap him up and take him with you. Otherwise, let the bell or phone ring.

- **Leave toilet lids down, and/or install toilet lid locks.**

- **Always cover and lock a hot tub or spa.**

- **Purchase an alarm for your pool that will sound if anything (or anyone) falls in.**

- **Don't count on floating devices to safeguard Baby.** Floating devices — even those designed specifically for babies — aren't intended to be a substitute for adult supervision. Baby can flip himself upside down under water very quickly, and if you're not right there to flip him right-side up, he could drown.

- **Learn infant CPR.**

Bathtubs pose another safety hazard — scalding. Make sure your hot water heater is turned down to 120 degrees and always feel the bath water before putting Baby in the tub. Never allow older babies or toddlers to play with the faucets — they may accidentally turn on the hot water full-force.

Hazards on the Go

You can't put Baby in a bubble to protect her from every hazard (wouldn't that make your life easy?), but you can take care to prevent some of the most common injuries, like those sustained in car accidents and with ride-on toys. And no, you can't slap a helmet on her head to protect her, either — they don't come in teeny infant sizes. Diligent observation is the only solution.

Keeping safe in the car

The first trip in the car with Baby along for the ride is sometimes a transformative experience: Previously wild drivers suddenly hit the brakes, driving with the care of an elderly soul behind the wheel. It's normal to feel this way; after all, your child's life is in your hands. There's more to keeping Baby safe in the car than driving at a turtle's pace, though. This section offers some tips on making sure everyone arrives at your destination safe and sound.

If you're at a complete loss as to how to install Baby's seat in your car, find a car-seat safety checkpoint. Call your local police station, hospital, automobile club, or pediatrician to find out when and where the next safety check will be. (And don't feel like a ding-dong: Some reports suggest that many, many, many car seats are installed improperly. You're just making sure your child is safe.)

A car seat is only as good as it's allowed to be. Everyone needs to be strapped into a seat when the car is moving, including Mom and Dad, so make sure you're setting a good example by buckling up every time you set out on a trip to the grocery store, the park, or on vacation.

Baby should be kept in a rear-facing car seat until she's 20 pounds *and* 1 year old (she must meet *both* qualifications before her seat gets turned toward the front). Studies have shown that infants under the age of 1 year lack the neck strength to survive a significant impact of this manner if they are facing forward — even if they're belted into a car seat. They're safest situated in the back seat (the middle rear seat is safest for protecting Baby in side collisions), facing the rear of the car.

Never put Baby in the front seat of a car, especially one with a passenger-side airbag. These cars have warnings on the passenger-side visor advising of the risk of injury and death to an infant riding in this seat. The airbag deployment is so swift and violent in nature that your child's car seat can't protect her from the force of it — in fact, the car seat itself could actually be a lethal weapon, even in a low-speed impact. No excuses, no one-time exceptions: Baby is a backseat rider 100 percent of the time.

Concentrate on driving. Sometimes things just happen while you're behind the wheel — Baby starts to cry, or whine, or scream — and there's not a whole lot you can do but try to tune it out until you reach your destination (assuming you're headed to the corner store and not across the country). If you find yourself becoming flustered or irritated, take ten deep breaths and tell yourself that Baby is going to be fine for the next few minutes. Don't try to grab the pacifier from the diaper bag on the passenger side floor or mix a bottle of formula while you're driving. This is just pure insanity, and a surefire way to make sure you run a red light or rear-end another driver. If using a mirror to watch your back seat baby, don't look in it too much; watch your rear-view mirror for cars instead!

Keep a tape of Baby's favorite music in the car for times like these. Make sure she has her comfort objects when you buckle her into her seat. Give Baby her pacifier, her blanket, her bottle — whatever makes her happy and lets you keep your eyes on the road.

When putting Baby in the car, adjust the harness straps in her car seat, making sure they're tight enough to hold her snugly in position in the event of an accident.

Walking with Baby

Driveways, sidewalks, and parking lots can be as dangerous as roadways — after all, it only takes one car to cause major injury to your older, mobile baby or child. Follow these tips to ensure his safety:

- ✔ **If you're leaving the house without your child, always walk around the back of your car to make sure he isn't behind your vehicle.**

- ✔ **Always hold your child's hand when crossing a parking lot.** Drivers tend to become distracted when they're looking for a spot, and a small child is hard to see.

- ✔ **Keep your child next to you in a crosswalk.** Even though drivers should stop in both directions, they don't always. You don't want your child running ahead of you into harm's way.

Teach Baby from the earliest age to stop, look, and listen before he crosses the street — and make sure he does it (along with you) every single time.

Baby on wheels: Ride-on toys and walkers

Wheels make Baby more independent — and increase your blood pressure substantially. Ride-on toys are a blast for older babies, and walkers are still in vogue in some households. How safe are these vehicles?

Pediatricians generally discourage the use of *walkers* (seats and trays on wheels) these days. They're just too fast, too unpredictable, and they can cause serious injuries. Baby can scoot her way out of the kitchen and down the basement steps before you even know she's gone anywhere. Put her in an *exercise ring or saucer* (seats that rock and turn but don't actually go anywhere) instead. You know exactly where she is and what she's doing, and she can't hurt herself, no matter how much she rocks and spins.

A baby who can't stay on a ride-on toy shouldn't be on it at all. He'll just slip off and bump his head. Used indoors, these toys are as dangerous as walkers; outdoors, they should be used only with constant supervision (to prevent Baby from rolling into the street). Check the wheels regularly to make sure they're securely attached.

The mobile child

When baby starts walking, and then running, toward more independence, your job as his bodyguard has officially begun. Your child wants to do more, see more, know more — but he has an inconvenient lack of fear and precious little understanding of what's harmful and what isn't.

The mobile child requires constant supervision, especially outdoors. You can be fairly sure that Baby is secure while he's playing in the family room, but after you leave the safe haven you've created, you just don't know what hazards will pop up. Leaving him alone in the yard for just a couple of minutes — even if the yard is fenced — is risky. Remember, to your child, a poisonous mushroom may seem like a tasty treat, and a piece of glass may seem like an appropriate plaything.

As Baby moves toward his toddler years, he'll only become more curious and perhaps even less fearful, which means you have to become more vigilant. (No one told you this when you were pregnant, huh?) Trying to see the world through his eyes can be helpful if only to assess the dangers of any environment you happen to be in. For example, in the future when you see monkey bars, you may automatically envision your child climbing to the very highest point and hanging there. Just keep in mind that the hazards you don't think of are often the most dangerous — so be *very* creative in your thinking.

Never Shake a Baby!

Shaken Baby Syndrome (SBS) happens when an infant or young child is shaken violently and intentionally. Baby's brain and spinal cord can be severely and permanently damaged. SBS most often occurs when a caregiver has reached the point of maximum frustration with a child's behavior (usually crying), and loses his temper (shakers tend to be male).

Never shake a baby. The frustration that comes along with caring for a screaming child who never seems to sleep is understandable — but taking it out on your child isn't. Remember, part of parenting is learning to draw on your reserves of patience and understanding. Another part of parenting (and one that isn't discussed enough) is knowing that sometimes it's best for you and your child to give yourself a break.

If Baby is destroying your very last nerve with her crying and you feel like you're losing it, put her somewhere safe — in her crib or playpen — and leave her for a few minutes. Don't go far; just find a corner of the house where the crying is quieter and give yourself time to calm down. Get yourself some nourishment. Call your mom or your best friend if venting to them will help. When you're feeling ready to deal with Baby, it's safe to go get her. She may not be any happier than when you left her, but you'll be in a better state of mind, and in this case, that makes all the difference.

Never leave Baby with a sitter or relative who's known to have a short fuse. You love your child unconditionally, and even then, her screaming can drive you up the wall — think about how someone who isn't her mother may react to constant crying. Baby's safety comes first. If your choice is to leave her with your high-strung brother or to bring her along on your errands, bundle her up and take her with you.

Recognizing the risks of roughhousing

Grandpa loves to bounce Baby on his knee. Uncle Bob likes to toss Baby in the air and catch her. You're a nervous wreck. Where's the line when it comes to playing with Baby?

Generally speaking, playing rough with an infant or toddler is a no-no. Their necks can't handle powerful movements (such as those involved with being thrown up in the air and caught), and it's best not to take the chance. Furthermore, when Baby is tossed up in the air, there isn't a 100 percent guarantee that she's going to land safely in her uncle's arms — so tell Bob to cool it. Grandpa's bouncing, on the other hand, is probably a safe activity, as long as he's being gentle.

Part VII
The Part of Tens

The 5th Wave — By Rich Tennant

"I want a lens that's heavy enough to counterbalance the weight on my back."

In this part . . .

Feeling like you need a crash-course in surviving the first few weeks with Baby? This section includes some helpful advice for new parents during their introductory month with Baby, and a list of tips just for dads. You can also read about some good reasons to call your pediatrician in the middle of the night — along with reasons to wait till the morning. If only every aspect of raising a baby could be broken down into ten simple bits of advice!

Chapter 21

Ten Tips for Surviving the First Few Weeks

Settling into the first few weeks with Baby may be the very best experience you've ever had. Or it may be the stuff of nightmares — because no one ever told you that you were going to feel so lousy after delivery, plus your hormones are up and down, your breasts are throbbing, you're tired, and your baby doesn't believe in sleeping when it's dark outside.

Most women don't want to admit that bringing a baby into the home can be a really difficult adjustment. The best thing you can do during this time is be kind to yourself. This chapter offers advice on how to make the first few weeks easier for you (and therefore for your child and your mate, as well). It doesn't offer advice on loving and cuddling your child, because you're going to do that instinctively anyway. This chapter is all about taking care of *you*.

Listen to Your Body

What have you just been through? Labor, delivery, post-delivery repair (if you had a C-section or an episiotomy) — oh, and nine months of pregnancy. Your body is different now. Your body is doing things you never knew it was capable of doing, like producing milk whenever your baby cries. Your body is *tired*. Make a real effort to get some rest whenever you can. Don't look upon naps as laziness; they're as necessary to you as food is right now. If you can't sleep, at least lie down when your baby is quiet.

Send Spot to Camp

You love your pet, but you really don't need to be dealing with walking the dog, caring for your episiotomy, and breastfeeding your newborn all at once. Unless you have a pup that is happy to do nothing but sleep all day long (and who won't require any attention until your partner is available to help), send him to the kennel the week you come home from the hospital. Sure, you'll feel a little guilty about it, until you realize that you're able to lie down and rest when Baby falls asleep (instead of listening to the dog bark at cats and squirrels that happen to be passing by the window). If you have a pet that just can't be boarded, think about sending the animal to a friend's house for a couple of days — and don't leave your baby alone with your pet.

Steal a Shower when You Can

Nothing makes you feel less human — and by extension, less like getting on with the day — than realizing that you stink of breast milk, spit-up, and your baby's diaper. When your partner comes home at the end of the day or when your mother stops by on her lunch hour, take the opportunity to pamper yourself with a shower (funny how basic hygiene suddenly turns into a luxury after you have a baby). It'll invigorate you and make you feel like your old self — or almost.

Order Take-Out

Maybe you're really into health food, or you're opposed to paying top dollar for prepared foods. Put those opinions aside for the moment and realize that when you bring a new baby into your home, you're going to spend almost every moment concentrating on her — and when you're not completely absorbed in caring for her or thinking about her, you may just be thinking about yourself and/or your partner and how tired you are, how your life has changed in just a matter of days, and what tomorrow will bring. Note that you will most likely not be concentrating on what you're going to prepare for dinner. (At least not until things settle down a bit and all of you fall into something of a routine.) Have your partner swing by the drive-through on the way home.

Make a Deal with the Dust

You don't bother it, and it won't bother you. You have much better things to worry about than whether you could write your name in the dust on your bookshelves. Let it be. When Baby has settled in a bit and you're starting to feel like you're ready to take on the deep-down house cleaning again, make a promise to yourself to do it only once a week, and preferably on a day when your mate can lend a hand. If you can't stand to look at the mess, let your mom tackle the dirt, or hire a cleaning lady or a high school student to do it for you.

Take the Phone off the Hook

Is there anyone you really need to talk to that you haven't already called? Think about this: You're on maternity (or family) leave. You need your rest. You don't need to be fielding calls from telemarketers and friends who mean well but have no concept of what it means to be up four times during the night breastfeeding a little one. When you're resting during the day, silence the phone. If you want your spouse or your mom to be able to call, tell them to dial your cell phone — and leave it on vibrate mode.

Accept Offers of Help

Normally, you'd never dream of allowing your mother to fold your husband's boxer shorts, nor would you let your father-in-law wash the dishes in your sink. In the weeks after Baby comes home, however, you may be inundated with offers of assistance from some very unlikely sources. Roll with it. Let these kind souls ease your burden while you get your strength back and connect with your new child. Make it very clear to these good Samaritans that you don't need help taking care of Baby; you need help with the household chores. Soon enough, *you'll* be the one doing the dirty work while your parents and in-laws visit with Baby.

Be Assertive

On the other hand, don't be afraid to say when enough's enough. You do need your rest, and Baby needs his. Anyone who's had a baby anytime within recent memory will realize that sometimes the most helpful thing they can do is to leave you alone. But some folks either forget what it's like to have a baby in the house, or they've never been through the experience. Don't be afraid to tell people that although you really appreciate their help, you and Baby need some peace and quiet. And if your in-laws are the problem, let your partner deal with them.

Give Yourself Credit

Sure, you're happy to be home with your baby, but you may feel like you should be doing more, particularly if you're used to being at work. You could take a conference call. You could catch up on your e-mail. You could take a sneak peek at the project that's on hiatus. Stop. Let the work go and give yourself credit for what you're doing. Parenting really is the hardest job in the world and it requires all your attention right now. If you have the luxury of being able to be home for at least several weeks after Baby is born, savor every minute of it without feeling as though you're not doing enough.

Don't Expect Perfection

You've noticed a disturbing trend on your television set: Women in these shows give birth without ever looking bloated afterward or appearing as though they're about to drop from exhaustion. Their homes look perfect; they seem insanely happy; their babies seem to sleep all day; their bodies have returned to normal within a week. Real life just can't compete with that level of insane happiness, and you're left feeling as though something has gone awry in your own birthing experience. Realize that it takes time for Baby to settle into a schedule, for your body to adjust to breastfeeding and/or to return to a somewhat normal state — realize, too, that you may never again see your pre-pregnancy body. There will be times when you feel like bursting into tears because you're so tired and your hormones are all out of whack. Let yourself feel however you're really feeling.

Chapter 22

Ten Tips for Daddy Survival

In This Chapter

▶ Understanding your new role

▶ Doing your part to ensure family harmony

▶ Making time for your Baby and your lady

▶ Cutting yourself some slack

*S*eems that everyone loves to focus on what happens to a new mother when Baby enters the picture. Dad is supposed to be in the picture as much or as little as Mom (or Grandma) wants or allows him to be (this goes for married couples as well as couples who aren't living under the same roof), and somehow, he's expected to glean enough information by his peripheral involvement in Baby's care to snag Father of the Year.

Although plenty of fathers throw themselves into Baby's first year with every-thing they've got, just as many are completely unsure of what they're supposed to be doing. This chapter offers advice for new dads who may be feeling a little out of the loop.

Accept Your New Role

You have been given the greatest gift in the world. The daddy-child bond is priceless, and something every child needs. Don't spend your days thinking about how great life was when you had no responsibilities, or how you'd love to go buy that new car but can't — because that money is earmarked for Baby's college fund. Life changes completely when Baby comes on the scene. Accept that your child and family must come first from here on out, and that your own needs and wants come second. Fighting this reality makes life very difficult and depressing for a dad, and you'll find very little support from friends and family if you choose to look out for yourself before you tend to the needs of your child and partner.

Help Mom

There's an old saying: If Mom's not happy, nobody's happy. Truer words were never spoken, especially when you're talking about life during Baby's first year. Your partner is learning to care for a child while simultaneously caring for a home — and regardless of which century we're living in, these tasks tend to fall to the woman of the household. Whether she's working outside of the home or not, there's a lot of work to be done around the house, so pitch in. Make dinner. Sweep the floor. Fold some laundry. Find something that will make her day a little easier — and don't wait for her to ask you to do it.

Don't Shy Away from the Dirty Work

Dirty diapers. Middle-of-the-night feedings. Soothing a colicky baby. As unpleasant as these things seem when you're dealing with them day after day and night after night, the truth is that this time flies by. Before you know it, your child will be out of diapers and on the school bus. Becoming a hands-on dad right from the start can make the transition from being a childless man to becoming a parent much more natural than, say, waiting until Baby is 1 year old before you make your way over to the changing table. In order to truly establish a bond with your child, you've got to get in the trenches — and the earlier, the better.

Catch the Highlights at 11

Sitting and watching a game on the tube while your partner is soothing a crying Baby doesn't win *you* any fans. Even if you can't really do anything, making an effort is sometimes all your partner really wants. So turn off that TV and pay attention to the family. You can ensure that you won't be getting the silent treatment for the next several days.

Talk the Talk

First-time parents — especially dads — sometimes feel silly talking to their babies. Spend some time alone with your child and talk to her in a sing-songy voice. You may feel ridiculous at first, but you won't believe how natural it starts to feel after you let yourself go. A young infant prefers soft, high voices (probably because she's so used to hearing her mother's voice in the womb), so she's much more likely to focus on you if you make the effort to speak to her in a tone of voice that she's comfortable with. And after she sets her sights on you, you're a goner. You're wrapped around her little finger for the rest of time.

Cut the Calendar back

You've seen it happen a hundred times: A guy's wife has a baby, and the rest of the guys never see him again. You've sworn that this won't happen to you. You can balance family and fun, right? Well, sadly, you really can't. Not when you have a baby in the house. Your partner needs your help, a baby needs his dad, and disregarding your family's needs in a quest for fun is going to land you in the doghouse. Big time. (Plus, it's a vicious cycle: You go out with the guys, you come home late, you're tired the next day, and unable to help your partner the way you should.) Scale back your social life after Baby makes his appearance — maybe not forever, but at least for now.

Take a Breather

Know when to put your child down in his crib and take a breather. Dealing with a colicky infant or a cranky, teething baby isn't easy. The crying can go on and on and on, and can be incredibly frustrating, especially if you've done everything you can think of to comfort your child and he's still miserable. Sometimes, you just have to put him in his crib or playpen and take a couple of minutes to calm *yourself.* Baby will be fine for a few minutes by himself and you'll feel better knowing that you've collected yourself enough to try again.

And of course, you should never, ever strike or shake a baby. Even one shake can hurt an infant.

Let the Family in

Maybe your parents are a pain. Maybe your in-laws are a pain. When Baby comes home, everyone wants to see her — but *you* may not want to see everybody. Realize that these people are your child's family now, too. Regardless of your feelings about them, you don't want to deny Baby the joy of having grandparents, aunts, uncles, and cousins around. Unless they're felons, put aside your family differences for the sake of your child. The upside is this: You may be surprised at how nice it is to have some help from your family during Baby's first year.

Take Care of Your Relationship

Make sure you take time to nurture your relationship with your partner. Baby's first year is a time of adjustment — your wife is so wrapped up in the baby that you've been put on the back burner. You're both so tired, sex is the last thing on either of your minds. And your wife doesn't trust anyone to watch the baby, so the two of you can never go out for an adult evening on the town. The danger is that your relationship will dwindle to little more than roommate status if this goes on for too long — so take the reins and get creative. If your partner doesn't want to go out, plan to have a nice dinner at home after Baby has settled down for the night (and don't make your spouse cook it!). Make the effort to talk about something other than the baby. Remind her every so often that although Baby is the apple of your eye, your wife is the love of your life. This can mean the difference between feeling safe and secure in your relationship and feeling like a ship lost at sea.

Go Easy on Yourself

Keep in mind that no one is *born* a father. It's a learning process, just like everything else in life. There will be days when you feel like you have no idea what you're doing (when you put Baby's diaper on backwards for instance), and you can't believe that anyone would allow you to raise a child. You're responsible for your child from the day she's born — but really *feeling* like a parent (and not just a caregiver) may take some time. Don't feel guilty about it. Before long, you won't remember what it was like *not* to be a parent.

Chapter 23

Ten Reasons to Call Your Pediatrician

In This Chapter

▶ Fighting the urge to report every sniffle

▶ Differentiating between the real deal and a false alarm

▶ Taking the signs of trouble seriously

Determining what warrants a call to the pediatrician can be tricky, especially during the first year when Baby is unable to tell you if something hurts — and particularly if this is your first child (because you have no previous experience to base your decisions on). This chapter covers some of the more urgent matters that may arise during the first year. For more detailed information on Baby's health, take a look at Part VI of this book.

If you have any lingering doubt about whether to call the doctor or to let something go, *call*. It's always better to know for sure that Baby is okay.

Fever

You needn't freak out over a fever; it's just a sign of illness, and usually isn't dangerous. You can call the doctor during regular office hours to make an appointment for Baby to be seen; meanwhile, use acetaminophen or ibuprofen to keep the fever down. For information on how to take Baby's temperature, see Chapter 20.

Call the doctor when:

✔ Your baby is 3 months old or younger and has a temperature (taken rectally) over 100.5 degrees — unless she has had a DTaP shot in the previous 24 hours. A fever is sometimes a side effect of immunizations.

✔ Your child has a fever over 105 and is listless (to the point of being unable to rouse him) or has a seizure (and he's never had one in the past).

✔ Baby has a fever with a stiff neck (Baby screams in pain when you try to move his chin toward his chest); this can be a sign of meningitis.

✔ Baby has a fever in conjunction with signs of dehydration (covered in more detail later in this chapter).

Respiratory Problems

A lot of viruses can cause a wheezing sound when Baby breathes. This isn't always a sign of serious illness, though it may be if it's heard in conjunction with other symptoms. If he is wheezing and showing serious signs of not being able to catch his breath — you can see his skin drawing in between his ribs or in the pit of his chest, or his color looks off (he's pale or his lip are appear to be bluish) call your doctor right away. Also look for respiratory rates greater than 60 (count for a minute!). Take a look at Chapter 20 for more information on various ailments Baby may have.

Vomiting

Babies spit up all the time. Normal spit-up looks a lot like the milk that just went into Baby's mouth, although it may be a bit thicker and/or stringy with mucous (yes, it's pretty gross). If your infant is projectile vomiting — shooting it halfway across the room — or the vomit is dark in color, call your doctor right away. Your baby may have a bowel obstruction.

Dehydration

Your nursing newborn may be experiencing dehydration if she isn't getting enough to eat. An older baby may become dehydrated if she has had diarrhea or has been vomiting. In either case, be on the lookout for signs of dehydration, which include:

✔ Fewer wet diapers (she should be wetting at least every six to eight hours)

✔ No tears when she cries

✔ Sunken eyes

✔ Crankiness

✔ Dry mouth

✔ A decrease in an older baby's activity level

Call your pediatrician immediately if Baby is exhibiting these symptoms. Dehydration can cause serious *electrolyte imbalances,* which can lead to organ failure.

Long-Term Cough or Stuffy Head

Kids catch a lot of colds. Baby doesn't need to be rushed to the doctor for every single virus. However, if he has a productive cough that just won't go away after ten days to two weeks or that seems to be getting worse, he should be evaluated in the doctor's office to make sure that the cough hasn't turned into a respiratory infection. Same thing with a stuffy head — if it hasn't cleared up after a couple of weeks and Baby is showing signs of feeling lousy (irritable, sleepy, not eating well), schedule an appointment to rule out a sinus infection.

Head Injuries

Not every bump to the head requires a doctor's visit. But if Baby lost consciousness after hitting his head or is showing signs of a concussion (unusual pallor, loss of motor skills, extreme irritability or lethargy, vomiting, or dilated or uneven pupils) or skull fracture (discharge from ears), call your doctor or take Baby to the emergency room for evaluation. For more information on head injuries, see Chapter 19.

Deep Cuts

An older, active baby will likely suffer his fair share of cuts — most will be small and easy-to-care for. Call the doctor if:

- The bleeding is profuse.
- You aren't able to at least slow the bleeding after applying direct pressure for ten minutes.
- The cut is a puncture wound (from a nail or another sharp, thin object, or from an animal bite).
- The cut has jagged edges (which are unlikely to close by themselves).
- The cut is deep and on his face, or if it's in an area where it's simply unlikely to stay closed (on a knee or an elbow, for example).

Baby may need a stitch or two to mend the wound. For more information on cuts, see Chapter 19.

Extreme Changes of Behavior

A radical difference in Baby's behavior may indicate that something is going on inside her body, whether it's an illness or injury. Call the doctor right away if your child:

- Is difficult to rouse
- Cries inconsolably
- Isn't able to do the things she usually does (she's been crawling well for weeks, and suddenly she's unable to hoist herself up off the ground)

Rashes

Children are prone to all kinds of rashes. Some of them are contagious; many aren't; some are symptoms of a virus or other illness. Most are uncomfortable for Baby. If your child breaks out in spots, or has a rash that is spreading or is itchy, call your doctor *to confirm a diagnosis* and to get advice on how to care for it. Diaper rash is usually not cause for concern, however. Most often, it can be cleared up with ointment. If a diaper rash starts to look red, swollen, and meaty (you'll know when you see it), it may be a yeast infection (even in a little boy). Call the doctor for diagnosis and antibiotic treatment. For more on rashes, see Chapter 18.

Seizures

A seizure is one of the most frightening things for a parent to see: Your child is on the floor or in the crib, body tensed up, eyes rolled back — and there's nothing you can do to help except to lay him on his side to prevent choking on spit-up or saliva, and to clear the area around him so that he doesn't hurt himself. If your child has been diagnosed with a seizure disorder (he has seizures when he has a fever, for example), you will already have been given instructions on when to call the doctor. If your child has never had a seizure before, call right away.

Chapter 24

Ten Reasons Not to Run to Your Pediatrician

In This Chapter

▶ Identifying a mild illness

▶ Nursing those bumps and bruises

▶ Keeping your cool and playing Dr. Mom

Although you need to know when to call the doctor, you also need to know when *not* to call — or when to simply wait until the morning. Sometimes, the best cure is Mom's love. Other times, you have to take a wait-and-see attitude, particularly with mild illnesses like a cold. Sometimes, you just have to sit back and let nature take its course.

Please remember that although your doctor is on call, she is with her family, helping with homework, bathing kids, putting them to bed, and trying to get a good night's sleep herself. Please call for emergencies, not routine questions! For more information on Baby's health, see Part VI of this book.

Low-Grade Fever

Although any fever should be evaluated in an infant who is less than 3 months old, a temperature in an older baby that's slightly over normal (98.6 degrees) but below 101 degrees isn't usually serious. After 3 months, almost all fevers can wait a day or two before being evaluated by the doctor, especially if Baby has no other symptoms (like a cough, a decrease in appetite, difficulty breathing, or pulling or swatting at the ears). Call during regular office hours for advice on pain reliever dosages. The fever may subside on its own; if it doesn't after several days, make an appointment with your pediatrician. For information on when to take a fever more seriously, flip to Chapter 23.

A fever is sometimes a side effect of immunizations. In lieu of other, serious symptoms (difficulty breathing, unusual and severe listlessness), a fever following a shot is not cause for concern at any age. For information on how to take Baby's temperature, see Chapter 18.

Manageable Crankiness

Babies who don't feel well sometimes show their discomfort by being very disagreeable. If your child is easily soothed (by being rocked or simply be being held), she's probably just not feeling tip-top. If nothing comforts her for over one hour and she cries continuously for that period of time, call your pediatrician.

Runny Nose

A simple cold doesn't need to be evaluated by the doctor. If Baby has a runny and/or stuffy nose and a little cough and no fever, let the virus run its course. A cold that just won't go away after a couple of weeks, a severe cough, wheezing, or difficulty breathing, the development of a worrisome fever, and/or extreme, inconsolable irritability are symptoms that warrant a call to the doctor's office.

Just a Little Lethargy

If Baby is feeling a little under the weather, expect him to be less active. Worrisome lethargy means that you aren't able to wake him, or that he's completely out of it. If he simply isn't bouncing off the walls when he has a cold, that's normal.

You don't want to do your normal activities with the same energy and excitement when you're sick either (although you do them because your name is Mommy).

Loss of Appetite

A breastfed infant shouldn't go more than three to four hours between feedings; bottlefed babies go slightly longer sometimes. When Baby is becoming more active (learning to move, finding that he can manipulate toys, exploring the kitchen cabinets), it's normal for his appetite to drop. He simply has other things to do. If he seems healthy and happy and he's just not eating as much as he normally does, his loss of interest in eating and/or nursing is probably just due to his increased interest in the rest of the world.

Babies experience a loss of appetite when sick, just like you do. As long as she wets her diaper every 8 to 12 hours, she's okay.

Increase in Appetite

As Baby grows, he needs to eat more to keep his energy levels up. Don't be surprised — and resist the urge to cut him off — if he suddenly wants to nurse more at 3 weeks, 6 weeks, and 6 months. Babies typically go through a growth spurt at these ages. When he's on solids, let him determine how much he wants to eat. *He'll* know when he's full.

Constipation

Its normal for babies to poop less often as they get older, even skipping one to three days between stools. It's also normal for Baby to grunt, push, and have a red face when pooping. (*You* try pooping while you're lying down — it ain't easy!) If baby hasn't pooped for several days and seems uncomfortable — she's drawing her legs up, she's crying, and has a decreased appetite, try a pediatric glycerin suppository, or try taking a rectal temperature to stimulate a bowel movement. This usually does the trick. You can call the doctor's office during regular office hours to find out how to keep this from happening repeatedly.

Teething

There's nothing your pediatrician can do for Baby's sore gums except offer you the same advice you'll find in most baby books: Pain relievers. Teething rings. Extra attention. And patience.

Scrapes, Bruises, Bumps

Most injuries that children sustain aren't serious. Wash a scrape out. Put ice on a bump. Bandage an open cut. You don't need to call the doctor for these minor wounds. However, if bleeding is profuse or a cut is deep or jagged, or if Baby has bumped his head and is showing signs of having a serious head injury (loss of consciousness, vomiting, large or uneven pupils, loss of motor function), call your doctor right away. For more on treating minor injuries, see Chapter 19.

Mild Allergic Reactions

Unless your child is showing signs of a moderate to severe allergic reaction to something (a rash that covers her body, swelling of the eyes and lips, difficulty breathing), removal of the offensive agent is usually enough to stop the reaction. If you've washed Baby's clothes with regular detergent and she develops a little rash on her stomach, discontinue its use. If you're trying out a new veggie and her cheeks turn pink, stop feeding it to her. If Baby does develop symptoms of a serious reaction, call your doctor immediately. For more information on allergic reactions, turn to Chapter 18.

Index

• G •

BUSINESS, CAREERS & PERSONAL FINANCE

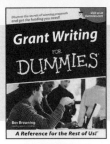

0-7645-5307-0

0-7645-5331-3 *†

Also available:

- Accounting For Dummies †
  0-7645-5314-3
- Business Plans Kit For Dummies †
  0-7645-5365-8
- Cover Letters For Dummies
  0-7645-5224-4
- Frugal Living For Dummies
  0-7645-5403-4
- Leadership For Dummies
  0-7645-5176-0
- Managing For Dummies
  0-7645-1771-6

- Marketing For Dummies
  0-7645-5600-2
- Personal Finance For Dummies *
  0-7645-2590-5
- Project Management For Dummies
  0-7645-5283-X
- Resumes For Dummies †
  0-7645-5471-9
- Selling For Dummies
  0-7645-5363-1
- Small Business Kit For Dummies *†
  0-7645-5093-4

HOME & BUSINESS COMPUTER BASICS

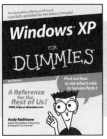

0-7645-4074-2

0-7645-3758-X

Also available:

- ACT! 6 For Dummies
  0-7645-2645-6
- iLife '04 All-in-One Desk Reference
  For Dummies
  0-7645-7347-0
- iPAQ For Dummies
  0-7645-6769-1
- Mac OS X Panther Timesaving
  Techniques For Dummies
  0-7645-5812-9
- Macs For Dummies
  0-7645-5656-8

- Microsoft Money 2004 For Dummies
  0-7645-4195-1
- Office 2003 All-in-One Desk Reference
  For Dummies
  0-7645-3883-7
- Outlook 2003 For Dummies
  0-7645-3759-8
- PCs For Dummies
  0-7645-4074-2
- TiVo For Dummies
  0-7645-6923-6
- Upgrading and Fixing PCs For Dummies
  0-7645-1665-5
- Windows XP Timesaving Techniques
  For Dummies
  0-7645-3748-2

FOOD, HOME, GARDEN, HOBBIES, MUSIC & PETS

0-7645-5295-3

0-7645-5232-5

Also available:

- Bass Guitar For Dummies
  0-7645-2487-9
- Diabetes Cookbook For Dummies
  0-7645-5230-9
- Gardening For Dummies *
  0-7645-5130-2
- Guitar For Dummies
  0-7645-5106-X
- Holiday Decorating For Dummies
  0-7645-2570-0
- Home Improvement All-in-One
  For Dummies
  0-7645-5680-0

- Knitting For Dummies
  0-7645-5395-X
- Piano For Dummies
  0-7645-5105-1
- Puppies For Dummies
  0-7645-5255-4
- Scrapbooking For Dummies
  0-7645-7208-3
- Senior Dogs For Dummies
  0-7645-5818-8
- Singing For Dummies
  0-7645-2475-5
- 30-Minute Meals For Dummies
  0-7645-2589-1

INTERNET & DIGITAL MEDIA

0-7645-1664-7

0-7645-6924-4

Also available:

- 2005 Online Shopping Directory
  For Dummies
  0-7645-7495-7
- CD & DVD Recording For Dummies
  0-7645-5956-7
- eBay For Dummies
  0-7645-5654-1
- Fighting Spam For Dummies
  0-7645-5965-6
- Genealogy Online For Dummies
  0-7645-5964-8
- Google For Dummies
  0-7645-4420-9

- Home Recording For Musicians
  For Dummies
  0-7645-1634-5
- The Internet For Dummies
  0-7645-4173-0
- iPod & iTunes For Dummies
  0-7645-7772-7
- Preventing Identity Theft For Dummies
  0-7645-7336-5
- Pro Tools All-in-One Desk Reference
  For Dummies
  0-7645-5714-9
- Roxio Easy Media Creator For Dummies
  0-7645-7131-1

* Separate Canadian edition also available

† Separate U.K. edition also available

Available wherever books are sold. For more information or to order direct: U.S. customers visit www.dummies.com or call 1-877-762-2974.
U.K. customers visit www.wileyeurope.com or call 0800 243407. Canadian customers visit www.wiley.ca or call 1-800-567-4797.

 WILEY

SPORTS, FITNESS, PARENTING, RELIGION & SPIRITUALITY

0-7645-5146-9

0-7645-5418-2

Also available:
- Adoption For Dummies
  0-7645-5488-3
- Basketball For Dummies
  0-7645-5248-1
- The Bible For Dummies
  0-7645-5296-1
- Buddhism For Dummies
  0-7645-5359-3
- Catholicism For Dummies
  0-7645-5391-7
- Hockey For Dummies
  0-7645-5228-7

- Judaism For Dummies
  0-7645-5299-6
- Martial Arts For Dummies
  0-7645-5358-5
- Pilates For Dummies
  0-7645-5397-6
- Religion For Dummies
  0-7645-5264-3
- Teaching Kids to Read For Dummies
  0-7645-4043-2
- Weight Training For Dummies
  0-7645-5168-X
- Yoga For Dummies
  0-7645-5117-5

TRAVEL

0-7645-5438-7

0-7645-5453-0

Also available:
- Alaska For Dummies
  0-7645-1761-9
- Arizona For Dummies
  0-7645-6938-4
- Cancún and the Yucatán For Dummies
  0-7645-2437-2
- Cruise Vacations For Dummies
  0-7645-6941-4
- Europe For Dummies
  0-7645-5456-5
- Ireland For Dummies
  0-7645-5455-7

- Las Vegas For Dummies
  0-7645-5448-4
- London For Dummies
  0-7645-4277-X
- New York City For Dummies
  0-7645-6945-7
- Paris For Dummies
  0-7645-5494-8
- RV Vacations For Dummies
  0-7645-5443-3
- Walt Disney World & Orlando For Dummies
  0-7645-6943-0

GRAPHICS, DESIGN & WEB DEVELOPMENT

0-7645-4345-8

0-7645-5589-8

Also available:
- Adobe Acrobat 6 PDF For Dummies
  0-7645-3760-1
- Building a Web Site For Dummies
  0-7645-7144-3
- Dreamweaver MX 2004 For Dummies
  0-7645-4342-3
- FrontPage 2003 For Dummies
  0-7645-3882-9
- HTML 4 For Dummies
  0-7645-1995-6
- Illustrator CS For Dummies
  0-7645-4084-X

- Macromedia Flash MX 2004 For Dummies
  0-7645-4358-X
- Photoshop 7 All-in-One Desk
  Reference For Dummies
  0-7645-1667-1
- Photoshop CS Timesaving Techniques
  For Dummies
  0-7645-6782-9
- PHP 5 For Dummies
  0-7645-4166-8
- PowerPoint 2003 For Dummies
  0-7645-3908-6
- QuarkXPress 6 For Dummies
  0-7645-2593-X

NETWORKING, SECURITY, PROGRAMMING & DATABASES

0-7645-6852-3

0-7645-5784-X

Also available:
- A+ Certification For Dummies
  0-7645-4187-0
- Access 2003 All-in-One Desk
  Reference For Dummies
  0-7645-3988-4
- Beginning Programming For Dummies
  0-7645-4997-9
- C For Dummies
  0-7645-7068-4
- Firewalls For Dummies
  0-7645-4048-3
- Home Networking For Dummies
  0-7645-42796

- Network Security For Dummies
  0-7645-1679-5
- Networking For Dummies
  0-7645-1677-9
- TCP/IP For Dummies
  0-7645-1760-0
- VBA For Dummies
  0-7645-3989-2
- Wireless All In-One Desk Reference
  For Dummies
  0-7645-7496-5
- Wireless Home Networking For Dummies
  0-7645-3910-8

HEALTH & SELF-HELP

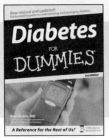

Diabetes FOR DUMMIES

0-7645-6820-5 *†

Low-Carb Dieting FOR DUMMIES

0-7645-2566-2

Also available:

- Alzheimer's For Dummies
  0-7645-3899-3
- Asthma For Dummies
  0-7645-4233-8
- Controlling Cholesterol For Dummies
  0-7645-5440-9
- Depression For Dummies
  0-7645-3900-0
- Dieting For Dummies
  0-7645-4149-8
- Fertility For Dummies
  0-7645-2549-2

- Fibromyalgia For Dummies
  0-7645-5441-7
- Improving Your Memory For Dummies
  0-7645-5435-2
- Pregnancy For Dummies †
  0-7645-4483-7
- Quitting Smoking For Dummies
  0-7645-2629-4
- Relationships For Dummies
  0-7645-5384-4
- Thyroid For Dummies
  0-7645-5385-2

EDUCATION, HISTORY, REFERENCE & TEST PREPARATION

Spanish FOR DUMMIES

0-7645-5194-9

The Origins of Tolkien's Middle-earth FOR DUMMIES

0-7645-4186-2

Also available:

- Algebra For Dummies
  0-7645-5325-9
- British History For Dummies
  0-7645-7021-8
- Calculus For Dummies
  0-7645-2498-4
- English Grammar For Dummies
  0-7645-5322-4
- Forensics For Dummies
  0-7645-5580-4
- The GMAT For Dummies
  0-7645-5251-1
- Inglés Para Dummies
  0-7645-5427-1

- Italian For Dummies
  0-7645-5196-5
- Latin For Dummies
  0-7645-5431-X
- Lewis & Clark For Dummies
  0-7645-2545-X
- Research Papers For Dummies
  0-7645-5426-3
- The SAT I For Dummies
  0-7645-7193-1
- Science Fair Projects For Dummies
  0-7645-5460-3
- U.S. History For Dummies
  0-7645-5249-X

Get smart @ dummies.com®

- **Find a full list of Dummies titles**
- **Look into loads of FREE on-site articles**
- **Sign up for FREE eTips e-mailed to you weekly**
- **See what other products carry the Dummies name**
- **Shop directly from the Dummies bookstore**
- **Enter to win new prizes every month!**

* Separate Canadian edition also available
† Separate U.K. edition also available

Available wherever books are sold. For more information or to order direct: U.S. customers visit www.dummies.com or call 1-877-762-2974.
U.K. customers visit www.wileyeurope.com or call 0800 243407. Canadian customers visit www.wiley.ca or call 1-800-567-4797.

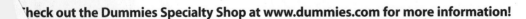